French

at your Fingertips

Contents

French
at your Fingertips

compiled by
LEXUS

with

Sabine Citron and Peter Terrell

Routledge & Kegan Paul
London

First published in 1986
by Routledge & Kegan Paul Ltd.

11 New Fetter Lane, London EC4P 4EE

Reprinted 1986

Set in Linotron Baskerville
by Morton Word Processing Ltd, Scarborough
and printed in Great Britain
by The Guernsey Press Co. Ltd, Guernsey, Channel Islands

British Library Cataloguing in Publication Data

French at your fingertips.—(Fingertips)

1. French language—Conversation and phrase books
I. Lexus   II.   Citron, Sabin   III. Terrell, Peter   IV. Series
448.3′421   PC2121

ISBN 0-7102-0724-7

Other titles in this series

French Pronunciation

Because you are likely to want to speak most of the French given in this book, rather than just to understand its meaning, an indication of the pronunciation has been given in square brackets. If you pronounce this as though it were English, the result will be clearly comprehensible to a French person.

In some cases, however, we have decided it was not necessary to give the entire pronunciation for a word or phrase. This may be because it would more or less duplicate the ordinary French spelling, or because the pronunciation of a particular word or words has already been given within the same entry. In these cases we have simply shown how to pronounce the problematic parts of the word or phrase.

Some comments on the pronunciation system used:

a when it occurs by itself	as in 'path', 'garden'
i	ee
j	as the 's' in 'composure'
o by itself or in combinations such as 'do' etc	as in 'go'
oo	similar to the 'u' sound in 'huge' or 'few'
uh	like the 'er' sound in 'butter' or the 'or' sound in 'manor'

The typical French nasal sounds written in French as 'on, om, an, am, en, em' have all been given as *on* in the pronunciation. If you say the 'ant' part of the word 'restaurant' leaving off the final 't' this is close to the correct sound.

French nasal sounds written as 'ain, aim, ein, in, im, un' have all been given as *an*. Say the English word 'an' leaving off the final 'n', as though you have a bad cold, to produce something approximating the correct sound.

English–French

A

a un, une *[an, œn]*; **50 francs a bottle** cinquante francs la bouteille

about: about 25 environ 25 *[onveeron]*; **see you about 6 o'clock** rendez-vous vers 6 heures *[vair]*; **is the manager about?** le directeur est-il là? *[eteel la]*; **I was just about to leave** j'étais sur le point de m'en aller *[jaytay sœr luh pwan]*; **how about a drink?** et si on allait prendre un verre? *[ay see on alay]*

above: en dessus *[on duhsœ]*; **above the village** au-dessus du village *[o-duhsœ]*

abroad à l'étranger *[a laytronjay]*

abscess un abscès *[absay]*

absolutely: it's absolutely perfect c'est parfait; **you're absolutely right** tu as tout à fait raison *[toota fay]*; **absolutely!** absolument! *[absolœmon]*

absorbent cotton du coton hydrophile *[koton eedrofeel]*

accelerator l'accélérateur *[axaylayraturr]*

accept accepter *[axeptay]*

accident un accident *[axeedon]*; **there's been an accident** il y a eu un accident *[eelya œ]*; **sorry, it was an accident** je suis désolé, je ne l'ai pas fait exprès *[juh nuh lay pa fay expray]*

accommodation(s): we need accommodation(s) for four nous aimerions des chambres pour quatre personnes *[nooz emreeon day shombr]*

accordion l'accordéon *[—ayon]*

accurate précis *[praysee]*

ache: I have an ache here j'ai mal ici *[jay mal ee-see]*; **my back aches** j'ai mal au dos *[o do]*

across: it's across the street c'est juste en face *[say jœst on fass]*

actor un acteur *[akturr]*

actress une actrice *[aktreess]*

adapter un adaptateur *[adaptaturr]*

address une adresse *[adress]*; **what's your address?** quelle est votre adresse? *[kel ay votr]*

address book le carnet d'adresses *[karnay dadress]*

admission: how much is admission? combien coûte l'entrée? *[komb-yan koot lontray]*

adore: I adore … j'adore … *[jador]*

adult un adulte *[adœlt]*

advance: I'll pay in advance je paierai d'avance *[payray davons]*

advertisement une publicité *[pœbleeseetay]*

advise: what would you advise? que conseillez-vous? *[kuh konsayay voo]*

affluent riche *[reesh]*

afraid: I'm afraid of heights j'ai peur du vide *[jay purr]*; **don't be afraid** ne crains rien *[nuh cran ree-an]*; **I'm not afraid** je n'ai pas peur; **I'm afraid I can't help you** je suis désolé, mais je ne peux pas vous aider *[swee dayzolay]*; **I'm afraid so** hélas, oui *[aylass wee]*; **I'm afraid not** malheureusement pas *[malurr-rurzmon pa]*

after: after you après vous *[apray]*; **after 9 o'clock** après 9 heures; **it was after 9 o'clock** il était passé 9 heures *[… passay …]*; **not until after 9 o'clock** pas avant 9 heures *[pa zavon]*

afternoon l'après-midi *[apray-meedee]*; **in the afternoon** l'après-midi; **good afternoon** bonjour *[bon-joor]*; **this afternoon** cet après-midi

aftershave un aftershave

after sun cream une crème après-soleil *[krem apray-solay]*

afterwards ensuite *[onsweet]*

again de nouveau *[duh noovo]*

against contre *[kontr]*

age l'âge *[ahj]*; **under age** mineur *[meenurr]*; **not at my age!** à mon âge!; **it takes ages** cela prend un temps fou *[suhla pron**

an tom foo]; **I haven't been here for ages** ça fait une éternité que je n'étais pas venu ici [sa fay œn aytairneetay kuh juh naytay pa vuhnœ ee-see]

agency une agence [ajons]

aggressive agressif

ago: a year ago il y a une année [eelya]; **it wasn't long ago** il n'y a pas longtemps [eel nya pa]

agony: it's agony c'est un vrai supplice [set an vray sœpleess]

agree: do you agree? êtes-vous d'accord?; **I agree** je suis d'accord [dakor]; **fish doesn't agree with me** je ne supporte pas le poisson [juh nuh sœport pa]

AIDS le SIDA [seeda]

air l'air; **by air** en avion [on avyon]

air conditioning la climatisation [kleemateezas-yon]

air hostess une hôtesse de l'air

airmail: by airmail par avion [avyon]

airmail envelope une enveloppe par avion [onvlop par avyon]

airplane un avion [avyon]

airport l'aéroport [airopor]

airport bus la navette de l'aéroport [navet duh lairopor]

airport tax les taxes d'aéroport

alarm l'alarme

alarm clock un réveil [rayvay]

alcohol l'alcool [alkol]

alcoholic: is it alcoholic? est-ce que c'est une boisson alcoolisée? [eskuhsay tœn bwasson alkoleezay]

Algeria l'Algérie [aljayree]

alive vivant [veevon]; **is he still alive?** est-ce qu'il vit encore? [eskeel vee tonkor]

all: all the hotels tous les hôtels [too]; **all my friends** tous mes amis; **all my money** tout mon argent [too]; **I ate all of it** je l'ai mangé tout entier [toot onteeay]; **all of them** tous [tooss]; **all right** d'accord [dakor]; **I'm all right** ça va [sa]; **that's all** c'est tout [say too]; **it's all changed** ce n'est plus comme avant [suh nay plœ kom avon]; **thank you — not at all** merci — de rien [duh ree-an]

allergic: I'm allergic to ... je suis allergique à ... [swee alairjeek]

allergy une allergie [alairjee]

all-inclusive tout compris [too kompree]

allowed: is it allowed? est-ce que c'est permis? [eskuh say pairmee]; **I'm not allowed to eat salt** je suis au régime sans sel [juh sweez an rayjeem son sel]

almost presque [presk]

alone seul [surl]; **are you alone?** êtes-vous seul? [et voo]; **leave me alone!** laissez-moi tranquille! [lessay mwa tronkeel]

already déjà [dayja]

also aussi [o-see]

alteration (to plans) une modification [modeefeekassyon]; (to clothes) une retouche [ruhtoosh]

alternative: is there an alternative? y a-t-il une autre possibilité? [yateel œn ohtr poseebeeleetay]; **we had no alternative** nous n'avions pas le choix [noo navyon pa luh shwa]

alternator un alternateur [altairnaturr]

although bien que [b-yan kuh]

altogether ensemble [onsombl]; **what does that come to altogether?** combien est-ce que ça fait en tout? [komb-yan eskuh sa fay on too]

always toujours [toojoor]

a.m.: at 8 a.m. à 8 heures du matin [dœ matan]

amazing (surprising) étonnant [aytonon]; (very good) remarquable [ruhmark-abl]

ambassador l'ambassadeur [ombasadurr]

ambulance une ambulance [ombœlons]; **get an ambulance!** appelez une ambulance!

America l'Amérique [amayreek]

American américain(e) [amayreekan, —ken]

American plan la pension complète [pons-yon komplet]

among parmi [parmee]

amp: a 15-amp fuse un fusible de 15 ampères [fœzeebl]

an(a)esthetic un anesthésique [anaystayzeek]

ancestor un ancêtre [onsetr]

anchor l'ancre [onkr]

anchovies des anchois [onshwa]

ancient ancien [onsyan]

and et [ay]

angina une angine de poitrine [onjeen duh pwatreen]

angry fâché [fashay]; **I'm very angry about it** je suis furieux [fœree-uh]

animal un animal [anee-mal]

ankle la cheville *[shuhvee]*

anniversary: it's our (wedding) anniversary today nous fêtons aujourd'hui notre anniversaire de mariage *[noo feton o-joordwee notr anneevairsair duh maree-ahj]*

annoy: he's annoying me il m'importune *[amportœn]*; **it's so annoying** c'est vraiment ennuyeux *[vraymon onwee-uh]*

anorak un anorak

another: can we have another room? est-ce que nous pouvons avoir une autre chambre? *[eskuh … avwa œn ohtr]*; **another bottle, please** encore une bouteille, s'il vous plaît *[onkor]*

answer: there was no answer on ne m'a pas répondu *[on nuh ma pa raypondœ]*; **what was his answer?** qu'a-t-il répondu? *[kateel]*

ant: ants des fourmis *[foormee]*

antibiotics des antibiotiques *[onteebee-oteek]*

anticlimax: what an anticlimax! quelle déception! *[kel dayseps-yon]*

antifreeze l'antigel *[onteejel]*

antihistamines des antihistaminiques *[ontee-eestameeneek]*

antique: is it an antique? est-ce un objet d'époque? *[objay daypok]*

antique shop un antiquaire *[onteekair]*

antisocial: don't be antisocial ne sois pas sauvage *[nuh swa pa so-vahj]*

any: have you got any rolls/milk? avez-vous des petits pains/du lait? *[… day … dœ …]*; **I haven't got any** je n'en ai pas *[juh non ay pa]*

anybody: can anybody help? est-ce que quelqu'un peut m'aider? *[kelkan]*; **there wasn't anybody there** il n'y avait personne *[pairson]*

anything: I don't want anything je n'ai besoin de rien *[ree-an]*; **don't you have anything else?** avez-vous autre chose? *[ohtr shohz]*

apart from sauf *[sohf]*

apartment un appartement *[apartmon]*

aperitif un apéritif

apology des excuses *[exkœz]*; **please accept my apologies** je vous prie de m'excuser *[juh voo pree duh mexkœzay]*

appalling effroyable *[efrwy-abl]*

appear: it would appear that … il semble que … *[eel sombl kuh]*

appendicitis l'appendicite *[apandeeseet]*

appetite: I've lost my appetite j'ai perdu l'appétit *[apaytee]*

apple une pomme *[pom]*

apple pie une tarte aux pommes *[o pom]*

application form (*for membership*) un formulaire d'inscription *[formœlair danskreepsyon]*

appointment un rendez-vous; **I'd like to make an appointment** j'aimerais prendre rendez-vous *[jemray prondr]*

appreciate: thank you, I appreciate it merci, c'est très aimable *[mairsee say trayz emabl]*

approve: she doesn't approve elle n'est pas d'accord *[el nay pa dakor]*

apricot un abricot *[abreeko]*

April avril *[avreel]*

aqualung un scaphandre autonome *[skafondr otonohm]*

Arab arabe *[a-rab]*

archaeology l'archéologie *[arkay-olojee]*

are *see page 113*

area: I don't know the area je ne connais pas la région *[rayjeeon]*

area code l'indicatif *[andeekateef]*

arm le bras *[bra]*

around *see* **about**

arrangement: will you make the arrangements? pouvez-vous organiser cela? *[poovay-voo organeezay suhla]*

arrest arrêter *[aretay]*; **he's been arrested** il a été arrêté *[eel a aytay]*

arrival l'arrivée *[areevay]*

arrive: when do we arrive? à quelle heure arrivons-nous? *[areevon]*; **has my parcel arrived yet?** mon colis est-il arrivé? *[eteel areevay]*; **let me know as soon as they arrive** avertissez-moi dès leur arrivée *[avairteesay-mwa]*; **we only arrived yesterday** nous ne sommes arrivés qu'hier *[kee-air]*

art l'art *[ar]*

art gallery un musée d'art *[mœzay]*

arthritis l'arthrite *[artreet]*

artificial artificiel *[arteefeesyel]*

artist un artiste *[arteest]*

as: as fast as you can aussi vite que possible *[o-see veet kuh poseebl]*; **as much as you can** autant que possible *[o-ton]*; **as you like** comme vous voulez *[kom]*; **as it's getting late** comme il se fait tard

ashore: to go ashore débarquer

[day-barkay]
ashtray un cendrier [sondreeay]
aside from à part [a par]
ask demander [duhmonday]; **that's not what I asked for** ce n'est pas ce que j'ai commandé [suh nay pa suh kuh jay komonday]; **could you ask him to phone me back?** pouvez-vous lui demander de me rappeler? [... lwee ... rapuhlay]
asleep: he's still asleep il dort encore [dor]
asparagus des asperges [aspairj]
aspirin une aspirine [aspeereen]
assault: she's been assaulted elle s'est fait agresser [el say fay tagressay]; **indecent assault** un attentat à la pudeur [atonta ala pœdurr]
assistant (helper) un assistant [asseeston]; (in shop) une vendeuse [vondurz]
assume: I assume that ... je suppose que ... [juh sœpohz kuh]
asthma l'asthme [as-muh]
astonishing étonnant [aytonon]
at: at the café au café [o]; **at the hotel** à l'hôtel; **at 8 o'clock** à 8 heures; **see you at dinner** à tout à l'heure, à table [a toota lurr, a tabl]
Atlantic l'Atlantique [atlonteek]
atmosphere l'atmosphère [atmossfair]
attractive: you're very attractive, Marie vous êtes très jolie, Marie [tray jolee]; **you're very attractive, Paul** je vous trouve séduisant, Paul [saydweezon]
aubergine une aubergine [obairjeen]
auction une vente aux enchères [vont o zonshair]

audience le public [pœbleek]
August août [oo]
aunt: my aunt ma tante [tont]
au pair (girl) une jeune fille au pair [jurn fee]
Australia l'Australie [ostralee]
Australian australien(ne) [ostraleean, —en]
Austria l'Autriche [otreesh]
authorities les autorités [otoreetay]
automatic automatique [otomateek]; (car) une voiture automatique [vwatœr]
automobile une automobile [oto—]
autumn l'automne [oton]; **in the autumn** en automne [on]
available: when will the car be available? quand est-ce que la voiture sera prête? [konteskuh la vwatœr suhra pret]; **when will he be available?** quand est-ce qu'il sera disponible? [deesponeebl]
avenue une avenue
average: the average Frenchman le Français moyen [mwy-an]; **an above average hotel** un hôtel de catégorie supérieure [sœpayreeurr]; **a below average hotel** un hôtel de catégorie inférieure [anfayreeurr]; **the food was only average** la nourriture était médiocre [maydeeokr]; **on average** en moyenne [on mwy-en]
awake: is she awake yet? est-elle éveillée? [etel ayvayay]
away: go away! allez-vous en! [alay-voo zon]
awful affreux [afruh]
axle l'essieu [es-yuh]

B

baby un bébé [baybay]
baby-carrier un porte-bébé [port-baybay]
baby-sitter un(e) baby-sitter; **can you get us a baby-sitter?** pouvez-vous nous trouver un baby-sitter? [poovay voo noo troovay]

bachelor un célibataire [seleebatair]
back: I've got a bad back je souffre du dos [juh soofr dœ do]; **at the back** à l'arrière [a laree-air]; **in the back of the car** sur le siège arrière [sœr luh see-ej]; **I'll be right back** je reviens dans un instant [juh ruhvee-yan don zan anston]; **when do you**

want it back? pour quand l'aimeriez-vous? *[poor kon lemuhree-ay voo]*; **can I have my money back?** est-ce que vous pouvez me rendre mon argent? *[eskuh voo poovay muh rondr]*; **come back!** revenez! *[ruhvuh-nay]*; **I go back home tomorrow** je rentre à la maison demain *[rontr]*; **we'll be back next year** nous reviendrons l'année prochaine *[noo ruhvee-andron]*; **when is the last bus back?** pour le retour, à quelle heure part le dernier bus? *[poor luh ruhtoor, a kel urr par luh dairnyay boos]*; **he backed into me** il m'est rentré dedans (en marche arrière) *[eel may rontray duh-don]*

backache des maux de reins *[mo duh ran]*
back door la porte arrière *[port aree-air]*
backgammon le trictrac
backpack un sac à dos *[sak ah do]*
back seat le siège arrière *[see-ej aree-air]*
back street une petite rue *[puhteet roo]*
bacon le bacon; **bacon and eggs** des oeufs au bacon *[uh o]*
bad (*quality*) mauvais *[movay]*; **this meat's bad** cette viande est avariée *[avaree-ay]*; **a bad headache** un violent mal de tête *[veeolon]*; **it's not bad** ce n'est pas mal; **too bad!** tant pis! *[ton pee]*
badly: he's been badly injured il est grièvement blessé *[gree-evmon blessay]*
bag un sac *[sak]*
baggage les bagages *[bagahj]*
baggage allowance le poids maximum de bagages autorisé *[pwa maxeemum duh bagahj otoreezay]*
baggage check (*at station*) la consigne *[kon-seen]*
bakery une boulangerie *[boolonjree]*
balcony le balcon; **a room with a balcony** une chambre avec balcon; **on the balcony** sur le balcon
bald chauve *[shohv]*
ball un ballon
ballet le ballet
ball-point pen un stylo à bille *[steelo a bee]*
banana une banane *[banan]*
band (*mus*) un orchestre *[orkestr]*
bandage le pansement *[ponsmon]*
bandaid un pansement adhésif *[ponsmon adayzeef]*
bank (*money*) une banque *[bonk]*; **when**

are the banks open? quelles sont les heures d'ouverture des banques? *[kel son layz urr doovairtoor]*
bank account un compte en banque
bar un bar; **let's meet in the bar** rendez-vous au bar; **a bar of chocolate** une tablette de chocolat *[tablet duh shokola]*
barbecue un barbecue
barber le coiffeur *[kwafurr]*
bargain: it's a real bargain c'est une bonne affaire *[set oon bon afair]*
barmaid la serveuse *[sairvurz]*
barman le barman
barrette une barrette
bartender le barman
basic: the hotel is rather basic l'hôtel est plutôt rudimentaire *[roodeemontair]*; **will you teach me some basic phrases?** pouvez-vous m'apprendre quelques expressions de base? *[… kelkuh … duh baz]*
basket un panier *[panyay]*
bath un bain *[ban]*; **can I take a bath?** est-ce que je peux prendre un bain? *[eskuh juh puh prondr an ban]*; **could you give me a bath towel?** pouvez-vous me donner une serviette de bain?
bathing la baignade *[ben-yad]*
bathing costume un maillot de bain *[my-o duh ban]*
bathrobe un peignoir *[pen-nwa]*
bathroom la salle de bain *[sal duh ban]*; **a room with a private bathroom** une chambre avec salle de bain; **can I use your bathroom?** où sont les toilettes, s'il vous plaît? *[oo son lay twalet seel voo-play]*
bath salts des sels de bain *[sel duh ban]*
battery (*torch etc*) une pile *[peel]*; **the battery's flat** (*car*) la batterie est à plat *[batuhree et a pla]*
bay la baie *[bay]*
be être *[etr]*; **be reasonable** soyez raisonnable *[swy-yay]*; **don't be lazy** ne soyez pas si paresseux; **where have you been?** où étiez-vous? *[oo aytee-ay voo]*; **I've never been to Nice** je ne suis jamais allé à Nice *[swee jamay zalay]*; *see* **I, you, he** *etc*
beach la plage *[plahj]*; **on the beach** à la plage; **I'm going to the beach** je vais à la plage *[vay]*
beach ball un ballon de plage *[plahj]*
beach café un café sur la plage *[plahj]*

beach mat une natte *[nat]*
beach towel une serviette de bain *[ban]*
beach umbrella un parasol
beads *(necklace)* un collier *[kol-yay]*
beans des haricots *[areeko]*; **broad beans** des fèves *[fev]*
beard la barbe *[barb]*
beautiful beau (belle) *[bo, bel]*; **thank you, that's beautiful** merci, c'est parfait *[say parfay]*
beauty salon un salon de beauté *[bo-tay]*
because parce que *[pars-kuh]*; **because of the weather** à cause du mauvais temps *[a kohz]*
bed un lit *[lee]*; **single bed** un lit pour une personne; **double bed** un lit pour deux personnes; **you haven't made my bed** vous n'avez pas fait mon lit *[voo navay pa fay mon lee]*; **I'm going to bed** je vais me coucher *[vay muh kooshay]*; **he's still in bed** il n'est pas encore levé *[eel nay pa zonkor luhvay]*
bed and breakfast la chambre et le petit déjeuner *[la shombr ay luh ptee day-juhnay]*
bed clothes la literie *[leetree]*
bed linen les draps *[dra]*
bedroom la chambre à coucher *[shombr a kooshay]*
bee une abeille *[abay]*
beef du bœuf *[burf]*
beer de la bière *[bee-air]*; **two beers, please** deux bières, s'il vous plaît
before: before breakfast avant le petit déjeuner *[avon]*; **before I leave** avant mon départ; **I haven't been here before** c'est la première fois que je viens ici *[say la prum-yair fwa kuh juh v-yan zee-see]*
begin: when does it begin? à quelle heure est-ce que ça commence? *[sa kom-mons]*
beginner un débutant *[daybooton]*; **I'm just a beginner** je suis un simple débutant *[sam-pl]*
beginner's slope la piste pour débutants
beginning: at the beginning au début *[o dayboo]*
behaviour le comportement *[—mon]*
behind derrière *[dairyair]*; **the car behind me** la voiture derrière moi
beige beige *[bej]*
Belgian belge *[belj]*
Belgium la Belgique *[beljeek]*
believe: I don't believe you je ne vous

crois pas *[krwa]*; **I believe you** je vous crois
bell *(door)* la sonnette; *(church)* la cloche *[klosh]*
belly-flop un plat-ventre *[pla-vontr]*
belong: that belongs to me c'est à moi *[set a mwa]*; **who does this belong to?** à qui est ceci? *[a kee]*
belongings: all my belongings toutes mes possessions *[posess-yon]*
below en dessous *[on duh-soo]*; **below the knee** au-dessous du genou *[o-duh-soo]*
belt une ceinture *[santœr]*
bend *(in road)* un virage *[veerahj]*
berries des baies *[bay]*
berth *(on ship)* une couchette *[kooshet]*
beside: beside the church à côté de l'église *[a kotay duh]*; **sit beside me** asseyez-vous à côté de moi *[assayay voo]*
besides: besides that de plus *[duh ploss]*
best: the best ... le meilleur ... *[may-yurr]*; **the best hotel in town** le meilleur hôtel de la ville; **that's the best meal I've ever had** c'est le meilleur repas que j'aie jamais mangé *[kuh jay jamay monjay]*
bet: I bet you 500 francs je vous parie 500 francs *[juh voo paree]*
better meilleur *[may-yurr]*; **that's better** c'est mieux *[say m-yuh]*; **are you feeling better?** est-ce que vous vous sentez mieux? *[eskuh voo voo sontay m-yuh]*; **I'm feeling a lot better** je me sens beaucoup mieux *[bo-koo]*; **I'd better be going now** il faut que je m'en aille *[eel fo kuh juh mon eye]*
between entre *[ontr]*
beyond plus loin que *[ploo lwan kuh]*; **beyond the mountains** au-delà des montagnes *[o-dla]*
bicycle une bicyclette *[beeseeklet]*; **can we rent bicycles here?** pouvons-nous louer des bicyclettes ici?
bidet le bidet
big grand *[gron]*; **a big one** un grand; **that's too big** c'est trop grand; **it's not big enough** ce n'est pas assez grand
bigger plus grand *[ploo gron]*
bike une bicyclette *[beeseeklet]*; *(motorbike)* une moto
bikini un bikini
bill l'addition *[adeess-yon]*; **could I have the bill, please?** l'addition, s'il vous plaît
billfold un portefeuille *[portfuh-ee]*

billiards un billard [bee-yar]

binding (ski) la fixation [feexas-yon]

bingo le loto

bird un oiseau [wazo]

biro (tm) un stylo-bille [steelo-bee]

birthday l'anniversaire [aneevairsair]; **it's my birthday** c'est mon anniversaire; **when is your birthday?** c'est quand, votre anniversaire? [say kon]; **happy birthday!** joyeux anniversaire! [jwy-yurz]

biscuit un biscuit [beeskwee]

bit: just a little bit for me pas trop pour moi [pa tro poor mwa]; **a big bit** un gros morceau [gro morso]; **a bit of that cake** un morceau de ce gâteau; **it's a bit too big for me** c'est un peu grand pour moi [set an puh]; **it's a bit cold today** il fait plutôt froid aujourd'hui [eel fay plooto frwa]

bite (by flea etc) un piqûre [peekoor]; **I've been bitten** (by insect) je me suis fait piquer [juh muh swee fay peekay]; **do you have something for bites?** avez-vous quelque chose contre les piqûres d'insecte? [avay-voo kelkuh shohz kontr lay peekoor dansekt]

bitter (taste etc) amer [amair]

bitter lemon un bitter lemon

black noir [nwahr]

black and white (photograph) en noir et blanc [on nwahr ay blon]

blackout: he's had a blackout il a perdu connaissance [eel a pairdoo konaysons]

bladder la vessie [vesee]

blanket une couverture [koovairtoor]; **I'd like another blanket** j'aimerais une couverture supplémentaire

blast! zut! [zoot]

blazer un blazer [blazair]

bleach (for toilet) de l'eau de Javel [ohd javel]

bleed saigner [sayn-yay]; **he's bleeding** il saigne [sayn]

bless you! santé! [sontay]

blind aveugle [avurgl]

blinds les stores [stor]

blind spot l'angle mort [longl mor]

blister une ampoule [ompool]

blocked (road) barré [baray]; (pipe) bouché [booshay]

block of flats un immeuble [eemurbl]

blond blond

blonde une blonde

blood le sang [son]; **his blood group is ...** son groupe sanguin est ... [son groop son-ghan ay]; **I have high blood pressure** j'ai de l'hypertension [eepair-tonsee-yon]

bloody mary un bloody mary

blouse un chemisier [shumeez-yay]

blow-dry un brushing

blue bleu [bluh]

blusher du rouge à joues [rooj a joo]

board: full board la pension complète [pons-yon komplet]; **half-board** la demi-pension

boarding house une pension [pons-yon]

boarding pass la carte d'embarquement [dombarkuh-mon]

boat un bateau [bato]

body le corps [kor]

boil (on skin) un furoncle [fooronkl]; (water) faire bouillir [fair booyeer]

boiled egg un oeuf à la coque [urf ala kok]

boiling hot bouillant [booyon]

bomb une bombe

bone un os [oss]

bonnet (of car) le capot [kapo]

book un livre [leevr]; **I'd like to book a table for two** j'aimerais réserver une table pour deux [jemray rayzairvay]

bookshop, bookstore une librairie [lee-brairee]

boot une botte [bot]; (of car) le coffre [kofr]

booze des boissons [bwasson]; **I had too much booze** j'ai trop bu [jay tro boo]

border (of country) la frontière [frontyair]

bored: I'm bored je m'ennuie [juh mon-nwee]

boring ennuyeux [onweeyuh]

born: I was born in 1960 je suis né en 1960 [swee nay on]

borrow: may I borrow ...? puis-je emprunter ...? [omprantay]

boss le patron [pa-tron]

both les deux [lay duh]; **I'll take both of them** je prends les deux; **we'll both come** nous viendrons tous deux [too duh]

bother: sorry to bother you je suis désolé de vous déranger [duh voo dayron-jay]; **it's no bother** sans problème [son prob-lem]; **it's such a bother** c'est vraiment ennuyeux [say vraymon onweeyuh]

bottle une bouteille [bootay]; **a bottle of wine** une bouteille de vin; **another**

bottle, please encore une bouteille, s'il vous plaît

bottle-opener un ouvre-bouteille *[oovr-bootay]*

bottom *(of person)* le derrière *[dairyair]*; **at the bottom of the hill** au pied de la colline *[o pyay duh la koleen]*

bottom gear la première

bouncer le videur *[veedurr]*

bowels les intestins *[an-testan]*

bowling *(ten pin)* le bowling

bowling green le terrain de bowling *[terran]*

bowls *(game)* les boules *[bool]*

box une boîte *[bwat]*

box lunch le casse-croûte *[kas-kroot]*

box office le guichet *[gheeshay]*

boy un garçon *[garson]*

boyfriend: my boyfriend mon ami *[amee]*

bra un soutien-gorge *[sootyan-gorj]*

bracelet un bracelet *[braslay]*

brake fluid du liquide pour freins *[leekeed poor fran]*

brake lining la garniture de frein *[duh fran]*

brakes les freins *[fran]*; **there's something wrong with the brakes** les freins ne fonctionnent pas bien *[nuh fonks-yon pa b-yan]*; **can you check the brakes?** est-ce que vous pouvez vérifier les freins?; **I had to brake suddenly** j'ai dû freiner brusquement *[jay doo frenay brooskuhmon]*

brandy le cognac

brave courageux *[koorahj-uh]*

bread du pain *[pan]*; **could we have some bread and butter?** est-ce que vous pouvez nous apporter du pain et du beurre? *[nooz aportay doo pan ay doo burr]*; **some more bread, please** encore un peu de pain, s'il vous plaît; **white bread** du pain blanc *[blon]*; **brown bread** du pain noir *[nwar]*; **wholemeal bread** du pain complet *[komplay]*; **rye bread** du pain de seigle *[segl]*

break casser *[kassay]*; **I think I've broken my ankle** je crois que je me suis cassé la cheville *[juh muh swee kassay]*; **it keeps breaking** il n'arrête pas de se casser *[eel naret pa duh suh]*

breakdown une panne *[pan]*; **I've had a breakdown** je suis tombé en panne *[juh*

swee tombay on pan]; **nervous breakdown** une dépression nerveuse *[daypres-yon nairvurz]*

breakfast le petit déjeuner *[ptee dayjuhnay]*; **English/full breakfast** le petit déjeuner anglais *[onglay]*; **continental breakfast** le petit déjeuner

break in: somebody's broken in il y a eu un cambriolage *[eel ya oo an kombree-olahj]*

breast le sein *[san]*

breast-feed nourrir au sein *[nooreer]*

breath le souffle *[soofl]*; **out of breath** essoufflé *[esooflay]*

breathe respirer *[respeeray]*; **I can't breathe** j'ai de la peine à respirer *[jay duh la pen a …]*

breathtaking *(view etc)* superbe *[soopairb]*

breeze une petite brise *[pteet breez]*

breezy *(fresh, cool)* frais *[fray]*

bridal suite la suite réservée aux jeunes mariés *[rayzairvay o jurn maree-yay]*

bride la mariée *[maree-yay]*

bridegroom le marié *[maree-yay]*

bridge un pont *[pon]*; *(card game)* le bridge

brief bref *(brève)* *[bref, brev]*

briefcase une serviette

bright *(light etc)* éclatant *[ayklaton]*; **bright red** rouge vif *[veef]*

brilliant *(idea, person)* génial *[jayneeal]*

bring apporter *[aportay]*; **could you bring it to my hotel?** pourriez-vous me le faire livrer à l'hôtel? *[… muh luh fair leevray …]*; **I'll bring it back** je le rapporterai *[raportuhray]*; **can I bring a friend too?** puis-je amener un(e) ami(e)? *[amenay an/oon amee]*

Britain la Grande-Bretagne *[grond-bruhtan]*

British britannique *[breetaneek]*

brochure un prospectus *[—toos]*; **do you have any brochures on …?** avez-vous des prospectus sur …?

broke: I'm broke je suis fauché *[fohshay]*

broken cassé *[kassay]*; **you've broken it** vous l'avez cassé; **it's broken** c'est cassé; **broken nose** le nez cassé *[… nay …]*

brooch une broche *[brosh]*

brother: my brother mon frère *[frair]*

brother-in-law: my brother-in-law mon beau-frère *[bo-frair]*

brown marron; *(hair)* brun *[bran]*; *(suntanned)* bronzé *[bronzay]*; **I don't go**

brown je ne bronze pas facilement *[juh nuh bronz pa faseelmon]*

brown paper du papier d'emballage *[papee-yay dombalahj]*

browse: may I just browse around? j'aimerais regarder *[jemray ruhgarday]*

bruise un bleu *[bluh]*

brunette une brune *[broon]*

brush une brosse *[bross]*; (*artist's*) un pinceau *[pan-so]*

Brussels sprouts des choux de Bruxelles *[shoo duh broosel]*

bubble bath un bain moussant *[ban mooson]*

bucket un seau

buffet le buffet *[boofay]*

bug (*insect*) une punaise *[poonez]*; **she's caught a bug** elle a attrapé un microbe *[el a atrapay an meekrohb]*

building un bâtiment *[bateemon]*

bulb une ampoule *[ompool]*; **we need a new bulb** nous avons besoin d'une nouvelle ampoule

bump: I bumped my head je me suis cogné la tête *[muh swee kon-yay la tet]*

bumper le pare-chocs *[par-shok]*

bumpy (*road*) cahoteux *[ka-otuh]*

bunch of flowers un bouquet de fleurs *[bookay duh flurr]*

bungalow le bungalow

bunion un oignon *[on-yon]*

bunk une couchette *[kooshet]*

bunk beds des lits superposés *[lee soopair-pozay]*

buoy une bouée *[boo-ay]*

burglar un cambrioleur *[kombree-olurr]*

burn: do you have an ointment for burns? avez-vous de la pommade pour les brûlures? *[brooloor]*

burnt: this meat is burnt cette viande est carbonisée *[karboneezay]*; **my arms are so burnt** j'ai un horrible coup de soleil sur les bras *[jay an orreebl kood solay soor lay bra]*

burst: a burst pipe un tuyau crevé *[twee-o krevay]*

bus le bus *[boos]*; **is this the bus for ...?** est-ce le bus pour ...? *[es]*; **when's the next bus?** à quelle heure part le prochain autocar? *[a kel urr par luh proshan otokar]*

bus driver le conducteur *[kondookturr]*

business les affaires *[afair]*; **I'm here on business** je suis ici pour affaires *[juh swee zee-see]*

bus station la gare routière *[gar rootyair]*

bus stop l'arrêt d'autobus *[aray dotoboos]*; **will you tell me which bus stop I get off at?** pouvez-vous m'indiquer où descendre? *[poovay-voo mandeekay oo dessondr]*

bust la poitrine *[pwatreen]*

bus tour une excursion en autocar

busy (*street*) animé *[aneemay]*; **I'm busy this evening** ce soir, je suis pris(e) *[juh swee pree/preez]*; **the line was busy** la ligne était occupée *[leen aytayt okoopay]*

but mais *[may]*; **not ... but ...** pas ..., mais ...

butcher la boucherie *[booshree]*

butter du beurre *[burr]*

butterfly un papillon *[papeeyon]*

button un bouton *[booton]*

buy: I'll buy it j'aimerais l'acheter *[jemray lashtay]*; **where can I buy ...?** où puis-je acheter ...? *[oo pweej]*

by: by train/plane en train/avion *[on]*; **who's it written by?** qui en est l'auteur? *[kee on ay loturr]*; **it's by Picasso** c'est un tableau de Picasso *[set an tablo duh]*; **I came by myself** je suis venu(e) tout(e) seul(e) *[too(t) surl]*; **a seat by the window** une place près de la fenêtre *[pray duh]*; **by the sea** près de la mer; **can you do it by Wednesday?** pouvez-vous le faire pour mercredi? *[poor]*

bye-bye au revoir

bypass (*road*) une route de contournement *[root duh kontoornuhmon]*

C

cab (*taxi*) un taxi
cabaret un spectacle de variétés [*spek-takl duh varee-aytay*]
cabbage un chou [*shoo*]
cabin une cabine [*kabeen*]
cable (*elec*) un câble [*kabl*]
cablecar un téléphérique [*taylayfayreek*]
café un café
caffeine la caféine [*kafay-een*]
cake un gâteau [*gato*]; **a piece of cake** une tranche de gâteau [*œn tronsh*]
calculator une calculette
calendar le calendrier [*kalondree-ay*]
call: what is this called? comment ça s'appelle? [*komon sa sa-pel*]; **call the manager!** appelez le patron! [*aplay*]; **I'd like to make a call to England** j'aimerais téléphoner en Angleterre [*jemray taylayfonay*]; **I'll call back later** (*come back*) je reviendrai plus tard [*ruhvee-andray*]; (*phone back*) je rappelerai [*ra-pelray*]; **I'm expecting a call from London** j'attends un téléphone de Londres [*jaton zan taylayfon*]; **would you give me a call at 7.30 tomorrow morning?** pouvez-vous me réveiller à 7 heures 30 demain matin? [*poovay-voo muh ray-vayay*]; **the trip has been called off** l'excursion a été annulée [*... a aytay anœlay*]
call box une cabine téléphonique [*kabeen taylayfoneek*]
calm calme; **calm down!** calmez-vous! [*kalmay-voo*]
Calor gas (*tm*) du butagaz
calories les calories
camera un appareil-photo [*aparay—*]
camp: is there somewhere we can camp? connaissez-vous un endroit où nous pouvons camper? [*konessay-voo an ondrwa oo noo poovon kompay*]; **can we camp here?** est-ce qu'on peut camper ici? [*eskon puh*]

campbed un lit de camp [*lee duh kon*]
camping le camping [*kompeeng*]
campsite un terrain de camping [*terran duh kompeeng*]
can: a can of ... une boîte de ... [*bwat duh*]; **a can of beer** une bière en boîte [*bee-air on bwat*]
can: can I ...? puis-je ...? [*pweej*]; **can you ...?** pouvez-vous ...? [*poovay-voo*]; **can he ...?** peut-il ...? [*puhteel*]; **can we ...?** pouvons-nous ...? [*poovon-noo*]; **can they ...?** peuvent-ils (elles) ...? [*puhvteel, puhvtel*]; **I can't ...** je ne peux pas ... [*juh nuh puh pa*]; **he can't ...** il ne peut pas ... [*puh*]; **can I keep it?** est-ce que je peux le garder?; **if I can** si possible [*see poseebl*]; **that can't be right** ce n'est pas possible [*suh nay pa*]
Canada le Canada
Canadian canadien(ne) [*kanadeean, —ee-en*]
canal le canal
cancel annuler [*anœlay*]; **can I cancel my reservation?** puis-je annuler ma réservation? [*pweej*]; **I'd like to cancel dinner for tonight** j'aimerais décommander le dîner de ce soir [*jemray daykomonday luh deenay*]; **I cancelled it** je l'ai annulé [*juh lay anœlay*]
cancellation l'annulation [*anœlasyon*]
candle une bougie [*boo-jee*]
candy des bonbons [*bonbon*]; **a piece of candy** un bonbon
canoe un canoë [*kano-ay*]
can-opener un ouvre-boîte [*oovr-bwat*]
cap (*yachting etc*) la casquette [*kasket*]; (*of bottle*) la capsule; (*of radiator*) le bouchon [*booshon*]; **bathing cap** le bonnet de bain [*bonay duh ban*]
capital city la capitale [*kapeetal*]
capital letters les majuscules [*majœskœl*]
capsize: it capsized il s'est retourné [*eel say ruhtoornay*]

captain le capitaine *[kapeeten]*

car une voiture *[vwatœr]*

carafe une carafe ·

carat: is it 9/14 carat gold? est-ce de l'or à 9/14 carats? *[es duh lor a nurf/katorz kara]*

caravan une caravane

caravan site un camping pour caravanes *[kompeeng poor]*

carbonated gazeux *[gazuh]*

carburet(t)or le carburateur *[karbœraturr]*

card: do you have a (business) card? avez-vous une carte de visite? *[avay voo œn kart duh veeseet]*

cardboard box un carton *[kar-ton]*

cardigan un gilet *[jeelay]*

cards les cartes *[kart]*; **do you play cards?** est-ce que vous jouez aux cartes? *[eskuh voo jooay o kart]* ·

care: will you take care of this bag for me? pouvez-vous me garder ce sac, s'il vous plaît? *[poovay-voo muh garday]*; **care of ...** chez ... *[shay]*

careful: be careful soyez prudent *[swyyay prœdon]*

careless: that was careless of you vous auriez dû faire attention *[voo zoreeay dœ fair atonsee-on]*

careless driving la conduite imprudente *[kondweet amprœdont]*

car ferry un ferry

car hire la location de voitures *[lokas-yon duh vwatœr]*

car keys les clefs de la voiture *[klay duh la vwatœr]*

carnation un œillet *[uhee-yay]*

carnival le carnaval

car park le parking *[parkeeng]*

carpet un tapis *[tapee]*

car rental la location de voitures *[lokas-yon duh vwatœr]*

carrot une carotte

carry porter *[portay]*; **could you carry this for me?** pouvez-vous porter ceci pour moi? *[poovay-voo portay suhsee poor mwa]*

carry-all un fourre-tout *[foortoo]*

carry-cot un porte-bébé *[port-baybay]*

car-sick: I get car-sick je suis malade en voiture *[swee malad on vwatœr]*

carton *(of cigarettes)* une cartouche *[kartoosh]*; **a carton of milk** un carton de lait

carving une sculpture *[skœlp-tœr]*

carwash *(place)* un lave-auto *[lav-oto]*

case *(suitcase)* une valise *[valeez]*; **in any case** de toute façon *[duh toot fasson]*; **in that case** dans ce cas *[don suh ka]*; **it's a special case** c'est un cas spécial; **in case he comes back** au cas où il reviendrait *[o ka oo eel ruhvee-andray]*; **I'll take two just in case** je vais en prendre deux, on ne sait jamais *[on nuh say jamay]*

cash de l'argent liquide *[arjon leekeed]*; **I don't have any cash** je n'ai pas d'argent sur moi *[juh nay pa darjon sœr mwa]*; **I'll pay cash** je paierai en liquide *[juh payray]*; **will you cash a cheque/check for me?** est-ce que vous pouvez me donner de l'argent contre un chèque? *[eskuh voo poovay muh donay duh larjon kontr an shek]*

cashdesk la caisse *[kess]*

cash dispenser un distributeur automatique de billets de banque *[deestreebœturr otomateek duh beeay duh bonk]*

cash register la caisse *[kess]*

casino un casino

cassette une cassette

cassette player un lecteur de cassettes *[lekturr]*

cassette recorder un magnétophone à cassettes *[man-yetofon]*

castle un château *[shato]*

casual: casual clothes des vêtements décontractés *[vetmon daykontraktay]*

cat un chat *[sha]*

catamaran un catamaran *[—ron]*

catastrophe une catastrophe *[katastrof]*

catch: where do we catch the bus? où est-ce qu'on peut prendre le bus? *[weskon puh prondr luh bœs]*; **he's caught some illness** il a attrapé une maladie *[eel a atrapay œn maladee]*

catching: is it catching? est-ce contagieux? *[es kontaj-ee-uh]*

cathedral la cathédrale *[katay-dral]*

Catholic catholique *[kato-leek]*

cauliflower un chou-fleur *[shoo-flurr]*

cause la cause *[kohz]*

cave une grotte *[grot]*

caviar le caviar

ceiling le plafond *[plafon]*

celebrations les festivités *[festeeveetay]*

celery du céleri en branche *[saylree on bronsh]*

cellophane du cellophane

cemetery le cimetière *[seemtee-air]*

center le centre *[sontr]*; *see also* **centre**

centigrade centigrade *[sonteegrad]*; *see page 121*

centimetre, centimeter un centimètre *[sonteemetr]*; *see page 119*

central central *[son-tral]*; **we'd prefer something more central** nous préférons quelque chose de plus central *[noo pray-fairon kelkuh shohz duh plœ]*

central heating le chauffage central *[shofahj son-tral]*

central station la gare principale *[gar pransee-pal]*

centre le centre *[sontr]*; **how do we get to the centre?** pouvez-vous m'indiquer comment aller dans le centre? *[poovay-voo mandeekay komon alay don]*; **in the centre** (*of town*) en ville *[on veel]*

century le siècle *[see-ekl]*; **in the 19th century** au XIXe *[o deeznufee-em]*

ceramics des objets en céramique *[dayz objay on sayrameek]*

certain certain *[sair-tan]*; **are you certain?** est-ce que vous en êtes sûr? *[eskuh voo zon et sœr]*; **I'm absolutely certain** j'en suis certain *[jon swee]*

certainly certainement *[sairten-mon]*; **certainly not** certainement pas *[pa]*

certificate un certificat *[sairteefeeka]*; **birth certificate** un acte de naissance *[akt duh nessons]*

chain la chaîne *[shen]*

chair une chaise *[shez]*

chairlift un télésiège *[taylaysee-ej]*

chalet un chalet

chambermaid la femme de chambre *[fam duh shombr]*

champagne du champagne *[shompan]*

chance: quite by chance tout à fait par hasard *[toota fay par azar]*; **no chance!** certainement pas! *[sairten-mon pa]*

change: could you change this into francs? est-ce que vous pouvez me changer ça en francs? *[eskuh voo poovay muh shonjay sa on fron]*; **I haven't any change** je n'ai pas de monnaie *[juh nay pa duh monay]*; **can you give me change for a 100 franc note?** pouvez-vous me faire la monnaie de 100 francs? *[muh fair la monay duh]*; **do we have to change (trains)?** est-ce qu'il faut changer?

[eskeel fo]; **for a change** pour changer; **you haven't changed the sheets** vous n'avez pas changé les draps *[... shon-jay ...]*; **the place has changed so much** cet endroit a tellement changé *[set ondrwa a telmon]*; **do you want to change places with me?** voulez-vous changer de place avec moi? *[voolay-voo shon-jay duh plas avek mwa]*; **can I change this for ...?** j'aimerais échanger ceci contre ... *[jemray ayshonjay suhsee]*

changeable (*weather*) variable *[varee-abl]*; (*person*) lunatique *[lœnateek]*

channel: the English Channel la Manche *[monsh]*

Channel Islands les îles anglo-normandes *[eel onglo-normond]*

chaos le chaos *[ka-o]*

chap le type *[teep]*; **the chap at reception** le monsieur de la réception *[muh-syuh]*

chapel la chapelle *[sha-pel]*

charge: is there an extra charge? y a-t-il un supplément? *[yateel an sœplay-mon]*; **what do you charge?** combien est-ce que ça va coûter? *[komb-yan eskuh sa va kootay]*; **who's in charge here?** je voudrais parler au patron *[juh voodray parlay o pa-tron]*

charmer: he's a real charmer c'est un charmeur *[sharmurr]*

charming charmant *[sharmon]*

chart un tableau

charter flight un vol charter *[shartair]*

chassis le chassis

cheap bon marché *[bon marshay]*; **do you have something cheaper?** avez-vous quelque chose de meilleur marché? *[avay-voo kelkuh shohz duh may-yurr marshay]*

cheat: I've been cheated je me suis fait avoir *[juh muh swee fay avwahr]*

check: will you check? est-ce que vous pouvez vérifier? *[eskuh voo poovay vay-reef-yay]*; **will you check the steering?** pouvez-vous vérifier la direction?; **I've checked it** j'ai vérifié *[jay]*

check (*money*) un chèque *[shek]*; **will you take a check?** acceptez-vous les chèques? *[axeptay-voo lay]*

check (*bill*) l'addition *[adeess-yon]*; **may I have the check please?** l'addition, s'il vous plaît

checkbook le carnet de chèques *[kar-*

nay duh shek]

checked (*shirt*) à carreaux *[a karo]*

checkers le jeu de dames *[juh duh dam]*

check-in (*at airport*) l'enregistrement des bagages *[onrejeestruh-mon day bagahj]*

checkroom le vestiaire *[vest-yair]*

cheek la joue *[joo];* **what a cheek!** quel culot! *[kel kœlo]*

cheeky effronté *[efrontay]*

cheerio au revoir! *[o ruh-vwa]*

cheers (*thank you*) merci *[mairsee];* (*toast*) santé *[sontay]*

cheer up! courage! *[koorahj]*

cheese du fromage *[fromahj]*

chef le chef

chemist une pharmacie *[farmasee]*

cheque un chèque *[shek];* **will you take a cheque?** acceptez-vous les chèques? *[axeptay-voo lay shek]*

cheque book le carnet de chèques *[karnay duh shek]*

cheque card la carte d'identité bancaire *[kart deedonteetay bonkair]*

cherry la cerise *[suhreez]*

chess les échecs *[layz ayshek]*

chest la poitrine *[pwatreen]*

chewing gum du chewing-gum *[shween-gom]*

chicken du poulet *[poolay]*

chickenpox la varicelle *[vareesel]*

child un enfant *[on-fon];* **children** les enfants

child minder un(e) gardien(ne) d'enfants *[gardyan, —yen]*

child minding service un service de garde d'enfants *[sairvees duh gard donfon]*

children's playground un terrain de jeux *[terran duh juh]*

children's pool la piscine pour enfants *[peeseen poor onfon]*

children's portion une portion pour enfants *[pors-yon poor onfon]*

children's room la chambre d'enfants *[shombr donfon]*

chilled (*wine*) rafraîchi *[rafreshee];* **it's not properly chilled** il n'est pas bien frais *[eel nay pa b-yan fray]*

chilly (*weather*) frisquet *[freeskay]*

chimney la cheminée *[shuhmeenay]*

chin le menton *[monton]*

china la porcelaine; (*adjective*) en porcelaine

chips des frites *[freet];* (**potato**) **chips** des chips *[cheeps]*

chiropodist le pédicure *[paydeekœr]*

chocolate du chocolat *[shokola];* **a chocolate bar** une tablette de chocolat *[tab-let];* **a box of chocolates** une boîte de chocolats *[bwat];* **hot chocolate** un chocolat chaud *[sho]*

choke (*car*) le starter *[startair]*

choose: it's hard to choose j'ai de la peine à choisir *[jay duh la pen a shwazeer];* **you choose for us** choisissez pour nous *[shwazeesay poor noo]*

chop: pork/lamb chop une côtelette de porc/d'agneau *[kot-let duh por/danyo]*

Christian name le prénom *[praynom]*

Christmas Noël *[no-el];* **merry Christmas!** joyeux Noël! *[jwy-uh]*

church une église *[aygleez];* **the Protestant Church** le temple *[tompl];* **the Catholic Church** l'église catholique

cider du cidre *[seedr]*

cigar un cigare *[see-gar]*

cigarette une cigarette *[see—];* **tipped/plain cigarettes** des cigarettes filtre/ordinaires *[feeltr/ordeenair]*

cigarette lighter un briquet *[breekay]*

cine-camera une caméra *[kamayra]*

cinema un cinéma *[seenayma]*

circle un cercle *[sairkl];* (*theatre: seats*) le balcon *[bal-kon]*

citizen le citoyen *[see-twy-an];* **I'm a British/American citizen** je suis britannique/américain(e)

city une ville *[veel]*

city centre, city center le centre-ville *[sontr-veel]*

claim (*insurance*) une demande de remboursement *[duhmond duh romboorsuhmon]*

claim form (*insurance*) le formulaire de déclaration de sinistres *[dayklaras-yon duh seeneestr]*

claret du bordeaux rouge

clarify clarifier *[klareefyay]*

classical classique *[klasseek]*

clean (*adjective*) propre *[propr];* **our apartment hasn't been cleaned today** notre appartement n'a pas été nettoyé aujourd'hui *[… na pa zaytay net-wy-ay …];* **it's not clean** ce n'est pas propre; **can you clean this for me?** (*clothes*) pouvez-vous me nettoyer ceci? *[poovay-voo muh net-*

wy-ay suhsee]

cleaning solution (*for contact lenses*) une solution de nettoyage *[solœss-yon duh net-wy-ahj]*

cleansing cream de la crème démaquillante *[krem daymakeeyont]*

clear: it's not very clear (*meaning*) ce n'est pas clair *[suh nay pa klair]*; **ok, that's clear** (*understood*) d'accord, je comprends *[dakor, juh kom-pron]*

clever intelligent *[antayleejon]*

cliff la falaise *[falez]*

climate le climat *[kleema]*

climb: it's a long climb to the top l'ascension est très longue *[lason-see-yon ay tray long]*; **we're going to climb ...** nous allons escalader ... *[nooz alon eskaladay]*

climber un alpiniste *[alpeeneest]*

climbing boots des chaussures d'escalade *[shohsœr deskalad]*

climbing holiday des vacances d'alpinisme *[vakons dalpeeneesm]*

clinic une clinique *[kleeneek]*

clip (*ski*) l'attache *[latash]*

cloakroom (*for coats*) le vestiaire *[vesteeair]*; (*WC*) les toilettes *[twalet]*

clock une horloge *[orloj]*

close: is it close? est-ce près d'ici? *[es pray deesee]*; **close to the hotel** près de l'hôtel; **close by** tout près d'ici; (*weather*) lourd *[loor]*

close: when do you close? quand est-ce que vous fermez? *[konteskuh voo fairmay]*

closed fermé *[fairmay]*; **they were closed** c'était fermé

closet une armoire *[armwahr]*

cloth (*material*) du tissu *[teesœ]*; (*rag etc*) un chiffon

clothes les vêtements *[vetmon]*

clothes line une corde à linge *[kord a lanj]*

clothes peg, clothespin une pince à linge *[panss a lanj]*

cloud un nuage *[nœ-ahj]*; **it's clouding over** le temps se couvre *[luh tom suh koovr]*

cloudy nuageux *[nwajuh]*

club le club

clubhouse le club

clumsy maladroit *[maladrwa]*

clutch (*car*) l'embrayage *[ombray-ahj]*;

the clutch is slipping l'embrayage patine *[pateen]*

coach un autocar *[otokar]*

coach party un groupe voyageant en autocar *[vwy-ahjon on otokar]*

coach trip une excursion en autocar *[ex-kœrss-yon on otokar]*

coast la côte *[koht]*; **at the coast** au bord de la mer *[o bor duh la mair]*

coastguard le garde-côte *[gard-koht]*

coat (*overcoat etc*) un manteau *[monto]*; (*jacket*) une veste

coathanger un cintre *[santr]*

cobbled street une rue pavée *[rœ pavay]*

cobbler un cordonnier *[kordonyay]*

cockroach un cafard *[kafar]*

cocktail un cocktail

cocktail bar le bar

cocoa (*drink*) du cacao *[kakow]*

coconut une noix de coco *[nwa duh]*

code: what's the (dialling) code for ...? quel est l'indicatif pour ...? *[kelay landeekateef poor]*

coffee un café; **white coffee** un café crème *[krem]*; (*with boiled milk*) un café au lait *[o lay]*; **black coffee** un café (noir) *[nwahr]*; **two coffees, please** deux cafés, s'il vous plaît

coin une pièce de monnaie *[p-yess duh monay]*

Coke (*tm*) un coca

cold froid *[frwa]*; **I'm cold** j'ai froid *[jay]*; **I have a cold** j'ai pris froid *[jay pree]*

coldbox (*for carrying food*) une glacière *[glasyair]*

cold cream de la crème de beauté *[krem duh bo-tay]*

collapse: he's collapsed il s'est effondré *[eel set ayfondray]*

collar le col

collar bone la clavicule *[klaveekœl]*

colleague: my colleague mon (ma) collègue *[koleg]*; **your colleague** votre collègue

collect: I've come to collect ... je suis venu chercher ... *[juh swee vuhnœ shairshay]*; **I collect ...** (*stamps etc*) je collectionne les ... *[koleksee-on]*; **I want to call New York collect** j'aimerais téléphoner à New York en PCV *[jemray taylayfonay ... on pay-say-vay]*

collect call une communication en PCV *[—kasyon on pay-say-vay]*

college l'Université *[œneevairseetay]*

collision une collision *[koleez-yon]*

cologne de l'eau de Cologne

colo(u)r la couleur *[koolurr]*; **do you have any other colours?** l'avez-vous en d'autres teintes? *[lavay voo on dohtr tant]*

colo(u)r film un film couleurs *[feelm koolurr]*

comb un peigne *[pen]*

come venir *[vuhneer]*; **I come from London** je viens de Londres *[juh v-yan]*; **where do you come from?** d'où êtes-vous? *[doo et-voo]*; **when are they coming?** quand arrivent-ils? *[kont areevteel]*; **come here!** venez ici! *[vuhnayz ee-see]*; **come with me** venez avec moi; **come back!** revenez! *[ruhvuhnay]*; **I'll come back later** je reviens tout à l'heure *[juh ruhv-yan tõota lurr]*; **come in!** entrez! *[ontray]*; **he's coming on very well** (*improving*) il fait beaucoup de progrès *[eel fay bokoo duh prog-ray]*; **it's coming on nicely** ça se présente bien *[sa suh prayzont b-yan]*; **come on!** allons! *[alon]*; **do you want to come out this evening?** voulez-vous sortir avec moi ce soir? *[voolay-voo sorteer avek mwa suh swahr]*; **these two pictures didn't come out** ces deux photos ne sont pas sorties *[say duh foto nuh son pa sortee]*; **the money hasn't come through yet** l'argent n'est pas encore arrivé *[larjon nay pa zonkor areevay]*

comfortable confortable *[komfort-abl]*; **it's not very comfortable** ce n'est pas très confortable

Common Market le Marché commun *[marshay koman]*

company (*firm*) une société *[sosyay-tay]*

comparison: there's no comparison il n'y a pas de comparaison possible *[eel nya pa de komparez-on poseebl]*

compartment (*train*) le compartiment *[komparteemon]*

compass une boussole *[boosol]*

compensation des dommages et intérêts *[domahj ay anteray]*

complain se plaindre *[suh plandr]*; **I want to complain about my room ...** c'est incroyable ma chambre ... *[sayt ankrwa-yabl]*

complaint une réclamation *[rayklamas-yon]*

complete complet *[komplay]*; **the complete set** toute la série *[toot la sayree]*; **it's a complete disaster** c'est une vraie catastrophe *[vray katas-trof]*

completely (*finished*) complètement *[kompletmon]*; (*different*) entièrement *[ontee-airmon]*

complicated: it's very complicated c'est très compliqué *[tray kompleekay]*

compliment: my compliments to the chef mes compliments au chef *[may kompleemon zo]*

comprehensive (*insurance*) tous risques *[too reesk]*

compulsory obligatoire *[obleegatwahr]*

computer un ordinateur *[ordeenaturr]*

concern: we are very concerned nous sommes très inquiets *[noo som trayz ankee-ay]*

concert un concert *[konsair]*

concussion une commotion cérébrale *[komos-yon sayray-bral]*

condenser (*car*) le condensateur *[kondonsaturr]*

condition la condition *[kondeesee-on]*; **in very good condition** en très bon état *[on tray bon ayta]*

conditioner (*for hair*) du baume après-shampooing *[bohm apray-shompwan]*

condom un préservatif *[prayzairvateef]*

conductor (*train*) le chef de train *[shef duh tran]*

conference une conférence *[konfay-rons]*

confirm: can you confirm that? pouvez-vous me confirmer cela? *[muh konfeermay]*

confuse: it's very confusing je ne m'y retrouve plus *[juh nuh mee ruhtroov plõo]*

congratulations! félicitations! *[fayleeseetas-yon]*

conjunctivitis une conjonctivite *[konjonkteeveet]*

connecting flight le vol qui assure la correspondance *[... kee asõor ...]*

connection la correspondance

connoisseur un connaisseur

conscious conscient *[kons-yon]*

consciousness: he's lost consciousness il a perdu connaissance *[konay-sons]*

constipation la constipation *[konsteepas-yon]*

consul le consul [kon-sœl]

consulate le consulat [konsœ-la]

contact: how can I contact ...? comment est-ce que je peux contacter ...? [komont eskuh juh puh kontaktay]; **I'm trying to contact ...** j'essaie de contacter ... [jessay]

contact lenses des lentilles de contact [lontee]

continent: on the continent en Europe continentale [on uhrop konteenon-tal]

contraceptive un contraceptif [kontrasepteef]

convenient pratique [prateek]

cook: it's not properly cooked c'est mal cuit [say mal kwee]; **it's beautifully cooked** c'est absolument délicieux [sayt absolœmon daylees-yuh]; **he's a good cook** il cuisine très bien [eel kweezeen tray b-yan]

cooker la cuisinière [kweezeenyair]

cookie un biscuit [beeskwee]

cool frais (fraîche) [fray, fresh]

corduroy du velours côtelé [kotlay]

cork le bouchon [booshon]

corkscrew le tire-bouchon [teerbooshon]

corn (foot) un cor au pied [kor o p-yay]

corner: on the corner au coin de la rue [kwan]; **in the corner** dans le coin; **a corner table** une table tranquille

cornflakes des cornflakes

coronary un infarctus [anfarktœs]

correct exact; **please correct me if I make a mistake** corrigez-moi si je fais des fautes [koreejay-mwa see juh fay day foht]

corridor le corridor

corset le corset [korsay]

cosmetics des produits de beauté [prodwee duh botay]

cost: what does it cost? combien ça coûte? [komb-yan sa koot]

cot un lit d'enfant [lee donfon]

cotton du coton [kot-on]

cotton buds des cotons-tiges [kot-on-teej]

cotton wool du coton hydrophile [kot-on eedrofeel]

couch un canapé [kanapay]

couchette une couchette

cough la toux [too]

cough drops des bonbons pour la toux [bonbon poor la too]

cough medicine un sirop contre la toux [seero kontr la too]

could: could you ...? pourriez-vous ...? [pooreeay-voo]; **could I have ...?** j'aimerais ... [jemray]; **I couldn't find it** je n'ai pas réussi à le trouver [juh nay pa ray-œsee a]

country un pays [payee]; **in the country** à la campagne [ala kompan]

countryside la campagne [kompan]

couple (man and woman) un couple [koopl]; **a couple of ...** quelques ... [kelkuh]

courier le guide [gheed]

course (of meal) le plat [pla]; **of course** bien sûr [b-yan sœr]; **of course not** bien sûr que non [kuh non]

court (law) la cour [koor]; (tennis) le court [koor]

courtesy bus (hotel to airport etc) la navette de l'hôtel [navet duh lotel]

cousin: my cousin mon cousin (ma cousine) [koozan, koozeen]

cover charge le couvert [koovair]

cow une vache [vash]

crab un crabe [krab]

cracked (plate etc) fissuré [feesœray]

cracker un biscuit salé [beeskwee salay]

craftshop une boutique d'artisanat [arteezana]

cramp (in leg etc) une crampe [kromp]

crankshaft le vilebrequin [veelbruhkan]

crash: there's been a crash il y a eu une collision [eelya œ œn koleez-yon]

crash course un cours intensif [koor antonseef]

crash helmet un casque [kask]

crawl (swimming) le crawl [krol]

crazy fou (folle) [foo, fol]

cream de la crème [krem]; (colo(u)r) crème

cream cheese du fromage blanc [fromahj blon]

crèche une crèche

credit card une carte de crédit [kart duh kraydee]

crib (for baby) un lit d'enfant [lee donfon]

crisis la crise [kreez]

crisps des chips [cheeps]

crockery de la vaisselle [vess-el]

crook: he's a crook c'est un escroc [set an eskro]

crossing (by sea) la traversée [travairsay]

crossroads un carrefour [karfoor]

crosswalk un passage pour piétons [pasahj poor pee-ay-ton]

crowd la foule *[fool]*
crowded bondé *[bonday]*
crown (*on tooth*) une couronne *[kooron]*
crucial: it's absolutely crucial c'est absolument essentiel *[set absolœmon esonsee-el]*
cruise une croisière *[krwaz-yair]*
crutch la béquille *[baykee]*; (*of body*) l'entre-jambes *[ontr-jomb]*
cry pleurer *[plurray]*; **don't cry** ne pleurez pas *[nuh plurray pa]*
cucumber le concombre *[konkombr]*
cuisine la cuisine
cultural culturel *[kœltœrel]*
cup une tasse *[tass]*; **a cup of coffee** un café
cupboard une armoire *[armwahr]*
cure: have you got something to cure it? avez-vous quelque chose contre cette maladie? *[avay-voo kelkuh shohz kontr set maladee]*
curlers des bigoudis *[beegoodee]*
current le courant *[kooron]*
curry le curry
curtains les rideaux *[reedo]*

curve le virage *[veerahj]*
cushion un coussin *[koosan]*
custom la coutume *[kootœm]*
customs la douane *[dwan]*
cut: I've cut myself je me suis coupé *[juh muh swee koopay]*; **could you cut a little off here?** pouvez-vous couper un peu par ici? *[poovay-voo koopay]*; **we were cut off** nous avons été coupés *[nooz avon zaytay]*; **the engine keeps cutting out** le moteur a des ratés *[luh moturr a day rahtay]*
cutlery les couverts *[kouvair]*
cutlet une côtelette *[kot-let]*
cycle: can we cycle there? est-ce qu'on peut y aller en vélo? *[eskon puh ee alay on vaylo]*
cycling le cyclisme *[seekleesm]*
cyclist un(e) cycliste *[seekleest]*
cylinder (*car*) le cylindre *[seelandr]*; (*for gas*) la bouteille *[bootay]*
cylinder-head gasket un joint de culasse *[jwan duh kœlass]*
cynical cynique *[seeneek]*
cystitis une cystite *[seesteet]*

D

damage: you've damaged it vous l'avez endommagé *[voo lavay ondoma-jay]*; **it's damaged** c'est abîmé *[set abeemay]*; **there's no damage** il n'y a pas de dégâts *[eel nya pa duh dayga]*
damn! zut! *[zœt]*
damp humide *[œ-meed]*
dance une danse *[dons]*; **do you want to dance?** voulez-vous danser avec moi? *[voolay-voo dansay avek mwa]*
dancer: he's a good dancer il danse très bien *[eel dons tray b-yan]*
dancing: we'd like to go dancing nous aimerions aller danser *[nooz aymuhree-on alay donsay]*
dandruff des pellicules *[peleekœl]*
dangerous dangereux *[donj-ruh]*
dare: I don't dare je n'ose pas *[juh

aohz pa]*
dark sombre *[sombr]*; **dark blue** bleu foncé *[fonsay]*; **when does it get dark?** quand est-ce que la nuit tombe? *[konteskuh la nwee tomb]*; **after dark** après la tombée de la nuit *[tombay]*
darling chéri *[shayree]*
darts les fléchettes *[flayshet]*
dashboard le tableau de bord *[tablo duh bor]*
date: what's the date? quel jour sommes-nous? *[kel joor som-noo]*; **on what date?** à quelle date? *[kel dat]*; **can we make a date?** est-ce que nous pouvons fixer un rendez-vous? *[eskuh noo poovon feexay an ronday-voo]*
dates (*to eat*) des dattes *[dat]*
daughter: my daughter ma fille *[fee]*

daughter-in-law la belle-fille [bel-fee]

dawn l'aurore [oror]; **at dawn** au lever du jour [o luhvay dœ joor]

day un jour [joor]; **the day after** le lendemain [londman]; **the day after tomorrow** après-demain [apray-duhman]; **the day before** la veille [vay]; **every day** chaque jour; **one day** un jour; **can we pay by the day?** pouvons-nous payer à la journée? [joornay]; **have a good day!** bonne journée! [bon]

daylight robbery du vol organisé [organeezay]

day trip une excursion d'une journée [ex-kœrs-yon dœn joornay]

dead mort [mor]

deaf sourd [soor]

deaf-aid un appareil acoustique [aparay akoosteek]

deal (business) une affaire; **it's a deal!** d'accord! [dakor]; **will you deal with it?** est-ce que vous pouvez vous en occuper? [eskuh voo poovay voo zon okœpay]

dealer (agent) un concessionnaire

dear cher [shair]; **Dear Sir** Monsieur; **Dear Madam** Madame; **Dear Alain/ Barbara** (formal) Cher Monsieur/Chère Madame; (to a friend) Cher Alain/Chère Barbara

death la mort [mor]

decadent décadent [daykadon]

December décembre [daysombr]

decent: that's very decent of you c'est très aimable [say trayz em-abl]

decide: we haven't decided yet nous n'avons pas encore décidé [noo navon pa zonkor dayseeday]; **you decide for us** décidez pour nous [dayseeday poor noo]; **it's all decided** c'est tout décidé

decision la décision [dayseez-yon]

deck le pont [pon]

deckchair une chaise longue [shez long]

declare: I have nothing to declare je n'ai rien à déclarer [juh nay ree-an na dayklaray]

decoration (in room) la décoration [daykoras-yon]

deduct déduire [daydweer]

deep profond [profon]; **is it deep?** est-ce que c'est profond? [eskuh say]

deep-freeze le congélateur [konjaylaturr]

definitely certainement [sairten-mon]; **definitely not** certainement pas

degree (university) un diplôme; (temperature) le degré [duhgray]

dehydrated (person) déshydraté [dayzeedratay]

de-icer le dégivreur [day-jeevrurr]

delay: the flight was delayed le vol avait du retard [avay dœ ruhtar]

deliberately exprès [expray]

delicacy: a local delicacy une spécialité de la région [spayss-yaleetay duh la rayjeeon]

delicious délicieux [daylees-yuh]

deliver: can you deliver it? est-ce que vous faites les livraisons? [eskuh voo fet lay leevrezon]

delivery: is there another mail delivery? y a-t-il une seconde distribution? [yateel œn suhgond deestreebœs-yon]

de luxe de luxe [lœx]

denims des jeans

Denmark le Danemark [danmark]

dent: there's a dent in it il est cabossé [eel ay kabossay]

dental floss du fil dentaire [feel dontair]

dentist le dentiste [don-teest]

dentures un dentier [dont-yay]

deny: he denies it il le nie [nee]

deodorant un déodorant [dayodoron]

department store un grand magasin [gron maga-zan]

departure le départ [daypar]

departure lounge le hall de départ [al duh daypar]

depend: it depends ça dépend [sa daypon]; **it depends on ...** ça dépend de ...

deposit (downpayment) un acompte [akont]

depressed déprimé [daypreemay]

depth la profondeur [profondurr]

description la description [deskreepsyon]

deserted (beach etc) désert [dayzair]

dessert le dessert [desair]

destination la destination [desteenasyon]

detergent un détergent [daytair-jon]

detour un détour [daytoor]

devalued dévalué [dayvalœay]

develop: could you develop these films? pouvez-vous développer ces films? [poovay-voo dayv-lopay say feelm]

diabetic diabétique [deeabayteek]

diagram le diagramme [dee—]

dialect le dialecte [dee—]

dialling code l'indicatif [andeekateef]

diamond un diamant [dyamon]

diaper la couche [koosh]

diarrhoea, diarrhea la diarrhée [deea-ray]; **do you have something to stop diarrhoea?** avez-vous quelque chose contre la diarrhée?

diary un agenda [ajonda]

dictionary un dictionnaire [deex-yonair]; **a French/English dictionary** un dictionnaire français/anglais

didn't see **not** and page 116

die mourir [mooreer]; **I'm absolutely dying for a drink** je meurs de soif [juh murr duh swaf]

diesel (fuel) du gas-oil

diet un régime [ray-jeem]; **I'm on a diet** je suis au régime [juh sweez o]

difference la différence [deefayrons]; **what's the difference between …?** quelle différence y a-t-il entre …?; **it doesn't make any difference** peu importe [puh amport]

different: it's different from this one il est différent de l'autre [deefayron]; **may we have a different table?** pourrions-nous avoir une autre table? [pooreeon-noo avwahr oon ohtr]; **they are different** ils ne se ressemblent pas [eel nuh suh ruhsombl pa]; **they are very different** ils ne se ressemblent pas du tout; **ah well, that's different** ah bon, ça change tout [sa shonj too]

difficult difficile [deefeeseel]

difficulty la difficulté [deefeekooltay]; **without any difficulty** sans problème [son prob-lem]; **I'm having difficulties with …** … me pose des problèmes [muh pohz]

digestion la digestion [deejest-yon]

dinghy (rubber) le canot pneumatique [kano pnuhmateek]; (sailing) le dériveur [dayreevurr]

dining car le wagon-restaurant [vagon]

dining room la salle à manger [sala monjay]

dinner le dîner [deenay]

dinner jacket un smoking

dinner party un dîner [deenay]

dipped headlights les phares en code [far on kod]

dipstick la jauge [johj]

direct direct [deerekt]; **does it go direct?** est-ce qu'il est direct? [eskeelay]

direction la direction [deereks-yon]; **in which direction is it?** dans quelle direction est-ce? [es]; **is it in this direction?** est-ce par là?

directory: telephone directory un annuaire du téléphone [annooair doo taylayfon]

directory enquiries les renseignements [ronsen-yuhmon]

dirt la saleté [sal-tay]

dirty sale [sal]

disabled handicapé [ondeekapay]

disagree: it disagrees with me (food) je ne le supporte pas [juh nuh luh sooport pa]

disappear disparaître [deesparetr]; **it's just disappeared** il s'est volatilisé [eel say volateeleezay]

disappointed: I was disappointed ça m'a déçu [sa ma daysoo]

disappointing décevant [day-svon]

disaster un désastre [day-zastr]

discharge (pus) les pertes [pairt]

disc jockey le disc-jockey

disco une discothèque

disco dancing la danse disco [dons]

discount un rabais [rabay]

disease une maladie

disgusting dégoûtant [daygooton]

dish un plat [pla]

dishcloth le torchon à vaisselle [torshon a ves-el]

dishwashing liquid du lave-vaisselle [lav-ves-el]

disinfectant un désinfectant [dayzanfekton]

disk (of film) le disque [deesk]

dislocated shoulder une épaule démise [aypol daymeez]

dispensing chemist une pharmacie

disposable nappies des couches à jeter [koosh a juhtay]

distance la distance [deestons]; **what's the distance from … to …?** quelle distance y a-t-il entre … et …? [kel … yateel ontr]; **in the distance** au loin [o lwan]

distilled water de l'eau distillée [o deesteelay]

distributor (car) le delco

disturb: the disco is disturbing us la discothèque nous dérange [noo dayronj]

diversion (traffic) la déviation [dayveeas-yon]

diving board le plongeoir [plon-jwar]

divorced divorcé [deevorsay]

dizzy: I feel dizzy j'ai la tête qui tourne [jay la tet kee toorn]

dizzy spells des étourdissements [aytoor-deess-mon]

do faire [fair]; **what shall I do?** que faire? [kuh fair]; **what are you doing tonight?** qu'est-ce que vous faites ce soir? [keskuh voo fet suh swahr]; **how do you do it?** comment est-ce que vous faites? [komont eskuh voo fet]; **will you do it for me?** est-ce que vous pouvez le faire pour moi? [eskuh voo poovay]; **who did it?** qui est le coupable? [kee ay luh koopabl]; **the meat's not done** la viande n'est pas bien cuite [pa b-yan kweet]; **what do you do?** (job) qu'est-ce que vous faites dans la vie? [kes kuh voo fet don la vee]; **do you have …?** avez-vous …? [avay-voo]

docks les docks [dok]

doctor un médecin [maydsan]; **he needs a doctor** il faut appeler un médecin [eel foht]; **can you call a doctor?** pouvez-vous appeler un médecin? [poovay-voo aplay]

document un document [dokœmon]

dog un chien [shee-an]

doll une poupée [poopay]

dollar un dollar

donkey un âne [ahn]

don't! non! see **not** and page 119

door (of room) la porte [port]; (of car) la portière [port-yair]

doorman le portier [port-yay]

dormobile (tm) un camping-car

dosage la dose [dohz]

double: double room une chambre pour deux [shombr poor duh]; **double bed** un grand lit [gron lee]; **double brandy** un double cognac [doobl]; **double r** (in spelling name) deux r [duhz]; **it's all double dutch to me** je n'y comprends rien [juh nee kompron ree-an]

doubt: I doubt it j'en doute [jon doot]

douche la douche

doughnut un beignet [benyay]

down: get down! descendez! [duh-sonday]; **he's not down yet** (out of bed) il n'est pas encore levé [pa zonkor luhvay]; **further down the road** plus loin sur cette route [plœ lwan sœr set root]; **I paid**

20% down j'ai payé 20% d'acompte [jay payay van poor son dakont]

downmarket (restaurant etc) simple [sam-pl]

downstairs en bas [on ba]

dozen une douzaine [doozen]; **half a dozen** une demi-douzaine

drain le tuyau d'écoulement [twee-yo day-koolmon]

draughts (game) les dames [dam]

draughty: it's rather draughty il y a un courant d'air [eelya an kooron dair]

drawing pin une punaise [pœnez]

dreadful épouvantable [aypoovontabl]

dream un rêve [rev]; **it's like a bad dream** c'est un véritable cauchemar [set an vayree-tabl kohshmar]; **sweet dreams!** faites de beaux rêves! [fet duh bo rev]

dress (woman's) une robe [rob]; **I'll just get dressed** je vais aller m'habiller [juh vay zalay mabeeyay]

dressing (for wound) un pansement [pons-mon]; (for salad) la vinaigrette

dressing gown une robe de chambre [rob duh shombr]

drink boire [bwahr]; **can I get you a drink?** aimeriez-vous boire quelque chose? [emreeay voo bwahr kelkuh shohz]; **I don't drink** je ne bois pas d'alcool [juh nuh bwa pa dalkol]; **a long cool drink** un grand verre d'une boisson glacée [gron vair dœn bwasson glassay]; **may I have a drink of water?** puis-je avoir un verre d'eau? [pweej avwahr an vair do]; **drink up!** finissez votre verre! [feeneesay votr vair]; **I had too much to drink** j'ai trop bu [jay tro bœ]

drinkable (water) potable [pot-abl]

drive: we drove here nous sommes venus en voiture [noo som vuhnœ on vwatœr]; **I'll drive you home** je vais vous reconduire [juh vay voo ruhkondweer]; **do you want to come for a drive?** voulez-vous venir faire un tour en voiture? [… fair an toor …]; **is it a very long drive?** est-ce très loin d'ici? [es tray lwan dee-see]

driver (of car) le conducteur [kon-dœkturr]; (of bus) le chauffeur

driver's license le permis de conduire [pairmee duh kondweer]

drive shaft l'arbre de transmission [arbr

duh tronsmeess-yon]

driving licence le permis de conduire [pairmee duh kondweer]

drizzle: it's drizzling il bruine [eel brween]

drop: just a drop une petite goutte [œn pteet goot]; **I dropped it** je l'ai laissé tomber [juh lay lessay tombay]; **drop in some time** venez me voir [vuhnay muh vwar]

drown: he's drowning il est en train de se noyer [eel et on tran duh suh nwy-yay]

drug un médicament [maydeekamon]

drugstore une pharmacie (general goods are not sold here)

drunk ivre [eevr]

drunken driving la conduite en état d'ivresse [kondweet on ayta deevress]

dry sec (sèche) [sek, sesh]

dry-clean nettoyer à sec [netwy-yay a sek]

dry-cleaner le teinturier [tantœreeay]

duck le canard [kanar]

due: when is the bus due? quand est-ce que le bus doit arriver? [kont eskuh luh bœs dwat areevay]

dumb muet [mœay]; (stupid) bête [bet]

dummy (for baby) la tétine [tayteen]

durex (tm) un préservatif [prayzairvateef]

during pendant [pondon]

dust la poussière [pooss-yair]

dustbin la poubelle [poo-bel]

Dutch hollandais [olonday]

Dutchman un Hollandais [olonday]

Dutchwoman une Hollandaise [olondez]

duty-free (goods) hors taxe [or tax]

duvet la couette [kwet]

dynamo la dynamo [deenamo]

dysentery la dysenterie [deesantree]

E

each: each of them tous [toos]; **one for each of us** un par personne [an par pairson]; **how much are they each?** combien est-ce qu'ils sont la pièce? [komb-yan eskeel son la pee-es]; **each time** chaque fois [shak fwa]; **we know each other** nous nous connaissons [noo noo konesson]

ear l'oreille [oray]

earache le mal d'oreille [doray]

early tôt [toh]; **early in the morning** tôt le matin; **it's too early** c'est trop tôt; **a day earlier** un jour plus tôt [plœ toh]; **half an hour earlier** une demi-heure plus tôt; **I need an early night** je vais aller me coucher tôt [juh vay zalay muh kooshay toh]

early riser: I'm an early riser je suis un lève-tôt [juh swee zan levto]

earring une boucle d'oreille [bookl doray]

earth la terre [tair]

earthenware la poterie [potree]

earwig un perce-oreille [pairs oray]

east l'est [est]; **to the east** vers l'est

Easter Pâques [pak]

easy facile [faseel]; **easy with the cream!** pas trop de crème! [pa tro duh krem]

eat manger [monjay]; **something to eat** quelque chose à manger [kelkuh shohz]; **we've already eaten** nous avons déjà mangé [noo zavon dayja monjay]

eau-de-Cologne de l'eau de Cologne

eccentric original [oreejeenal]

edible mangeable [mon-jabl]

efficient (staff) capable [kap-abl]; (hotel) bien organisé [b-yan organeezay]

egg un œuf [urf]

eggplant une aubergine [obairjeen]

Eire l'Irlande du Sud [eerlond dœ sœd]

either: either ... or ... soit ..., soit ... [swa]; **I don't like either of them** je n'aime ni l'un ni l'autre [nee lan nee lohtr]

elastic élastique [aylasteek]

elastic band un élastique [aylasteek]

Elastoplast (tm) un pansement adhésif [ponsmon adayzeef]

elbow le coude [kood]

electric électrique [aylektreek]

electric blanket une couverture chauffante [koovairtœr shohfont]

electric cooker une cuisinière électrique [kweezeen-yair aylektreek]

electric fire un radiateur électrique [radyaturr aylektreek]

electrician un électricien [aylektreess-yan]

electricity l'électricité [aylektreeseetay]

electric outlet une prise [preez]

elegant élégant [aylaygon]

elevator l'ascenseur [asonsurr]

else: something else quelque chose d'autre [kelkuh shohz dohtr]; **somewhere else** ailleurs [eye-yurr]; **let's go somewhere else** allons ailleurs [alon]; **what else?** quoi d'autre? [kwa]; **nothing else, thanks** c'est tout, merci [say too]

embarrassed gêné [jenay]

embarrassing gênant [jaynon]

embassy l'ambassade [ombasad]

emergency une urgence [œrjons]; **this is an emergency** il s'agit d'une urgence [eel sajee dœn]

emery board une lime à ongles en carton [leem a ongl on kar-ton]

emotional (person) émotif [aymoteef]

empty vide [veed]

end la fin [fan]; **at the end of the street** au bout de la rue [o boo duh la rœ]; **when does it end?** quand est-ce que ça finit? [konteskuh sa feenee]

energetic plein d'énergie [plan daynair-jee]

energy l'énergie [aynairjee]

engaged (toilet, telephone) occupé [okœpay]; (person) fiancé [f-yonsay]

engagement ring une bague de fiançailles [bag duh f-yons-eye]

engine le moteur [moturr]

engine trouble des ennuis mécaniques [on-nwee maykaneek]

England l'Angleterre [ongluhtair]

English anglais [onglay]; **the English** les Anglais [layz]; **I'm English** je suis anglais(e); **do you speak English?** parlez-vous l'anglais? [parlay voo]

English woman une Anglaise [onglez]

enjoy: I enjoyed it very much j'ai beaucoup aimé [jay bo-koop aymay]; **enjoy yourself!** amusez-vous bien! [amœzay voo b-yan]

enjoyable très agréable [trayz agrayabl]

enlargement (of photo) un agrandissement [agrondeesmon]

enormous énorme [aynorm]

enough assez [asay]; **there's not enough ...** il n'y a pas assez de ... [eel nya pa]; **it's not big enough** ce n'est pas assez grand; **thank you, that's enough** merci, ça suffit [sœfee]

entertainment: what sort of entertainment is there? qu'y a-t-il à faire? [kyateel a fair]

enthusiastic enthousiaste [ontoozeeast]

entrance l'entrée [ontray]

envelope une enveloppe [onvlop]

epileptic un épileptique

equipment (diving etc) du matériel [matayree-el]

eraser une gomme [gom]

erotic érotique [ayroteek]

error une erreur [errurr]

escalator un escalier roulant [eskalyay roolon]

especially spécialement [spays-yalmon]

espresso un express

essential essentiel [aysons-yel]

estate agent une agence immobilière [ajons eemobeelyair]

ethnic (restaurant etc) typiquement français [teepeekmon fronsay]

Eurocheque un eurochèque [uhroshek]

Eurocheque card une carte eurochèque [kart uhroshek]

Europe l'Europe [uhrop]

European européen(ne) [uhropay-an, —en]

European plan la demi-pension [duh-mee pons-yon]

even: even the French même les Français [mem]; **even if ...** même si ...

evening le soir [swahr]; **good evening** bonsoir; **this evening** ce soir; **in the evening** le soir; **evening meal** le repas du soir

evening dress la tenue de soirée [tuhnœ duh swaray]; (woman's) une robe du soir [rob dœ swahr]

eventually finalement [feenalmon]

ever: have you ever been to Boston? est-ce que vous êtes déjà allé à Boston? [eskuh voo zet dayja alay a]; **if you ever come to Britain** si un jour vous venez en Grande-Bretagne [see an joor *voo vuhnay]*

every chaque *[shak]*; **every day** chaque jour

everyone tout le monde *[tool mond]*

everything tout *[too]*

everywhere partout *[partoo]*

exactly! exactement! *[exaktuhmon]*

exam un examen *[examan]*

example un exemple *[exompl]*; **for example** par exemple

excellent excellent *[exsaylon]*

except sauf *[sohf]*; **except Sunday** sauf le dimanche

exception une exception *[exsepsyon]*; **as an exception** à titre exceptionnel *[a teetr exsepsyonel]*

excess un excès *[exsay]*

excess baggage un excédent de bagages *[exsaydon duh bagahj]*

excessive (*bill etc*) excessif; **that's a bit excessive** c'est vraiment exagéré *[say vraymon exajayray]*

exchange (*money*) le change *[shonj]*; (*telephone*) le central *[sontral]*; **in exchange** en échange *[ayshonj]*

exchange rate: what's the exchange rate? quel est le cours du change? *[kel ay luh koor dœ shonj]*

exciting passionnant *[pas-yonon]*

exclusive (*club etc*) sélect *[saylekt]*

excursion une excursion *[exkœrs-yon]*; **is there an excursion to ...?** y a-t-il une excursion organisée pour aller à ... *[ya-teel œn ...]*

excuse me pardon *[par-don]*

exhaust (*car*) le tuyau d'échappement *[twee-o dayshapmon]*

exhausted épuisé *[aypweezay]*

exhibition une exposition *[expozeess-yon]*

exist: does it still exist? (*café etc*) est-ce qu'il existe toujours? *[eskeel exeest too-joor]*

exit la sortie *[sortee]*

expect: I expect so je pense que oui *[juh pons kuh wee]*; **she's expecting** elle attend un enfant *[el aton an onfon]*

expensive cher *[shair]*

experience: an absolutely unforgettable experience une expérience inoubliable *[expayree-ons eenooblee-abl]*

experienced expérimenté *[expayree-montay]*

expert un expert *[expair]*

expire: it's expired il n'est plus valable *[eel nay plœ val-abl]*

explain expliquer *[expleekay]*; **would you explain that to me?** pouvez-vous m'expliquer? *[poovay-voo]*

explore explorer *[exploray]*; **I just want to go and explore** je veux partir à la découverte *[juh vuh parteer ala day-koovair]*

export l'exportation *[exportas-yon]*

exposure meter un posemètre *[pohz-metr]*

express (*mail*) par exprès

extra: can we have an extra chair? pouvons-nous avoir encore une chaise? *[...onkor œn ...]*; **is that extra?** est-ce un supplément? *[es on sœplaymon]*

extraordinary extraordinaire

extremely extrêmement *[extrem-mon]*

extrovert extraverti *[—vairtee]*

eye un œil *[uh-ee]*; **your eyes** vos yeux *[voz yuh]*; **will you keep an eye on it for me?** pouvez-vous me le garder, s'il vous plaît? *[poovay-voo muh luh garday]*

eyebrow le sourcil *[soorsee]*

eyebrow pencil un crayon à sourcils *[soorsee]*

eye drops des gouttes pour les yeux *[goot poor layz juh]*

eyeliner de l'eye-liner

eye shadow le fard à paupières *[far a pohp-yair]*

eye witness un témoin oculaire *[tay-mwan okœlair]*

F

fabulous fabuleux *[fabœoluh]*

face le visage *[veezahj]*

face mask (*diving*) un masque de plongée *[mask duh plonjay]*

face pack un masque de beauté *[mask duh bo-tay]*

facing: facing the sea avec vue sur la mer *[avek vœ]*

fact un fait *[fay]*

factory une usine *[œzeen]*

Fahrenheit *see page 121*

faint: she's fainted elle s'est évanouie *[el set ayvanwee]*; **I think I'm going to faint** je crois que je vais m'évanouir *[juh krwa kuh juh vay mayvanweer]*

fair la foire *[fwar]*; **it's not fair** ce n'est pas juste *[suh nay pa jœost]*; **ok, fair enough** bon, d'accord *[dakor]*

fake un faux *[fo]*

fall: he's had a fall il est tombé *[eel ay tombay]*; **he fell off his bike** il est tombé de son vélo *[vaylo]*; **in the fall** (*autumn*) en automne *[on oton]*

false faux (fausse) *[fo, fohs]*

false teeth un dentier *[dont-yay]*

family la famille *[famee]*

family hotel une pension de famille *[pons-yon duh famee]*

family name le nom de famille *[nom duh famee]*

famished: I'm famished je meurs de faim *[juh murr duh fam]*

famous célèbre *[saylebr]*

fan (*mechanical*) le ventilateur *[vonteela-tur]*; (*hand held*) un éventail *[ayvont-eye]*; (*football etc*) un fan

fan belt la courroie du ventilateur *[koorwa dœ vonteelaturr]*

fancy: he fancies you vous lui plaisez *[voo lwee plezay]*

fancy dress un déguisement *[daygheez-mon]*

fantastic fantastique *[fontasteek]*

far loin *[lwan]*; **is it far?** c'est loin d'ici? *[say lwan deessee]*; **how far is it to the Louvre?** est-ce que le Louvre est loin d'ici?; **as far as I'm concerned** quant à moi *[konta mwa]*

fare le prix du billet *[pree dœ beeyay]*; **what's the fare to ...?** combien coûte le billet pour ...? *[komb-yan koot]*

farewell party une fête d'adieu *[fet dad-yuh]*

farm une ferme *[fairm]*

farther plus loin *[plœ lwan]*; **farther than ...** plus loin que ...

fashion la mode *[mod]*

fashionable à la mode

fast rapide *[rapeed]*; **not so fast!** pas si vite! *[pa see veet]*

fat (*adjective*) gros (grosse) *[gro, gros]*; (*on meat*) le gras *[gra]*

father: my father mon père *[pair]*

father-in-law le beau-père *[bo-pair]*

fathom une brasse (*1,83 m*) *[brass]*

fattening: it's fattening ça fait grossir *[sa fay groseer]*

faucet le robinet *[robeenay]*

fault un défaut *[dayfo]*; **it was my fault** c'est de ma faute *[say duh ma foht]*; **it's not my fault** ce n'est pas de ma faute

faulty défectueux *[dayfektœo-uh]*

favo(u)rite préféré *[prayfay-ray]*; **that's my favourite** c'est mon préféré

fawn (*colour*) fauve *[fohv]*

February février *[fayvree-ay]*

fed up: I'm fed up j'en ai assez *[jon ay asay]*; **I'm fed up with ...** j'en ai par-dessus la tête de ... *[jon ay parduhsœ la tet duh]*

feeding bottle un biberon *[beebron]*

feel: I feel hot/cold j'ai chaud/froid *[jay sho/frwa]*; **I feel like a drink** j'ai envie de boire quelque chose *[jay onvee duh]*; **I don't feel like it** je n'en ai pas envie *[juh non ay pa zonvee]*; **how are you feeling**

today? comment vous sentez-vous aujourd'hui? *[komon voo sontay-voo ojoordwee]*; **I'm feeling a lot better** je me sens beaucoup mieux *[juh muh son bo-koo m-yuh]*

felt-tip (pen) un stylo-feutre *[steelo-furtr]*

fence la barrière *[baree-air]*

ferry le ferry; **what time's the last ferry?** à quelle heure part le dernier ferry? *[a kel urr]*

festival un festival *[festeeval]*

fetch: I'll go and fetch it je vais aller le chercher *[juh vayz alay luh shairshay]*; **will you come and fetch me?** est-ce que vous pouvez venir me chercher? *[eskuh voo poovay vuh-neer muh]*

fever la fièvre *[fee-evr]*

feverish: I'm feeling feverish je me sens fiévreux *[juh muh son fee-evruh]*

few: only a few pas trop *[pa troh]*; **a few minutes** quelques minutes *[kelkuh]*; **he's had a good few** (*to drink*) il a pas mal bu *[eel a pa mal bœ]*

fiancé: my fiancé mon fiancé *[fee-onsay]*

fiancée: my fiancée ma fiancée *[fee-onsay]*

fiasco: what a fiasco! quel désastre! *[kel dayzastr]*

field un champ *[shom]*

fifty-fifty moitié-moitié *[mwateeay]*

fight une bagarre *[bagar]*

figs des figues *[feeg]*

figure (*number*) un chiffre *[sheefr]*; **I have to watch my figure** je dois faire attention à ma ligne *[juh dwa fair atons-yon a ma leen]*

fill remplir *[rompleer]*; **fill her up please** le plein, s'il vous plaît *[luh plan]*; **will you help me fill out this form?** pouvez-vous m'aider à remplir ce formulaire? *[poovay-voo mayday]*

fillet un filet *[feelay]*

filling (*tooth*) un plombage *[plombahj]*

filling station une station-service *[stas-yon sairvees]*

film un film *[feelm]*; **do you have this type of film?** avez-vous ce genre de film? *[avay-voo]*; **16mm film** film 16 mm *[sez meeleemetr]*; **35mm film** film 24 × 36 *[vant-katr tront-seess]*

film processing le développement des films *[dayv-lopmon day feelm]*

filter un filtre *[feeltr]*

filter-tipped à bout filtre *[a boo feeltr]*

filthy (*room etc*) crasseux *[krassuh]*

find trouver *[troovay]*; **I can't find it** je n'arrive pas à le retrouver *[juh nareev pa a luh ruh—]*; **if you find it** si vous le trouvez; **I've found a …** j'ai trouvé un … *[jay troovay]*

fine: it's fine weather il fait beau *[eel fay bo]*; **a 50 francs fine** une amende de 50 francs *[amond]*; **thank you, that's fine** (*to waiter etc*) merci, ça va comme cela *[sa va kom suhla]*; **how are you? — fine, thanks** comment allez-vous? — bien, merci *[b-yan]*

finger le doigt *[dwa]*

fingernail un ongle *[ongl]*

finish: I haven't finished je n'ai pas fini *[juh nay pa feenee]*; **when I've finished** quand j'aurai terminé *[kon joray tair-meenay]*; **when does it finish?** à quelle heure est-ce que ça finit? *[a kel urr eskuh sa feenee]*; **finish off your drink** videz votre verre *[veeday votr vair]*

Finland la Finlande *[fanlond]*

fire: fire! au feu! *[o fuh]*; **may we light a fire here?** pouvons-nous faire du feu ici? *[poovon-noo fair dœ fuh]*; **it's on fire** il (elle) a pris feu *[eel a pree fuh]*; **it's not firing properly** l'allumage ne fonctionne pas bien *[lalœmahj nuh fonks-yon pa b-yan]*

fire alarm l'avertisseur d'incendie *[avair-teesurr dansondee]*

fire brigade, fire department les pompiers *[pomp-yay]*

fire escape la sortie de secours *[sortee duh suhkoor]*

fire extinguisher un extincteur *[extank-turr]*

firm (*company*) une entreprise *[ontruh-preez]*

first premier *[pruhm-yay]*; **I was first** (*in queue*) je suis arrivé avant vous *[juh sweez areevay avon voo]*; **at first** tout d'abord *[too dabor]*; **this is the first time** c'est la première fois *[… pruhm-yair …]*

first aid les premiers secours *[pruhm-yay suhkoor]*

first aid kit une trousse de premiers secours *[troos duh pruhm-yay suhkoor]*

first class (*travel*) en première classe *[on pruhm-yair klass]*

first name le prénom *[praynom]*

fish du poisson *[pwasson]*
fisherman un pêcheur *[peshurr]*
fishing la pêche *[pesh]*
fishing boat le bateau de pêche *[bato duh pesh]*
fishing net le filet *[feelay]*
fishing rod une canne à pêche *[kan a pesh]*
fishing tackle l'attirail de pêche *[ateer-eye duh pesh]*
fishing village un village de pêcheurs *[veelahj duh peshurr]*
fit (*healthy*) en bonne condition physique *[on bon kondees-yon feezeek]*; **I'm not very fit** je ne suis pas très en forme *[pa trayz on form]*; **a keep fit fanatic** un fana de culture physique; **it doesn't fit** ce n'est pas la bonne taille *[suh nay pa la bon t-eye]*
fix: can you fix it? (*arrange*) est-ce que vous pouvez organiser cela? *[eskuh voo poovay organeezay suhla]*; (*repair*) est-ce que vous pouvez le réparer? *[rayparay]*; **let's fix a time** fixons une heure; **it's all fixed up** c'est tout décidé *[say too day-seeday]*
fizzy mousseux *[moosuh]*
fizzy drink une boisson gazeuse *[bwasson gazurz]*
flab (*on body*) des bourrelets *[boor-lay]*
flag un drapeau *[drapo]*
flannel (*for washing*) un gant de toilette *[gon duh twalet]*
flash (*phot*) un flash
flashcube une ampoule de flash *[ompool]*
flashlight une lampe de poche *[lomp duh posh]*
flashy (*clothes*) tape-à-l'œil *[tap-a-luh-ee]*
flat (*adjective*) plat *[pla]*; **this beer is flat** cette bière est éventée *[set bee-air et ayvontay]*; **I've got a flat (tyre)** j'ai un pneu à plat *[jay an pnuh a pla]*; (*apartment*) un appartement *[apartuhmon]*
flatterer un flatteur *[flaturr]*
flatware les couverts *[koovair]*
flavo(u)r le goût *[goo]*
flea la puce *[pœss]*
flea powder de la poudre contre les puces *[poodr kontr lay pœss]*
flexible flexible *[flexeebl]*
flies (*on trousers*) la braguette *[braghet]*
flight un vol
flippers des palmes *[pal-m]*

flirt flirter *[flurtay]*
float flotter *[flotay]*
flood une inondation *[eenondas-yon]*
floor (*of room*) le plancher *[plonshay]*; (*storey*) l'étage *[aytahj]*; **on the floor** par terre *[par tair]*; **on the second floor** (*UK*) au second *[o suhgon]*; (*USA*) au premier *[o pruhm-yay]*
floorshow un spectacle de variétés *[spek-takl duh vareeaytay]*
flop (*failure*) un désastre *[dayzastr]*
florist le fleuriste *[flurreest]*
flour la farine *[fareen]*
flower la fleur *[flurr]*
flu la grippe *[greep]*
fluent: he speaks fluent French il parle couramment le français *[eel parl koo-ramon luh fronsay]*
fly voler *[volay]*; **can we fly there?** pou-vons-nous y aller en avion? *[alay on avyon]*
fly (*insect*) la mouche *[moosh]*
fly spray de l'insecticide *[ansekteeseed]*
foggy: it's foggy il y a du brouillard *[eelya dœ brooyar]*
fog light le phare antibrouillard *[far ontee-brooyar]*
folk dancing les danses folkloriques *[dons]*
folk music la musique folklorique
follow suivre *[sweevr]*; **follow me!** suivez-moi! *[sweevay-mwa]*
fond: I'm quite fond of ... j'aime beau-coup ... *[jem bo-koo]*
food la nourriture *[nooreetœr]*; **the food's excellent** la nourriture est excellente
food poisoning une intoxication alimen-taire *[antoxeekas-yon aleemontair]*
food store un magasin d'alimentation *[magazan daleemontas-yon]*
fool un imbécile *[ambayseel]*
foolish insensé *[ansonsay]*
foot le pied *[p-yay]*; **on foot** à pied; *see page 119*
football le football; (*ball*) le ballon de foot-ball
for: is that for me? est-ce pour moi? *[es poor mwa]*; **what's this for?** à quoi est-ce que ça sert? *[a kwa eskuh sa sair]*; **I've been here for a week** je suis ici depuis une semaine *[... duhpwee zoon ...]*; **a bus for ...** un bus pour ...
forbidden interdit *[antairdee]*

forehead le front [fron]

foreign étranger [aytronjay]

foreigner un étranger [aytronjay]

foreign exchange le change [shonj]

forest une forêt [foray]

forget oublier [ooblee-ay]; **I forget, I've forgotten** j'ai oublié [jay ooblee-ay]; **don't forget** n'oubliez pas [nooblee-ay pa]

fork une fourchette [foorshet]; (in road) un embranchement [ombronshmon]

form (document) un formulaire

formal (person) guindé [ganday]; (dress) de soirée [duh swaray]

fortnight quinze jours [kanz joor]

fortunately heureusement [urrurzmon]

fortune-teller une diseuse de bonne aventure [deezurz duh bon avontoor]

forward: could you forward my mail? est-ce que vous pouvez faire suivre mon courrier? [eskuh voo poovay fair sweevr mon koor-yay]

forwarding address une adresse pour faire suivre le courrier [poor fair sweevr luh koor-yay]

foundation cream du fond de teint [fon duh tan]

fountain une fontaine [fonten]

foyer (of cinema etc) le foyer

fracture une fracture [frak-toor]

fractured skull une fracture du crâne [frak-toor duh kran]

fragile fragile [fra-jeel]

frame (picture) un cadre

France la France [frons]

fraud une escroquerie [eskrokree]

free libre [leebr]; (no charge) gratuit [grat-wee]; **admission free** entrée libre

freeway l'autoroute [otoroot]

freezer un congélateur [konjaylaturr]

freezing: it's freezing cold il fait un froid de loup [eel fet an frwa duh loo]

French français(e) [fronsay, —ez]; (language) le français

French fries des frites [freet]

Frenchman un Français [fronsay]

Frenchwoman une Française [fronsez]

frequent fréquent [fraykon]

fresh frais (fraîche) [fray, fresh]; **don't get fresh with me** pas d'impertinences [pa dampairteenons]

fresh orange juice une orange pressée [oronj pressay]

friction tape du chatterton

Friday vendredi [vondruhdee]

fridge un frigo [freego]

fried egg un œuf sur le plat [urf soor luh pla]

friend un ami (une amie) [amee]

friendly amical [ameekal]

frog une grenouille [gruhnwee]

frogs' legs des cuisses de grenouille [kweess duh gruhnwee]

from: I'm from London/Chicago je viens de Londres/Chicago [juh v-yan duh]; **from here to the beach** d'ici à la plage [dee-see]; **the next boat from ...** le prochain bateau en provenance de ... [provnons duh]; **as from Tuesday** à partir de mardi [a parteer duh]

front le devant [duhvon]; **in front** devant; **in front of us** devant nous; **at the front** à l'avant [a lavon]

frost le gel [jel]

frostbite des gelures [juhloor]

frozen gelé [juhlay]

frozen food des aliments surgelés [aleemon soorjuhlay]

fruit des fruits [frwee]

fruit juice un jus de fruit [joo duh frwee]

fruit machine une machine à sous [soo]

fruit salad une salade de fruits [duh frwee]

frustrating: it's very frustrating c'est très frustrant [tray froostron]

fry frire [freer]; **nothing fried** pas de friture [pa duh freetoor]

frying pan une poêle [pwal]

full plein [plan]; **it's full of ...** c'est plein de ...; **I'm full** j'ai trop mangé [jay tro monjay]

full-board la pension complète [pons-yon komplet]

full-bodied (wine) qui a du corps [kee a doo kor]

fun: it's fun c'est amusant [set amoozon]; **it was great fun** je me suis bien amusé [juh muh swee b-yan amoozay]; **just for fun** seulement pour rire [surlmon poor reer]; **have fun!** amusez-vous bien! [amoozay voo b-yan]

funeral un enterrement [ontairmon]

funny drôle

furniture les meubles [murbl]

further plus loin [ploo lwan]; **it's 2 kilometres further** il y a encore deux kilomè-

tres *[eelya onkor]*; **further down the road** plus loin sur cette route *[root]*
fuse un fusible *[fœzeebl]*; **the lights have fused** les plombs ont sauté *[lay plom on sohtay]*

fuse wire le fusible *[fœzeebl]*
future le futur *[fœtœr]*; **in future** à l'avenir *[a lavneer]*

G

gale une tempête *[tompet]*
gallon un gallon *[ga-lon]*; *see page 121*
gallstone un calcul biliaire *[kalkœl beel-yair]*
gamble jouer *[jooay]*; **I don't gamble** je n'aime pas les jeux d'argent *[juh nem pa lay juh darjon]*
game le jeu *[juh]*; *(sport)* la partie *[partee]*
games room la salle de jeux *[sal duh juh]*
gammon du jambon *[jombon]*
garage un garage *[ga-rahj]*
garbage les ordures *[ordœr]*
garden le jardin *[jardan]*
garlic l'ail *[eye]*
gas le gaz; *(gasoline)* l'essence *[essonss]*
gas cylinder une bouteille de gaz *[boo-tay]*
gasket un joint *[jwan]*
gas pedal l'accélérateur *[axaylayraturr]*
gas permeable lenses des lentilles semi-rigides *[lontee suhmee-reejeed]*
gas station une station-service *[stas-yon-sairvees]*
gas tank le réservoir *[rayzairvwahr]*
gastroenteritis une gastro-entérite *[-ontayreet]*
gate le portail *[port-eye]*; *(at airport)* la porte *[port]*
gauge *(fuel etc)* la jauge *[johj]*
gay *(homosexual)* homosexuel
gear *(car)* la vitesse *[veetess]*; *(equipment)* le matériel *[matayree-el]*; **the gears stick** j'ai de la peine à passer les vitesses *[jay duh la pen a passay les veetess]*
gearbox la boîte de vitesses *[bwat duh veetess]*
gear lever, gear shift le levier de vitesses *[luhv-yay duh veetess]*
general delivery la poste restante

generous: that's very generous of you c'est vraiment très généreux de votre part *[say vraymon tray jaynayruh]*
gentleman: that gentleman over there ce monsieur -là-bas *[muh-syuh]*; **he's such a gentleman** c'est un vrai gentleman *[set an vray]*
gents les toilettes *[lay twalet]*
genuine authentique *[otenteek]*
German allemand *[almon]*
German measles la rubéole *[rœbayol]*
Germany l'Allemagne *[alman]*
get: have you got …? avez-vous …? *[avay-voo]*; **how do I get to …?** pouvez-vous m'indiquer comment aller à …? *[poovay-voo mandeekay komon alay]*; **where do I get them from?** où puis-je en trouver? *[oo pweej on troovay]*; **can I get you a drink?** puis-je vous offrir un verre? *[… ofreer …]*; **will you get it for me?** pouvez-vous me l'obtenir? *[muh lob-tuhneer]*; **when do we get there?** à quelle heure est-ce que nous arrivons? *[a kel urr eskuh noo zareevon]*; **I've got to go** il faut que je m'en aille *[eel fo kuh juh mon eye]*; **where do I get off?** où dois-je descendre? *[oo dwaj daysondr]*; **it's difficult to get to** ce n'est pas un endroit facile à atteindre *[suh nay pa zan ondrwa faseel a atandr]*; **when I get up** *(in morning)* à mon réveil *[rayvay]*
ghastly épouvantable *[aypoovont-abl]*
ghost un fantôme *[fontohm]*
gift un cadeau *[kado]*
gigantic gigantesque *[jeegontesk]*
gin du gin *[djeen]*; **a gin and tonic** un gin-tonic
girl une fille *[fee]*
girlfriend: my girlfriend mon amie

[amee]

give donner *[donay]*; **will you give me ...?** est-ce que vous pouvez me donner ...? *[eskuh voo poovay muh donay]*; **I gave it to him** je le lui ai donné *[juh luh lwee ay donay]*; **I'll give you 20 francs** je vous en donne 20 francs *[juh vay]*; **would you give this to ...?** pouvez-vous donner ceci à ..., s'il vous plaît? *[poovay-voo donay suhsee]*; **will you give it back?** est-ce que vous me le rendrez? *[muh luh rondray]*

glad content *[konton]*; **I'm so glad** je suis ravi *[ravee]*

glamorous superbe *[soopairb]*

gland la glande *[glond]*

glandular fever une mononucléose infectieuse *[mononooklayohz anfexee-urz]*

glass le verre *[vair]*; **a glass of water** un verre d'eau *[vair doh]*

glasses des lunettes *[loonet]*

gloves des gants *[gon]*

glue de la colle *[kol]*

gnat un moucheron *[mooshron]*

go aller *[alay]*; **we want to go to ...** nous aimerions aller à ... *[nooz emree-on alay a]*; **I'm going there tomorrow** j'y vais demain *[jee vay duhman]*; **when does it go?** *(leave)* à quelle heure part-il? *[a kel urr parteel]*; **where are you going?** où allez-vous? *[oo alay voo]*; **let's go!** allons-y! *[alonzee]*; **he's gone** *(left)* il est parti *[eel ay partee]*; **it's all gone** il n'y en a plus *[eel n-yon a ploo]*; **I went there yesterday** j'y suis allé hier *[jee swee zalay eeair]*; **a hotdog to go** un hot-dog à emporter *[a omportay]*; **go away!** allez-vous en! *[alay-voozon]*; **the milk has gone off** le lait a tourné; **we're going out tonight** nous sortons ce soir *[noo sorton]*; **do you want to go out tonight?** voulez-vous sortir ce soir? *[voolay-voo sorteer]*; **has the price gone up?** le prix a-t-il augmenté? *[luh pree ateel ohgmontay]*

goal *(sport)* un but *[boo]*

goat une chèvre *[shevr]*

goat's cheese du fromage de chèvre *[fromahj duh shevr]*

God Dieu *[d-yuh]*

goggles *(ski)* des lunettes de ski *[loonet]*; *(diving)* des lunettes de plongée *[plonjay]*

gold l'or

golf le golf

golf clubs des crosses de golf *[kross]*

golf course un terrain de golf *[terran]*

good bon (bonne) *[bon]*; **good!** très bien! *[tray b-yan]*; **that's no good** ça ne va pas *[sa nuh va pa]*; **good heavens!** grands dieux! *[gron d-yuh]*

goodbye au revoir! *[o rvwar]*

good-looking séduisant *[saydweezon]*

gooey *(food etc)* gluant *[gloo-on]*

goose une oie *[wa]*

gooseberries des groseilles à maquereau *[gro-zay a makro]*

gorgeous splendide *[splondeed]*; *(meal)* merveilleux *[mairvay-yuh]*

gourmet un fin gourmet *[fan]*

gourmet food de la bonne cuisine

government le gouvernement *[goovair-nuhmon]*

gradually peu à peu *[puh a puh]*

gram(me) un gramme; *see page 119*

grammar la grammaire

granddaughter la petite-fille *[pteet-fee]*

grandfather le grand-père *[gron-pair]*

grandmother la grand-mère *[gron-mair]*

grandson le petit-fils *[ptee-feess]*

grapefruit un pamplemousse *[pompluh-mooss]*

grapefruit juice un jus de pamplemousse *[joo duh pompluh-mooss]*

grapes du raisin *[rez-an]*

grass l'herbe *[airb]*

grateful reconnaissant *[ruhkonesson]*; **I'm very grateful to you** je vous suis très reconnaissant *[juh voo swee]*

gravy la sauce *[sohss]*

gray gris *[gree]*

grease *(on food)* la graisse *[gress]*; *(car)* le lubrifiant *[loobreefeeon]*

greasy *(cooking)* gras (grasse) *[gra, grass]*

great grand *[gron]*; *(very good)* fantastique *[fontasteek]*; **that's great!** c'est formidable! *[say formee-dabl]*

Great Britain la Grande-Bretagne *[grond-bruhtan]*

Greece la Grèce *[gress]*

greedy *(for food)* gourmand *[goormon]*

green vert *[vair]*

green card *(insurance)* la carte verte *[kart vairt]*

greengrocer un marchand de légumes *[marshon duh laygoom]*

grey gris *[gree]*

grilled grillé *[gree-yay]*

gristle *(meat)* le cartilage *[karteelahj]*

grocer une épicerie *[aypeesree]*
ground le sol; **on the ground** par terre *[par tair]*; **on the ground floor** au rez-de-chaussée *[rayd-shoh-say]*
ground beef du bœuf haché *[burf hashay]*
group un groupe *[groop]*
group insurance une assurance collective *[assœrons kolekteev]*
group leader le responsable *[respons-abl]*
guarantee une garantie *[garontee]*; **is it guaranteed?** y a-t-il une garantie? *[yateel]*
guardian le tuteur (la tutrice) *[tœtur,*

—treess]
guest un invité *[anveetay]*
guesthouse une pension *[pons-yon]*
guest room la chambre d'amis *[shombr damee]*
guide (*tourist*) le guide *[gheed]*
guidebook un guide *[gheed]*
guilty coupable *[koop-abl]*
guitar la guitare *[gheetar]*
gum (*in mouth*) la gencive *[jonseev]*
gun un revolver *[rayvol-vair]*; (*rifle*) un fusil *[fœzee]*
gymnasium le gymnase *[jeemnaz]*
gyn(a)ecologist un gynécologue *[jeenaykolog]*

H

hair les cheveux *[shuhvuh]*
hairbrush une brosse à cheveux *[bross a shuhvuh]*
haircut une coupe de cheveux *[koop duh shuhvuh]*; **just an ordinary haircut, please** une coupe simple, s'il vous plaît *[... sampl ...]*
hairdresser le coiffeur *[kwafurr]*
hairdryer un sèche-cheveux *[sesh-shuhvuh]*
hair foam de la mousse (pour les cheveux) *[poor lay shuhvuh]*
hair gel du gel (pour les cheveux) *[jel (poor lay shuhvuh)]*
hair grip une pince à cheveux *[panss a shuhvuh]*
hair lacquer de la laque *[lak]*
half la moitié *[mwateeay]*; **half an hour** une demi-heure *[duhmee-urr]*; **a half portion** une demi-portion *[duhmee-pors-yon]*; **half a litre** un demi-litre; **half as much** la moitié de cela; *see page 118*
halfway: halfway to Geneva à mi-chemin de Genève *[mee-shuhman]*
ham du jambon *[jombon]*
hamburger un hamburger *[omboorgair]*
hammer un marteau *[marto]*
hand la main *[man]*; **will you give me a**

hand? pourriez-vous me donner un coup de main? *[pooreeay-voo muh donay an koo duh man]*
handbag un sac à main *[a man]*
hand baggage les bagages à main *[bagahj a man]*
handbrake le frein à main *[fran a man]*
handkerchief un mouchoir *[mooshwar]*
handle (*door, cup*) la poignée *[pwanyay]*; **will you handle it?** est-ce que vous pouvez vous en charger? *[eskuh voo poovay voo zon sharjay]*
hand luggage les bagages à main *[bagahj a man]*
handmade fait à la main *[fay ala man]*
handsome beau (belle) *[bo, bel]*
hanger (*for clothes*) un cintre *[santr]*
hangover la gueule de bois *[gurl duh bwa]*; **I've got a terrible hangover** j'ai une gueule de bois épouvantable
happen: how did it happen? comment est-ce arrivé? *[komon es areevay]*; **what's happening** qu'est-ce qui se passe? *[keskee suh pas]*; **it won't happen again** ça ne se reproduira pas *[sa nuh suh ruhprodweera pa]*
happy heureux *[ur-ruh]*; **we're not happy with the room** la chambre ne nous

plaît pas *[nuh noo play pa]*
harbo(u)r le port *[por]*
hard dur *[dœr]*; (*difficult*) difficile *[dee-feeseel]*
hard-boiled egg un œuf dur *[urf dœr]*
hard lenses des lentilles rigides *[lontee reejeed]*
hardly à peine *[a pen]*; **hardly ever** presque jamais *[presk jamay]*
hardware store une quincaillerie *[kan-ky-ree]*
harm du mal
hassle: it's too much hassle c'est trop compliqué *[say tro kompleekay]*; **a hassle-free holiday** des vacances sans problèmes *[son prob-lem]*
hat un chapeau *[shapo]*
hatchback une familiale *[fameeleeal]*
hate: I hate ... je déteste ... *[daytest]*
have avoir *[avwahr]*; **do you have ...?** avez-vous ...? *[avay-voo]*; **can I have ...?** j'aimerais ... *[jemray]*; **can I have some water?** est-ce que je peux avoir de l'eau? *[eskuh juh puh]*; **I have ...** j'ai ... *[jay]*; **I don't have ...** je n'ai pas ... *[juh nay pa]*; **can we have breakfast in our room?** pouvez-vous nous monter le petit déjeuner? *[poovay-voo noo montay]*; **have another** (*drink etc*) encore un verre? *[on-kor an vair]*; **I have to leave early** je dois partir tôt *[juh dwa]*; **do I have to ...?** est-ce que je dois ...? *[eskuh juh dwa]*; **do we have to ...?** est-ce que nous devons ...? *[eskuh noo duhvon]*; *see page 113*
hay fever le rhume des foins *[rœm day fwan]*
he il *[eel]*; **is he here?** est-il ici? *[eteel]*; *see page 108*
head la tête *[tet]*; **we're heading for Amiens** nous sommes en route pour Amiens *[noo som zon root]*
headache un mal de tête *[mal duh tet]*
headlight le phare *[far]*
headphones des écouteurs *[aykooturr]*
head waiter le maître d'hôtel *[metr dotel]*
head wind un vent contraire *[von kon-trair]*
health la santé *[sontay]*; **your health!** à votre santé! *[votr]*
healthy bon pour la santé *[sontay]*; (*person*) bien portant *[b-yan porton]*
hear: can you hear me? m'entendez-vous? *[montonday-voo]*; **I can't hear**

you je ne vous entends pas *[juh nuh voo zonton pa]*; **I've heard about it** j'en ai entendu parler *[jon ay ontondœ parlay]*
hearing aid un appareil acoustique *[aparay akoosteek]*
heart le cœur *[kurr]*
heart attack une crise cardiaque *[kreez kardyak]*
heat la chaleur *[shalurr]*; **not in this heat!** pas avec cette chaleur!
heater (*in car*) le chauffage *[shohfahj]*
heating le chauffage *[shohfahj]*
heat rash une éruption due à la chaleur *[ayrœps-yon dœ ala shalurr]*
heat stroke un coup de chaleur *[koo duh shalurr]*
heatwave une vague de chaleur *[vag duh shalurr]*
heavy lourd *[loor]*
hectic trépidant *[traypeedon]*
heel le talon; **could you put new heels on these?** pouvez-vous refaire les talons? *[poovay-voo ruhfair lay talon]*
heelbar un talon-minute *[talon-meenœt]*
height (*of mountain*) l'altitude; (*of person*) la taille *[tie]*
helicopter un hélicoptère *[ayleekoptair]*
hell: oh hell! flûte! *[flœt]*; **go to hell!** allez au diable! *[alay zo dee-abl]*
hello bonjour *[bonjoor]*; (*in surprise*) tiens! *[t-yan]*; (*on phone*) allô
helmet (*motorcycle*) le casque *[kask]*
help aider *[ayday]*; **can you help me?** est-ce que vous pouvez m'aider? *[eskuh voo poovay mayday]*; **thanks for your help** merci de votre aide *[mairsee duh votr ed]*; **help!** au secours! *[o suhkoor]*
helpful: he was very helpful il a été très obligeant *[eel a aytay trayz obleejon]*; **that's helpful of you** c'est très aimable *[em-abl]*
helping (*of food*) une portion *[pors-yon]*
hepatitis une hépatite *[aypateet]*
her: I don't know her je ne la connais pas *[juh nuh la konay pa]*; **will you send it to her?** pouvez-vous le lui envoyer? *[luh lwee onvwy-ay]*; **it's her** c'est elle *[set el]*; **with her** avec elle; **that's her suitcase** c'est sa valise; *see pages 107, 108*
herbs des fines herbes *[feenz airb]*
here ici *[ee-see]*; **here you are** (*giving something*) voilà *[vwala]*; **here he comes** le voilà

hers: that's hers c'est à elle *[set a el]*; *see page 111*

hey! hé! *[hay]*

hiccups le hoquet *[okay]*

hide cacher *[kashay]*

hideous affreux *[afruh]*

high haut *[o]*

high beam: on high beam pleins feux *[plan fuh]*

highchair (*for baby*) une chaise haute *[shez oht]*

highlighter (*cosmetics*) une ombre à paupières *[ombr a pohpyair]*

highway l'autoroute *[otoroot]*

hiking la randonnée *[rondonay]*

hill une colline *[koleen]*; **it's further up the hill** c'est plus haut *[say plœ o]*

hillside le flanc de la colline *[flon duh la koleen]*

hilly vallonné *[valonay]*

him: I don't know him je ne le connais pas *[juh nuh luh konay pa]*; **will you send it to him?** pouvez-vous le lui envoyer? *[luh lwee onvwy-ay]*; **it's him** c'est lui; **with him** avec lui; *see page 108*

hip la hanche *[onsh]*

hire: can I hire a car? j'aimerais louer une voiture *[jemray looay]*; **do you hire them out?** est-ce que vous les louez? *[eskuh voo lay looay]*

his son (sa); **it's his drink** c'est son verre; **it's his** c'est à lui *[set a lwee]*; *see pages 107, 111*

history l'histoire *[eestwahr]*

hit: he hit me il m'a frappé *[frapay]*; **I hit my head** je me suis cogné la tête *[juh muh swee konyay la tet]*

hitch: is there a hitch? y a-t-il un problème? *[yateel an prob-lem]*

hitch-hike faire de l'auto-stop *[fair duh lotostop]*

hitch-hiker un auto-stoppeur (une auto-stoppeuse) *[otostopur, —purz]*

hit record un hit

Holland la Hollande *[olond]*

hole un trou *[troo]*

holiday les vacances *[vakonss]*; **I'm on holiday** je suis en vacances

home (*house*) la maison *[mezzon]*; **at home** chez moi *[shay mwa]*; (*in my own country*) dans mon pays *[don mon payee]*; **I go home tomorrow** je rentre demain *[juh rontr duhman]*

home address le domicile permanent *[domeeseel pairmanon]*

homemade fait maison *[fay mezzon]*

homesick: I'm homesick j'ai le mal du pays *[jay luh mal dœ payee]*

honest honnête *[onet]*

honestly? vraiment? *[vraymon]*

honey du miel *[mee-el]*

honeymoon la lune de miel *[lœn duh mee-el]*; **it's our honeymoon** nous sommes en voyage de noces *[noo som zon vwy-ahj duh nos]*; **a second honeymoon** une seconde lune de miel *[suhgond]*

honeymoon suite la suite pour jeunes mariés *[sweet poor jurn maree-ay]*

hoover (*tm*) un aspirateur *[aspeeraturr]*

hope espérer *[espairay]*; (*noun*) l'espoir *[espwahr]*; **I hope so** j'espère que oui *[jespair kuh wee]*; **I hope not** j'espère que non *[jespair kuh non]*

horn (*car*) le klaxon *[klaxon]*

horrible horrible *[oreebl]*

horse un cheval *[shuhval]*

horse riding l'équitation *[aykeetas-yon]*

hose (*car radiator*) un durit (*tm*) *[dœreet]*

hospital un hôpital *[opee-tal]*

hospitality l'hospitalité *[—ectay]*; **thank you for your hospitality** merci pour votre hospitalité

hostel le foyer; **youth hostel** l'auberge de jeunesse *[obairj duh jur-ness]*

hot chaud *[sho]*; (*curry etc*) épicé *[aypeesay]*; **I'm hot** j'ai chaud *[jay sho]*; **something hot to eat** quelque chose de chaud; **it's so hot today** il fait si chaud aujourd'hui *[eel fay see]*

hotdog un hot-dog

hotel un hôtel *[otel]*; **at my hotel** dans mon hôtel

hotel clerk le (la) réceptionniste *[raysepsyoneest]*

hotplate (*on cooker*) une plaque chauffante *[plak shohfont]*

hot-water bottle une bouillotte *[boo-yot]*

hour une heure *[urr]*; **on the hour** à l'heure juste

house une maison *[mezzon]*

housewife une ménagère *[maynajair]*

how comment *[komon]*; **how many?** combien? *[komb-yan]*; **how many …?** combien de …?; **how much?** combien?; **how often?** tous les combien? *[too lay]*; **how**

are you? comment allez-vous? *[komont alay-voo]*; **how do you do?** enchanté! *[onshontay]*; **how about a beer?** et si on allait prendre une bière? *[ay see on alay prondr]*; **how nice of you!** c'est vraiment aimable à vous! *[say vraymon em-abl]*; **would you show me how to?** pouvez-vous me montrer comment faire? *[poovay-voo muh montray komon fair]*

humid humide *[oo-meed]*

humidity l'humidité *[oomeedeetay]*

humo(u)r: where's your sense of humo(u)r? n'avez-vous pas le sens de l'humour? *[navay-voo pa luh sons duh loomoor]*

hundredweight *see page 120*

hungry: I'm hungry j'ai faim *[jay fam]*; **I'm not hungry** je n'ai pas faim *[juh nay pa fam]*

hurry: I'm in a hurry je suis pressé *[juh swee pressay]*; **hurry up!** dépêchez-vous! *[daypeshay-voo]*; **there's no hurry** ce n'est pas pressé *[suh nay pa pressay]*

hurt: it hurts ça fait mal *[sa fay mal]*; **my back hurts** j'ai mal aux reins *[jay mal o ran]*

husband: my husband mon mari *[ma-ree]*

hydrofoil un hydrofoil *[eedro—]*

I

I je *[juh]*; **I am English** je suis anglais(e) *[swee]*; *see page 108*

ice la glace *[glass]*; **with ice** avec des glaçons *[glasson]*

ice-cream une glace *[glass]*

ice-cream cone un cornet de glace *[kornay duh glass]*

iced coffee un café glacé *[glassay]*

idea idée *[eeday]*; **good idea!** bonne idée!

ideal idéal *[eeday-al]*

identity papers les papiers *[pap-yay]*

idiot idiot *[eedee-o]*

idyllic idyllique *[eedeeleek]*

if si *[see]*; **if you could** si vous pouviez *[poovee-ay]*; **if not** sinon *[seenon]*

ignition l'allumage *[aloomahj]*

ill malade *[malad]*; **I feel ill** je ne me sens pas bien *[juh nuh muh son pa b-yan]*

illegal illégal *[eelay-gal]*

illegible illisible *[eeleezeebl]*

illness une maladie *[maladee]*

imitation (*leather etc*) une imitation *[eemeetas-yon]*

immediately tout de suite *[toot sweet]*

immigration l'immigration *[eemeegras-yon]*

import importer *[amportay]*

important important *[amporton]*; **it's**

very important c'est très important *[say trayz]*; **it's not important** ça ne fait rien *[sa nuh fay ree-an]*

impossible impossible *[amposs-eebl]*

impressive impressionnant *[ampress-yonon]*

improve: the weather is improving le temps s'améliore *[samayleeor]*; **I want to improve my French** je veux améliorer mon français *[juh vuhz amayleeoray mon …]*

improvement des progrès *[prog-ray]*

in: in my room dans ma chambre *[don]*; **in the town centre** dans le centre-ville; **in London** à Londres; **in one hour's time** dans une heure; **in August** en août *[on]*; **in English** en anglais; **in French** en français; **is he in?** est-ce qu'il est là? *[eskeel ay la]*

inch un pouce *[pooss]*; *see page 119*

include: is that included in the price? est-ce compris dans le prix? *[es kompree]*; **does that include meals?** est-ce que les repas sont compris?

inclusive compris *[kompree]*

incompetent incompétent *[ankompay-ton]*

inconvenient inopportun *[eenoportan]*

increase une augmentation *[ohgmontas-yon]*

incredible incroyable *[ankrwy-abl]*

indecent indécent *[andayson]*

independent indépendant *[andaypon-don]*

India l'Inde *[and]*

Indian indien(ne) *[andee-an, —en]*

indicator le clignotant *[kleen-yoton]*

indigestion une indigestion *[andeejest-yon]*

indoor pool une piscine couverte *[pee-seen koovairt]*

indoors à l'intérieur *[lantay-ree-urr]*

industry l'industrie *[andœstree]*

inefficient inefficace *[eenefeekass]*

infection une infection *[anfex-yon]*

infectious contagieux *[kontahj-yuh]*

inflammation une inflammation *[an-flamas-yon]*

inflation l'inflation *[anflas-yon]*

informal simple *[sam-pl]*

information le renseignement *[ronsen-yuhmon]*

information desk les renseignements *[ronsen-yuhmon]*

information office le bureau de rensei-gnements *[bœro duh ronsen-yuhmon]*

injection une piqûre *[pee-kœr]*

injured blessé *[blessay]*; **she's been in-jured** elle est blessée

injury une blessure *[blessœr]*

in-law: my in-laws mes beaux-parents *[bo-paron]*

innocent innocent *[eenoson]*

inquisitive curieux *[kœree-uh]*

insect un insecte *[ansekt]*

insect bite une piqûre d'insecte *[peekœr dansekt]*

insecticide un insecticide *[ansekteeseed]*

insect repellent une crème anti-insecte *[krem ontee-ansekt]*

inside: inside the tent dans la tente *[don]*; **let's sit inside** allons nous asseoir à l'intérieur *[lantayree-urr]*

insincere hypocrite *[eepokreet]*

insist: I insist j'insiste *[janseest]*

insomnia l'insomnie *[ansomnee]*

instant coffee du café soluble *[solœbl]*

instead: I'll have that one instead dans ce cas, je prendrai celui-ci *[don suh ka]*; **instead of ...** au lieu de ... *[o l-yuh duh]*

insulating tape du chatterton

insulin l'insuline *[ansœleen]*

insult une injure *[anjœr]*

insurance une assurance *[asœrons]*; **write your insurance company here** écrivez le nom de votre assurance ici *[aykreevay]*

insurance policy une police d'assurance *[poleess dasœrons]*

intellectual un(e) intellectuel(le) *[an—]*

intelligent intelligent *[antayleejon]*

intentional: it wasn't intentional je ne l'ai pas fait exprès *[juh nuh lay pa fay expray]*

interest: places of interest les endroits à visiter *[ondrwa a veezeetay]*

interested: I'm very interested in ... je m'intéresse beaucoup à ... *[mantay-ress bo-koo]*

interesting intéressant *[antayresson]*; **that's very interesting** c'est très intéres-sant

international international *[antairnas-yonal]*

interpret faire l'interprète *[fair lantair-pret]*; **would you interpret?** pouvez-vous traduire? *[poovay-voo tradweer]*

interpreter un interprète *[antairpret]*

intersection un carrefour *[karfoor]*

interval (*in play etc*) un entracte *[ontrakt]*

into dans *[don]*; **I'm not into that** (*don't like*) ça ne m'intéresse pas *[sa nuh mantay-ress pa]*

introduce: may I introduce ...? puis-je vous présenter ...? *[pweej voo pray-zontay]*

introvert introverti *[antrovairtee]*

invalid un invalide *[anvaleed]*

invalid chair un fauteuil roulant *[fotuh-ee roolon]*

invitation une invitation *[anveetas-yon]*; **thank you for the invitation** merci pour votre invitation

invite inviter *[anveetay]*; **can I invite you out tonight?** puis-je vous inviter à sortir ce soir? *[pweej voo zanveetay a sorteer suh swahr]*

involved: I don't want to get involved in it je ne veux pas m'en mêler *[juh nuh vuh pa mon melay]*

iodine de l'iode *[yod]*

Ireland l'Irlande *[eerlond]*

Irish irlandais *[eerlonday]*

Irishman un Irlandais *[eerlonday]*

Irishwoman une Irlandaise *[eerlondez]*

iron (*for clothes*) un fer à repasser *[fair a ruh-passay]*; **can you iron these for me?** pouvez-vous me repasser ces vêtements? *[vetmon]*

ironmonger le quincailler *[kan-ky-ay]*

is *see page 113*

island une île *[eel]*; **on the island** sur l'île

isolated isolé *[eezolay]*

it ça *[sa]*; (*masculine*) il *[eel]*; (*feminine*) elle *[el]*; **it is ...** c'est ... *[say]*; **is it ...?** est-ce ...? *[es]*; **where is it?** (*a place etc*) où est-ce que c'est? *[weskuh say]*; (*object*) où est-il (elle)? *[oo eteel, —tel]*; **it's her** c'est elle *[set el]*; **it's only me** ce n'est que moi *[suh nay kuh mwa]*; **it was ...** c'était ... *[saytay]*; **that's just it!** justement! *[joostuhmon]*; **that's it** (*that's right*) c'est ça *[say sa]*; *see page 108*

Italian italien(ne) *[eetalyan, —en]*

Italy l'Italie *[eetalee]*

itch: it itches ça me démange *[sa muh daymonj]*

itinerary un itinéraire *[eeteenayrair]*

IUD le stérilet *[stayreelay]*

J

jack (*for car*) un cric *[kreek]*

jacket une veste *[vest]*

jacuzzi un jacousi

jam de la confiture *[konfeetoor]*; **traffic jam** un embouteillage *[ombootay-yahj]*; **I jammed on the brakes** j'ai freiné à bloc *[jay frenay a blok]*

January janvier *[jonveeay]*

jaundice la jaunice *[joneess]*

jaw la mâchoire *[mashwahr]*

jazz le jazz

jazz club un club de jazz

jealous jaloux *[jaloo]*

jeans des jeans

jellyfish une méduse *[maydooz]*

jet-setter: he is a jet-setter il fait partie du jet-set *[eel fay partee doo]*

jetty la jetée *[juhtay]*

Jew un Juif *[jweef]*

jewel(le)ry des bijoux *[beejoo]*

Jewish juif (juive) *[jweef, jweev]*

jiffy: just a jiffy! une seconde! *[suhgond]*

job un travail *[trav-eye]*; **just the job!** exactement ce qu'il nous faut *[exak-tuhmon suhkeel noo fo]*; **it's a good job you told me!** heureusement que vous me l'avez dit! *[ururzmon kuh voo'muh lavay dee]*

jog: I'm going for a jog je vais faire du jogging *[juh vay fair]*

jogging le jogging

join: I'd like to join je voudrais devenir membre *[juh voodray duhvneer mombr]*; **can I join you?** (*go with*) est-ce que je peux venir avec vous? *[eskuh juh puh vuhneer avek voo]*; (*sit with*) est-ce que je peux me joindre à vous? *[jwandr a voo]*

joint (*in bone*) une articulation *[ar-teekoolas-yon]*; (*to smoke*) un joint *[jwan]*

joke une plaisanterie *[plezzontree]*; **you've got to be joking!** vous plaisantez! *[voo plezzontay]*; **it's no joke** ce n'est pas drôle *[suh nay pa drohl]*

jolly: it was jolly good c'était fantastique *[saytay fontasteek]*; **jolly good!** très bien!

journey un voyage *[vwy-ahj]*; **have a good journey!** bon voyage!

jug un pot *[po]*; **a jug of water** une carafe d'eau *[do]*

July juillet *[jwee-yay]*

jump: you made me jump vous m'avez fait sursauter *[voo mavay fay soorsohtay]*; **jump in!** (*to car*) montez! *[montay]*

jumper un pull *[pool]*

jump leads un câble de raccordement (pour batterie) *[kahbl duh rakorduhmon (poor batree)]*

junction un croisement *[krwazmon]*

June juin *[jwan]*

junior: Mr Jones junior M. Jones fils
[feess]
junk du bric-à-brac
just: just one for me un seul pour moi *[an
surl]*; **it's just me** c'est moi *[say mwa]*;
just for me pour moi *[poor mwa]*; **just a
little** un petit peu *[an ptee puh]*; **just

here ici *[ee-see]*; **not just now** pas maintenant *[pa]*; **he just left** il vient de partir
[eel v-yan duh parteer]; **that's just right**
c'est parfait *[parfay]*; **it's just as good**
c'est tout aussi bien *[say toot o-see
b-yan]*; **that's just as well** tant mieux
[ton m-yuh]

K

kagul un suranorak *[soor—]*
keen: I'm not keen je n'en ai pas très envie
[juh non ay pa trayz onvee]
keep: can I keep it? est-ce que je peux le
garder? *[eskuh juh puh luh garday]*;
please keep it gardez-le *[garday-luh]*;
keep the change gardez la monnaie; **will
it keep?** *(food)* est-ce que ça se garde?
[eskuh sa suh gard]; **it's keeping me
awake** ça m'empêche de dormir *[sa
mompesh duh dormeer]*; **it keeps on
breaking** ça se casse sans arrêt *[sas kass
son zaray]*; **I can't keep anything down**
(food) je vomis tout ce que je mange *[juh
vomee tooskuh juh monj]*
kerb le bord du trottoir *[bor doo trotwahr]*
ketchup le ketchup
kettle une bouilloire *[boo-ee-wahr]*
key un clé *[klay]*
kid: the kids les enfants *[onfon]*; **I'm not
kidding** je ne plaisante pas *[juh nuh
plezzont pa]*
kidneys les reins *[ran]*; *(food)* les rognons
[ronyon]
kill tuer *[too-ay]*
kilo un kilo; *see page 120*
kilometre, kilometer un kilomètre
[keelo-metr]; *see page 119*
kind: that's very kind c'est très aimable
[say trayz em-abl]; **this kind of ...** ce

genre de ... *[suh jonr duh]*
kiss un baiser *[bezzay]*; *(verb)* embrasser
[ombrassay]
kitchen la cuisine *[kweezeen]*
kitchenette un coin-cuisine *[kwan-
kweezeen]*
Kleenex *(tm)* un kleenex
knackered crevé *[kruhvay]*
knee le genou *[jnoo]*
kneecap la rotule *[rotool]*
knickers le slip *[sleep]*
knife un couteau *[kooto]*
knitting le tricot *[treeko]*
knitting needles des aiguilles à tricoter
[aygwee a treekotay]
**knock: there's a knocking noise from
the engine** le moteur cogne *[luh mohturr
kon]*; **he's had a knock on the head** il a
reçu un coup sur la tête *[eel a ruhsoo an
koo soor la tet]*; **he's been knocked over**
il a été renversé (par une voiture) *[eel a
aytay ronvairsay]*
knot *(in rope)* un nœud *[nuh]*
know *(somebody)* connaître *[konetr]*;
(something) savoir *[savwahr]*; **I don't
know** je ne sais pas *[juh nuh say pa]*; **do
you know a good restaurant?** connaissez-vous un bon restaurant? *[ko-
nessay-voo]*; **who knows?** qui sait? *[kee
say]*

L

label une étiquette *[ayteeket]*

laces (*shoes*) les lacets *[lassay]*

lacquer de la laque *[lak]*

ladies' (room) les toilettes *[twalet]*

lady une dame *[dam]*; **ladies and gentlemen!** messieurs dames! *[mess-yuh dam]*

lager une bière *[bee-air]*; **lager and lime** doesn't exist as such but ask for 'un panaché' *[panashay]* (*lager with lemonade*)

lake un lac

lamb un agneau *[anyo]*

lamp une lampe *[lomp]*

lamppost un lampadaire *[lompadair]*

lampshade un abat-jour *[abajoor]*

land (*not sea*) la terre *[tair]*; **when does the plane land?** à quelle heure est-ce que l'avion atterrit? *[a kel urr eskuh lavyon atairee]*

landscape le paysage *[payeezahj]*

lane (*car*) la voie *[vwa]*; (*narrow road*) le chemin *[shuhman]*

language la langue *[long]*

language course un cours de langue *[koor duh long]*

large grand *[gron]*

laryngitis une laryngite *[laranjeet]*

last dernier *[dairnyay]*; **last year** l'année dernière *[dairnyair]*; **last Wednesday** mercredi passé *[passay]*; **last night** hier soir *[yair swahr]*; **when is the last bus?** à quelle heure part le dernier bus?; **one last drink** un dernier verre; **when I was last in Cannes** la dernière fois que je suis allé à Cannes *[fwa kuh juh swee zalay a]*; **at last!** enfin! *[onfan]*; **how long does … last?** combien de temps dure …? *[komb-yan duh tom door]*

last name le nom de famille *[famee]*

late: sorry I'm late je suis désolé d'être en retard *[juh swee dayzolay detr on ruhtar]*; **don't be late** venez à l'heure *[vuhnay za lurr]*; **the bus was late** l'autobus

avait du retard *[avay doo ruhtar]*; **we'll be back late** nous rentrerons tard *[noo rontruhron tar]*; **it's getting late** il se fait tard *[eel suh fay]*; **is it that late!** est-il déjà si tard? *[eteel dayja]*; **it's too late now** c'est trop tard; **I'm a late riser** je suis un(e) lève-tard *[juh swee zan (zoon) levtar]*

lately récemment *[raysamon]*

later plus tard *[ploo tar]*; **later on** plus tard; **I'll come back later** je reviendrai plus tard *[juh ruhveeandray]*; **see you later** à tout à l'heure *[a toota lurr]*; **no later than Tuesday** mardi au plus tard

latest: the latest news les dernières nouvelles *[dairnyair noovel]*; **at the latest** au plus tard *[o ploo tar]*

laugh rire *[reer]*; **don't laugh** ne riez pas *[nuh reeay pa]*; **it's no laughing matter** c'est très sérieux *[say tray sayreeuh]*

launderette, laundromat une laverie automatique *[lavree otomateek]*

laundry (*clothes*) la lessive *[lesseev]*; (*place*) la blanchisserie *[blonsheesree]*; **could you get the laundry done?** pouvez-vous faire laver ce linge? *[poovay-voo fair lavay suh lanj]*

lavatory les toilettes *[twalet]*

law la loi *[lwa]*; **against the law** illégal *[eelay-gal]*

lawn la pelouse *[puhlooz]*

lawyer un avocat *[avoka]*

laxative un laxatif *[laxateef]*

lay-by une aire de stationnement *[air duh stas-yonmon]*

laze around: I just want to laze around for a few days j'ai envie de passer quelques jours à ne rien faire *[jay onvee duh pasay kelkuh joor a nuh ree-an fair]*

lazy paresseux *[paressuh]*; **don't be lazy** ne soyez pas si paresseux *[nuh swy-ay pa]*; **a nice lazy holiday** des vacances tranquilles à ne rien faire *[vakonss tron-*

keel a nuh ree-an fair]

lead (*elec*) le fil *[feel]*; **where does this road lead?** où cette route mène-t-elle? *[oo set root mentel]*

leaf une feuille *[fuh-ee]*

leaflet un dépliant *[daypleeon]*; **do you have any leaflets on …?** avez-vous des dépliants sur …? *[avay-voo]*

leak une fuite *[fweet]*; **the roof leaks** il y a une fuite dans le toit *[eelya]*

learn: I want to learn … je veux apprendre … *[juh vuh zaprondr]*

learner: I'm just a learner je ne suis qu'un débutant *[kan daybooton]*

lease louer *[looay]*

least: not in the least pas du tout *[pa doo too]*; **at least 50** au moins 50 *[o mwan]*

leather du cuir *[kweer]*

leave: when does the bus leave? quand est-ce que le bus part? *[konteskuh … par]*; **I leave tomorrow** je m'en vais demain *[juh mon vay]*; **he left this morning** il est parti ce matin *[eel ay partee]*; **may I leave this here?** puis-je laisser ceci ici? *[pweej lessay suhsee ee-see]*; **I left my bag in the bar** j'ai oublié mon sac au bar *[jay oobleeay]*; **she left her bag here** elle a oublié son sac ici; **leave the window open please** laissez la fenêtre ouverte, s'il vous plaît *[lessay]*; **there's not much left** il ne reste presque rien *[eel nuh rest presk ree-an]*; **I've hardly any money left** je n'ai presque plus d'argent *[juh nay presk ploo]*; **I'll leave it up to you** à vous de décider *[a voo duh dayseeday]*

lecherous lubrique *[loobreek]*

left gauche; **on the left** à gauche

left-hand drive la conduite à gauche *[kondweet]*

left-handed gaucher *[gohshay]*

left luggage office la consigne *[konseen]*

leg la jambe *[jomb]*

legal légal *[lay-gal]*

legal aid l'assistance financière pour les frais judiciaires *[aseestonss feenonseeair poor lay fray joodeeseeair]*

lemon un citron *[seetron]*

lemonade de la limonade *[leemonad]*

lemon tea un thé citron *[tay seetron]*

lend: would you lend me your …? pourriez-vous me prêter votre …? *[pooreeay-voo muh pretay]*

lens (*phot*) l'objectif *[objekteef]*; (*contact*) la lentille *[lontee]*

lens cap le bouchon d'objectif *[booshon dobjekteef]*

Lent le Carême *[karem]*

lesbian une lesbienne

less: less than an hour moins d'une heure *[mwan]*; **less than that** moins que cela; **less hot** moins chaud

lesson la leçon *[luhson]*; **do you give lessons?** donnez-vous des leçons?

let: will you let me know? pouvez-vous me le faire savoir? *[poovay voo muh luh fair savwar]*; **I'll let you know** je vous préviendrai *[juh voo prayveeandray]*; **let me try** est-ce que je peux essayer? *[eskuh juh puh]*; **let me go!** lâchez-moi! *[lashay-mwa]*; **let's leave now** partons maintenant *[parton mantnon]*; **let's not go yet** ne partons pas tout de suite *[nuh parton pa toot sweet]*; **will you let me off at …?** pouvez-vous me laisser descendre à …, s'il vous plaît? *[… muh lessay duhsondr]*; **room to let** chambre à louer *[looay]*

letter une lettre *[letr]*; **are there any letters for me?** est-ce qu'il y a du courrier pour moi? *[eskeel ya doo kooreeay poor mwa]*

letterbox la boîte aux lettres *[bwat o letr]*

lettuce une salade

level crossing un passage à niveau *[pasahj a neevo]*

lever le levier *[luhvyay]*

liable responsable *[respons-abl]*

liberated: a liberated woman une femme libérée *[fam leebayray]*

library une bibliothèque

licence, license un permis *[pairmee]*

license plate la plaque minéralogique *[plak meenay-ralojeek]*

lid un couvercle *[koovairkl]*

lido une piscine en plein air *[peeseen on plan air]*

lie (*untruth*) un mensonge *[monsonj]*; **can she lie down for a while?** est-ce qu'elle peut s'étendre un moment? *[eskel puh saytondr an momon]*; **I want to go and lie down** j'aimerais aller m'étendre *[jem-ray alay maytondr]*

lie-in: I'm going to have a lie-in je vais faire la grasse matinée *[juh vay fair la grass mateenay]*

life la vie [vee]; **not on your life!** jamais de la vie! [jamay]; **that's life** c'est la vie! [say]

lifebelt une bouée de sauvetage [booay duh sohvtahj]

lifeboat le canot de sauvetage [kano duh sohvtahj]

lifeguard (on beach) le maître nageur [metr nahjurr]

life insurance une assurance-vie [asœronss-vee]

life jacket le gilet de sauvetage [jeelay duh sohvtahj]

lift (in hotel) un ascenseur [asonsurr]; **could you give me a lift?** pouvez-vous m'emmener? [poovay-voo momnay]; **do you want a lift?** est-ce que je peux vous emmener quelque part? [eskuh juh puh voo zomnay kelkuh par]; **thanks for the lift** merci de m'avoir accompagné [duh mavwahr akompanyay]; **I got a lift** on m'a ramené [on ma ramnay]

light la lumière [lœm-yair]; (not heavy) léger [lay-jay]; **the light was on** la lumière était allumée [alœmay]; **do you have a light?** avez-vous du feu? [avay-voo dœ fuh]; **a light meal** un repas léger; **light blue** bleu clair

light bulb une ampoule [ompool]

lighter (cigarette) un briquet [breekay]

lighthouse un phare [far]

light meter le posemètre [pohzmetr]

lightning les éclairs [ayklair]

like: I'd like a … j'aimerais un(e) … [jemray]; **I'd like to …** j'aimerais …; **would you like a …?** aimeriez-vous un(e) …? [emreeay-voo]; **would you like to come too?** voulez-vous nous accompagner? [voolay-voo]; **I like it** ça me plaît [sah muh play]; **I like you** vous me plaisez [voo muh plezzay]; **I don't like it** ça ne me plaît pas; **he doesn't like it** ça ne lui plaît pas; **do you like …?** aimez-vous …? [aymay-voo]; **I like swimming** j'aime nager [jem]; **OK, if you like** bon, d'accord, si vous voulez [dakor, see voo voolay]; **what's it like?** comment est-ce? [komon es]; **do it like this** faites comme ceci [fet kom suhsee]; **one like that** un comme ça [an kom sa]

lilo un matelas pneumatique [matla pnuhmateek]

lime cordial, lime juice un jus de citron vert [jœ duh seetron vair]

line (on paper, tel) la ligne [leen]; (of people) la file [feel]; **could you give me a line?** (tel) pouvez-vous me donner une ligne? [poovay-voo muh donay]

linen (for beds) les draps [dra]

linguist un(e) linguiste [langweest]; **I'm no linguist** je ne suis pas doué pour les langues [juh nuh swee pa dooay poor lay long]

lining la doublure [dooblœr]

lip la lèvre [levr]

lip brush un pinceau à lèvres [panso a levr]

lip gloss du brillant à lèvres [breeyon a levr]

lip pencil un crayon à lèvres [levr]

lip salve de la pommade pour les lèvres [levr]

lipstick du rouge à lèvres [rooj a levr]

liqueur une liqueur [leekurr]

liquor l'alcool [alkol]

liquor store un magasin de vins et spiritueux [magazan duh van zay spee-reetœ-uh]

list la liste [leest]

listen: I'd like to listen to … j'aimerais écouter … [jemray aykootay]; **listen!** écoutez! [aykootay]

liter, litre un litre [leetr]; see page 120

litter des ordures

little petit [ptee]; **just a little, thanks** un tout petit peu, s'il vous plaît [an too ptee puh]; **just a very little** un tout petit; **a little cream** un peu de crème; **a little more** un peu plus [plœss]; **a little better** un peu mieux; **that's too little** (not enough) ce n'est pas assez [suh nay pa zassay]

live vivre [veevr]; **I live in Manchester/Texas** je vis à Manchester/au Texas [juh vee]; **where do you live?** où est-ce que vous habitez? [weskuh voo zabeetay]; **where does he live?** où habite-t-il [oo abeeteel]; **we live together** nous vivons ensemble [noo veevon zonsombl]

lively vivant [veevon]; (person) plein de vitalité [plan duh veetaleetay]

liver le foie [fwa]

lizard le lézard [layzar]

loaf un pain [pan]

lobby (of hotel) le hall [al]

lobster une langouste [longoost]

local: a local wine un vin de pays [duh

payee]; **a local newspaper** un journal local *[lo-kal]*; **a local restaurant** un restaurant du quartier *[dœ kart-yay]*

lock une serrure *[sair-rœr]*; **it's locked** c'est fermé à clé *[fairmay a klay]*; **I've locked myself out of my room** je me suis enfermé dehors *[juh muh swee zon-fairmay duh-or]*

lockers (*for luggage etc*) la consigne *[konseen]*

log: I slept like a log j'ai dormi comme une souche *[jay dormee kom œn soosh]*

lollipop une sucette *[sœset]*

London Londres *[londr]*

lonely solitaire; **are you lonely?** vous sentez-vous seul? *[voo sontay-voo surl]*

long long (longue) *[lon, lon-g]*; **how long does it take?** combien de temps est-ce que ça prend? *[komb-yan duh tom eskuh sa pron]*; **is it a long way?** est-ce loin d'ici? *[es lwan dee-see]*; **a long time** long-temps *[lontom]*; **I won't be long** je reviens dans un instant *[juh ruhv-yan don zan anston]*; **don't be long** revenez bien-tôt *[ruhvnay b-yanto]*; **that was long ago** c'était il y a longtemps *[saytay eelya]*; **I'd like to stay longer** j'aimerais rester plus longtemps *[jemray restay plœ]*; **long time no see!** ça fait des âges! *[sa fay day zahj]*; **so long!** au revoir! *[o rvwar]*

long distance call un appel interurbain *[antair-œrban]*

loo: where's the loo? où sont les toilettes? *[oo son lay twalet]*; **I want to go to the loo** j'aimerais aller aux toilettes *[jemray alay o]*

look: that looks good ça a l'air bon *[sa a lair]*; **you look tired** vous avez l'air fatigué *[voo zavay]*; **I'm just looking, thanks** je ne fais que regarder *[juh nuh fay kuh ruhgarday]*; **you don't look your age** vous ne faites pas votre âge *[voo nuh fet pa]*; **look at him** regardez-le *[ruhgarday-luh]*; **I'm looking for …** je cherche … *[juh shairsh]*; **look out!** attention! *[atons-yon]*; **can I have a look?** puis-je regarder?; **can I have a look around?** puis-je regarder?

loose: it's loose (*button*) il se découd *[eel suh daykoo]*; (*handle etc*) il est mal fixé *[eel ay mal feexay]*

loose change de la petite monnaie *[pteet monay]*

lorry un camion *[kamyon]*

lorry driver un camionneur *[kamyonurr]*

lose perdre *[pairdr]*; **I've lost my …** j'ai perdu mon (ma) … *[jay pairdœ]*; **I'm lost** je me suis perdu *[juh muh swee pairdœ]*

lost property office, lost and found le bureau des objets trouvés *[objay troovay]*

lot: a lot, lots beaucoup *[bo-koo]*; **not a lot** pas beaucoup; **a lot of money** beaucoup d'argent; **a lot of women** beaucoup de femmes; **a lot cooler** bien plus frais *[b-yan plœ fray]*; **I like it a lot** ça me plaît beaucoup; **is it a lot further?** est-ce encore loin? *[es onkor lwan]*; **I'll take the (whole) lot** je prends le tout *[juh pron luh too]*

lotion une lotion *[lohsyon]*

loud fort *[for]*; **the music is rather loud** la musique est trop forte *[tro fort]*

lounge le salon

lousy infect *[anfekt]*; **I feel lousy** je suis mal fichu *[juh swee mal feeshœ]*

love: I love you je vous aime *[juh voo zem]*; **he's fallen in love** il est tombé amoureux *[eel ay tombay amooruh]*; **I love France** j'adore la France *[jador]*; **let's make love** voulez-vous faire l'amour avec moi? *[voolay-voo fair lamoor avek mwa]*

lovely ravissant *[raveeson]*

low bas *[ba]*

low beam les phares en code *[far on kod]*

LP un 33 tours *[trontwa toor]*

luck la chance *[shonss]*; **hard luck!** pas de chance! *[pa duh]*; **good luck!** bonne chance! *[bon shonss]*; **just my luck!** c'est bien ma veine! *[say b-yan ma ven]*; **it was pure luck** c'était vraiment de la chance *[saytay vraymon]*

lucky: that's lucky! quelle chance! *[kel shonss]*

lucky charm un porte-bonheur *[port-bonurr]*

luggage les bagages *[bagahj]*

lumbago un lumbago *[lambago]*

lump (*med*) une grosseur *[grossurr]*

lunch le déjeuner *[dayjuhnay]*

lungs les poumons *[poomon]*

Luxembourg le Luxembourg *[lœxom-boor]*

luxurious luxueux *[lœxœ-uh]*

luxury le luxe *[lœx]*

M

macho macho

mad fou (folle) [foo, fol]

madam Madame [ma-dam]

magazine un magazine

magnificent magnifique [man-yeefeek]

maid (in hotel) la femme de chambre [fam duh shombr]

maiden name le nom de jeune fille [nom duh jurn fee]

mail: is there any mail for me? est-ce qu'il y a du courrier pour moi? [eskeel ya dœ kooreeay poor mwa]

mailbox une boîte aux lettres [bwat o letr]

main principal [pranseepal]; **where's the main post office?** où est la poste principale?; **that's the main thing** c'est l'essentiel [say lessonsee-el]; **main road** la grand-route [gron-root]; (in the country) une grande route

make faire [fair]; **do you make them yourself?** les faites-vous vous-même? [lay fet-voo voo-mem]; **it's very well made** c'est très bien fait [tray b-yan fay]; **what does that make altogether?** combien est-ce que ça fait en tout? [komb-yan eskuh sa fay on too]; **I make it only 52 francs** d'après mes calculs, ça ne fait que 52 francs [dapray may kalkœl sa nuh fay kuh]

make-up le maquillage [makeeyahj]

make-up remover un démaquillant [daymakeeyon]

male chauvinist pig un phallocrate [fa-lokrat]

man un homme [om]

manager le directeur [deerekturr]; **may I see the manager?** puis-je parler au patron? [pweej parlay o pa-tron]

manageress la directrice [deerektreess]

manicure la manucure

many beaucoup [bo-koo]

map: a map of ... (town) un plan de ... [plon duh]; (area) une carte de ... [kart];

it's not on this map ce n'est pas sur cette carte [suh nay pa sœr set kart]

marble le marbre

March mars [marss]

marijuana la marijuana [maree-oo-anah]

mark: there's a mark on it il y a une tache [eelya œn tash]; **could you mark it on the map for me?** pourriez-vous me le marquer sur la carte? [pooreeay-voo muh luh markay]

market un marché [marshay]

marmalade de la confiture d'oranges [konfeetœr doronj]

married: are you married? êtes-vous marié? [et-voo mareeay]; **I'm married** je suis marié

mascara du mascara

mass: I'd like to go to mass je voudrais aller à la messe [alay ala mess]

mast le mât [ma]

masterpiece un chef-d'œuvre [shefdurvr]

matches des allumettes [alœmet]

material (cloth) du tissu [teesœ]

matter: it doesn't matter ça ne fait rien [sa nuh fay ree-an]; **what's the matter?** qu'est-ce qui se passe? [keskee suh pass]

mattress un matelas [matla]

maximum le maximum [maxeemum]

May mai [may]

may: may I have another beer? j'aimerais encore une bière [jemray]; **may I?** puis-je? [pweej]

maybe peut-être [puht-etr]; **maybe not** peut-être que non [kuh non]

mayonnaise de la mayonnaise

me: come with me venez avec moi [mwa]; **it's for me** c'est pour moi [say]; **it's me** c'est moi; **me too** moi aussi [mwa o-see]; see page 108

meal: that was an excellent meal quel excellent repas! [ruh-pa]

mean: what does this word mean? que signifie ce mot? [kuh seen-yeefee suh mo];

what does he mean? que veut-il dire? *[kuh vuhteel deer]*

measles la rougeole *[roojol]*; **German measles** la rubéole *[rœbayol]*

measurements les dimensions *[deemonsyon]*

meat de la viande *[veeond]*

mechanic: do you have a mechanic here? y a-t-il un mécanicien ici? *[yateel an maykan-eeseean ee-see]*

medicine (*drug*) un remède *[ruhmed]*

medieval médiéval *[maydeeayval]*

Mediterranean la Méditerranée *[maydeetairanay]*

medium moyen *[mwy-an]*

medium-rare (*steak*) à point *[pwan]*

medium-sized de taille moyenne *[tie mwy-en]*

meet: pleased to meet you enchanté *[onshontay]*; **where shall we meet?** où nous retrouverons-nous? *[oo noo ruhtroovron-noo]*; **let's meet up again** j'aimerais vous revoir *[jemray voo ruhvwar]*

meeting (*business etc*) une réunion *[rayœneeon]*

meeting place le lieu de rendez-vous *[l-yuh duh]*

melon un melon *[muhlon]*

member un membre *[mombr]*; **I'd like to become a member** je voudrais devenir membre *[juh voodray duhvneer mombr]*

mend: can you mend this? est-ce que vous pouvez réparer ceci? *[eskuh voo poovay rayparay suhsee]*

men's room les toilettes *[twalet]*

mention: don't mention it je vous en prie *[juh voo zon pree]*

menu la carte *[kart]*

mess la pagaille *[pag-eye]*

message: are there any messages for me? est-ce que quelqu'un a laissé un mot pour moi? *[eskuh kelkun a lessay un mo poor mwa]*; **I'd like to leave a message for ...** je voudrais laisser un message pour ... *[lessay an messahj]*

metal le métal *[may-tal]*

metre, meter un mètre *[metr]*; *see page 119*

midday: at midday à midi

middle: in the middle au milieu *[o meel-yuh]*; **in the middle of the road** au milieu de la route

Middle Ages: in the Middle Ages au

moyen âge *[mwy-an ahj]*

midnight: at midnight à minuit *[meenwee]*

might: I might want to stay another 3 days il est possible que je reste encore 3 jours *[eel ay poseebl kuh]*; **you might have warned me!** vous auriez pu m'avertir! *[voo zoreeay pœ]*

migraine une migraine *[meegren]*

mild doux (douce) *[doo, dooss]*

mile un mille *[meel]*; **that's miles away!** c'est drôlement loin! *[say drolmon lwan]*; *see page 119*

military militaire

milk du lait *[lay]*

milkshake un milk-shake

millimetre, millimeter un millimètre *[meelee-metr]*

minced meat de la viande hachée *[veeond ashay]*

mind: I don't mind ça ne me dérange pas *[sa nuh muh dayronj pa]*; (*either will do etc*) ça m'est égal *[sa met aygal]*; **would you mind if I ...?** est-ce que ça vous dérange si je ...? *[eskuh]*; **never mind** tant pis *[ton pee]*; **I've changed my mind** j'ai changé d'avis *[jay shonjay davee]*

mine: it's mine c'est à moi *[set a mwa]*; *see page 114*

mineral water de l'eau minérale *[o meenayral]*

minimum le minimum *[meeneemum]*

mint (*sweet*) un bonbon à la menthe *[mont]*

minus moins *[mwan]*; **minus 3 degrees** moins trois

minute une minute *[meenœt]*; **in a minute** dans un instant *[don zan anston]*; **just a minute** un instant

mirror un miroir *[meer-wahr]*

Miss Mademoiselle (Mlle) *[mad-mwazel]*

miss: I miss you vous me manquez *[voo muh monkay]*; **there is a ... missing** il manque un(e) ... *[eel monk]*; **we missed the bus** nous avons raté le bus *[noo zavon ratay]*

mist la brume *[brœm]*

mistake une erreur *[errurr]*; **I think there's a mistake here** je crois qu'il y a une erreur *[juh krwa keelya]*

misunderstanding un malentendu *[malontondœ]*

mixture le mélange *[maylonj]*

mix-up: there's been some sort of mix-up il y a une erreur *[eelya œn errurr]*

modern moderne *[modairn]*; **a modern art gallery** une galerie d'art moderne

moisturizer une crème hydratante *[krem eedratont]*

moment un moment *[momon]*; **I won't be a moment** je reviens dans un instant *[juh ruhv-yan don zan anston]*

monastery le monastère *[monastair]*

Monday lundi *[landee]*

money l'argent *[arjon]*; **I don't have any money** je n'ai pas d'argent *[juh nay pa]*; **do you take English/American money?** acceptez-vous l'argent anglais/américain? *[axeptay-voo]*

month le mois *[mwa]*

monument un monument *[monœmon]*

moon la lune *[lœn]*

moorings le mouillage *[mwee-ahj]*

moped un cyclomoteur *[seeklomoturr]*

more: may I have some more? (*of that*) puis-je en avoir un peu plus? *[pwee jon avwahr an puh plœss]*; (*of them*) puis-je en avoir encore quelques-uns? *[onkor kelkuh-zan]*; **more water, please** encore un peu d'eau, s'il vous plaît; **no more** ça suffit *[sa sœfee]*; **more expensive** plus cher *[plœ shair]*; **more than 50** plus de 50; **more than that** plus que ça *[kuh sa]*; **a lot more** beaucoup plus *[bo-koo]*; **I don't stay there any more** je n'habite plus ici *[juh nabeet plœ zee-see]*

morning le matin *[matan]*; **good morning** bonjour *[bon-joor]*; **this morning** ce matin; **in the morning** le matin

mosquito un moustique *[moosteek]*

most: I like this one most c'est celui (celle)-ci que je préfère *[prayfair]*; **most of the time/the hotels** la plupart du temps/des hôtels *[plœpar]*

mother: my mother ma mère *[mair]*

motif (*in patterns*) le motif *[moteef]*

motor le moteur *[moturr]*

motorbike une moto

motorboat un hors-bord *[or-bor]*

motorist un automobiliste *[otomo-beeleest]*

motorway une autoroute *[otoroot]*

motor yacht un yacht (à moteur) *[mo-turr]*

mountain une montagne *[montan]*; **up in the mountains** à la montagne; **a mountain village** un village de montagne

mouse une souris *[sooree]*

moustache une moustache *[moos-tash]*

mouth la bouche *[boosh]*

move: he's moved to another hotel il a changé d'hôtel *[eel a shonjay dotel]*; **could you move your car?** est-ce que vous pouvez déplacer votre voiture? *[es-kuh voo poovay dayplassay votr vwatœr]*

movie un film *[feelm]*; **let's go to the movies** allons au cinéma *[alon zo see-nayma]*

movie camera une caméra *[kamayra]*

movie theater un cinéma *[seenayma]*

moving: a very moving tune un air très émouvant *[trayz aymoovon]*

Mr Monsieur (M.) *[muh-syuh]*

Mrs Madame (Mme) *[ma-dam]*

Ms *no equivalent in French*

much beaucoup *[bo-koo]*; **much better** beaucoup mieux; **much cooler** beaucoup plus frais *[plœ]*; **not much** pas beaucoup *[pa]*; **not so much** pas tant que ça *[pa ton kuh sa]*

muffler (*on car*) le silencieux *[seelons-yuh]*

mug: I've been mugged j'ai été dévalisé *[jay aytay dayvaleezay]*

muggy lourd *[loor]*

mule une mule

murals des peintures murales *[pantœr mœral]*

muscle un muscle *[mœskl]*

museum un musée *[mœzay]*

mushroom un champignon *[shompeen-yon]*

music la musique *[mœzeek]*; **do you have the sheet music for ...?** avez-vous la partition de ...? *[avay-voo la parteess-yon duh]*

musician un musicien *[mœzeess-yan]*

mussels des moules *[mool]*

must: I must ... je dois ... *[juh dwa]*; **I mustn't drink** il ne faut pas que je boive *[eel nuh fo pa kuh]*; **you mustn't forget** n'oubliez surtout pas *[noobleeay sœrtoo pa]*

mustache une moustache *[mooz-tash]*

mustard de la moutarde *[mootard]*

my mon (ma); (*plural*) mes *[may]*; *see page 109*

myself: I'll do it myself je le ferai moi-même *[mwa-mem]*

N

nail (*finger*) un ongle [*ongl*]; (*wood*) un clou [*kloo*]

nail clippers une pince à ongles [*panss a ongl*]

nailfile une lime à ongles [*leem a ongl*]

nail polish du vernis à ongles [*vairnee a ongl*]

nail polish remover du dissolvant [*— von*]

nail scissors des ciseaux à ongles [*seezo a ongl*]

naked nu [*nœ*]

name le nom; **what's your name?** quel est votre nom? [*kel ay votr*]; **what's its name?** comment est-ce que ça s'appelle? [*komon eskuh sa sapel*]; **my name is …** je m'appelle … [*juh ma-pel*]

nap: he's having a nap il fait la sieste [*eel fay la see-est*]

napkin une serviette [*sairvyet*]

nappy la couche [*koosh*]

nappy-liners les protège-couches [*protej-koosh*]

narrow étroit [*aytrwa*]

nasty désagréable [*dayzagray-abl*]; (*weather, cut*) mauvais [*mo-vay*]

national national [*nas-yonal*]

nationality la nationalité [*nas-yona-leetay*]

natural naturel [*natœ-rel*]

naturally naturellement [*natœ-relmon*]

nature la nature [*natœr*]

naturist un naturiste [*natœreest*]

nausea la nausée [*no-zay*]

near: is it near here? est-ce près d'ici? [*es pray dee-see*]; **near the window** près de la fenêtre [*pray duh la funetr*]; **do you go near …?** est-ce que vous passez près de …? [*eskuh voo passay pray duh*]; **where is the nearest …?** où est le (la) … le (la) plus proche? [*plœ prosh*]

nearby tout près [*too pray*]

nearly presque [*presk*]

nearside (*wheel*) du côté droit [*kotay drwa*]

neat (*drink*) sec

necessary nécessaire [*naysesair*]; **is it necessary to …?** faut-il …? [*foteel*]; **it's not necessary** ce n'est pas nécessaire [*suh nay pa*]

neck le cou [*koo*]

necklace le collier [*kolyay*]

necktie la cravate

need: I need a … j'ai besoin d'un … [*jay buhzwan*]; **it needs more salt** ça manque de sel [*sa monk*]; **do I need to …?** dois-je …? [*dwaj*]; **there's no need** ce n'est pas nécessaire [*suh nay pa naysesair*]; **there's no need to shout!** ça ne sert à rien de crier [*sa nuh sair a ree-an*]

needle une aiguille [*aygwee*]

negative (*film*) le négatif [*naygateef*]

neighbo(u)r un(e) voisin(e) [*vwazan, —zeen*]

neighbo(u)rhood le voisinage [*vwazee-nahj*]

neither: neither of us ni lui (elle), ni moi [*nee*]; **neither one (of them)** ni l'un ni l'autre [*nee lun nee lohtr*]; **neither … nor …** ni …, ni …; **neither do I** moi non plus [*mwa non plœ*]

nephew: my nephew mon neveu [*nuh-vuh*]

nervous nerveux [*nairvuh*]

net (*fishing, tennis*) le filet [*feelay*]; **100 francs net** 100 francs net

nettle une ortie [*ortee*]

neurotic névrosé [*nevrozay*]

neutral: in neutral (gear) au point mort [*o pwan mor*]

never jamais [*jamay*]

new nouveau (nouvelle) [*noovo, noovel*]

news (*TV etc*) les nouvelles [*noovel*]; **is there any news?** y a-t-il du nouveau? [*yateel dœ noovo*]

newspaper un journal [*joor-nal*]; **do you**

have any English newspapers? est-ce que vous avez des journaux anglais? *[day joorno zonglay]*

newsstand un kiosque à journaux *[keeosk a joorno]*

New Year le Nouvel An *[noovel on]*; **Happy New Year!** bonne année!

New Year's Eve la Saint-Sylvestre *[san seelvestr]*

New Zealand la Nouvelle Zélande *[noovel zaylond]*

New Zealander un Néo-Zélandais *[nayo-zaylonday]*

next prochain *[proshan]*; **next to the post office** à côté de la poste *[a kotay duh]*; **the next to that** celui (celle) d'à côté; **it's at the next corner** c'est au prochain croisement; **next week** la semaine prochaine; **next Monday** lundi prochain

nextdoor à côté *[a kotay]*

next of kin le plus proche parent *[plœ prosh paron]*

nice (*person*) gentil *[jontee]*; (*meal*) délicieux *[daylees-yuh]*; (*town*) joli *[jolee]*; **that's very nice of you** c'est très aimable à vous *[say trayz em-abl a voo]*; **a nice cold drink** une boisson bien fraîche *[b-yan fresh]*

nickname le surnom *[sœrnom]*

niece: my niece ma nièce *[nee-ess]*

night la nuit *[nwee]*; **for one night** pour une nuit; **for three nights** pour trois nuits; **good night** bonne nuit; **at night** la nuit

nightcap (*drink*) une boisson avant d'aller se coucher *[bwasson avon dalay suh kooshay]*

nightclub la boîte de nuit *[bwat duh nwee]*

nightdress une chemise de nuit *[shuhmeez duh nwee]*

night flight le vol de nuit *[vol duh nwee]*

nightie la chemise de nuit *[shuhmeez duh nwee]*

night-life la vie nocturne *[vee noktœrn]*

nightmare un cauchemar *[kohshmar]*

night porter le gardien de nuit *[gardeean duh nwee]*

nit (*bug*) un pou *[poo]*

no non; **I've no money** je n'ai pas d'argent *[juh nay pa]*; **there's no more** il n'y en a plus *[eel n-yon a plœ]*; **no more than …** pas plus que …; **oh no!** (*upset*) ce n'est pas

possible! *[suh nay pa poseebl]*

nobody personne *[pairson]*

noise le bruit *[brwee]*

noisy bruyant *[brwee-on]*; **it's too noisy** c'est trop bruyant

non-alcoholic non alcoolisé *[alkoleezay]*

none aucun *[o-kan]*; **none of them** aucun d'entre eux *[dontr uh]*

nonsense des bêtises *[beteez]*

non-smoking non-fumeurs *[non fœmurr]*

non-stop sans arrêt *[son zaray]*

no-one personne *[pairson]*

nor: nor do I moi non plus *[mwa non plœ]*

normal normal *[nor-mal]*

north le nord *[nor]*; **to the north** vers le nord *[vair]*

northeast le nord-est *[nor-est]*; **to the northeast** vers le nord-est *[vair]*

Northern Ireland l'Irlande du Nord *[eerlond dœ nor]*

northwest le nord-ouest *[nor-west]*; **to the northwest** vers le nord-ouest *[vair]*

nose le nez *[nay]*

nosebleed: I have a nosebleed je saigne du nez *[juh sen dœ nay]*

not pas *[pa]*; **I don't smoke** je ne fume pas *[juh nuh fœm pa]*; **he didn't say anything** il n'a rien dit *[eel na ree-an]*; **it's not important** ce n'est pas important *[suh nay pa]*; **not that one** pas celui-ci; **not for me** pas pour moi

note (*bank note*) un billet (de banque) *[bee-ay duh bonk]*

notebook le bloc-notes *[blok-not]*

nothing rien *[ree-an]*

November novembre *[no-vombr]*

now maintenant *[mantnon]*; **not now** pas maintenant

nowhere nulle part *[nœl par]*

nudist un nudiste *[nœdeest]*

nudist beach une plage réservée aux nudistes *[plahj rayzairvay o nœdeest]*

nuisance: he's being a nuisance il nous importune *[eel nooz amportœn]*

numb engourdi *[ongoordee]*

number le numéro *[nœmayro]*; **what number?** quel numéro?

number plate la plaque minéralogique *[plak meenay-ralojeek]*

nurse une infirmière *[anfeerm-yair]*

nursery (*at airport etc*) la garderie d'enfants *[garduhree donfon]*

nursery slope une piste pour débutants
[peest poor daybooton]
nut la noisette [nwazet]; (for bolt) un

écrou [aykroo]
nutter: he's a nutter il est cinglé [eel ay
sanglay]

O

oar une rame [ram]
obligatory obligatoire [obleegatwahr]
oblige: much obliged merci beaucoup
[mairsee bo-koo]
obnoxious insupportable [ansooport-abl]
obvious: that's obvious c'est évident [set
ayveedon]
occasionally de temps en temps [duh
tomz on tom]
o'clock see page 118
October octobre [oktobr]
octopus un poulpe [poolp]
odd (number) impair [ampair]; (strange) bizarre
odometer le compteur kilométrique
[komturr keelomaytreek]
of de [duh]; **the name of the hotel** le nom
de l'hôtel; **have one of mine** prenez
un(e) des mien(ne)s [... day ...]; see page
106–107
off: it just broke off il s'est cassé [say
kassay]; **20% off** 20% de rabais [duh
rabay]; **the lights were off** la lumière
était éteinte [aytant]; **just off the main
road** tout près de la route principale [too
pray duh la root pranseepal]
offend: don't be offended ne vous vexez
pas [nuh voo vexay pa]
office le bureau [booro]
officer (said to policeman) monsieur l'agent
[muh-syuh lajon]
official un fonctionnaire [fonx-yonair]; **is
that official?** est-ce officiel? [es offeesee-
el]
off-season à la morte-saison [ala mort-
sezzon]
off-side (wheel) du côté gauche [kotay
gohsh]
often souvent [soovon]; **not often** pas
souvent [pa]

oil l'huile [weel]; **it's losing oil** elle perd
de l'huile; **will you change the oil?** est-
ce que vous pouvez me faire une vidange?
[muh fair oon veedonj]; **the oil light's
flashing** l'indicateur de niveau d'huile
clignote [landeekaturr duh neevo dweel
kleenyot]
oil painting une peinture à l'huile [pan-
toor a lweel]
oil pressure la pression d'huile [press-
yon dweel]
ointment une pommade
OK d'accord [dakor]; **are you OK?** ça va?
[sa va]; **that's OK thanks** merci, ça va
bien [mairsee sa va b-yan]; **that's OK by
me** ça me convient [sa muh konv-yan]
old vieux (vieille) [v-yuh, v-yay]; **how old
are you?** quel âge avez-vous? [kel ahj
avay-voo]
old-age pensioner un retraité [ruh-
tretay]
old-fashioned démodé [daymoday]
old town la vieille ville [v-yay veel]
olive une olive [oleev]
olive oil de l'huile d'olive [weel doleev]
omelet(te) une omelette
on sur [soor]; **on the beach** à la plage; **on
Friday** vendredi; **on television** à la télévision; **I don't have it on me** je ne l'ai
pas sur moi [juh nuh lay pa soor mwa];
this drink's on me c'est ma tournée [say
ma toornay]; **a book on Chamonix** un
livre sur Chamonix; **the warning light
comes on** l'avertisseur lumineux s'al-
lume [avairteesurr loomeenuh saloom];
the light was on la lumière était allumée
[aloomay]; **what's on in town?** qu'y a-t-il
à faire en ville? [kyateel a fair on veel]; **it's
just not on!** (not acceptable) c'est inacceptable [set eenaxept-abl]

once une fois *[œn fwa]*; **at once** tout de suite *[toot sweet]*

one un (une) *[an, œn]*; **that one** celui-ci (celle-ci) *[suhlwee-see, sel-see]*; **the green one** le (la) vert(e); **the one with the black dress on** celle avec la robe noire; **the one in the blue shirt** celui avec la chemise bleue

onion un oignon *[onyon]*

only: only one seulement un(e) *[surl-mon]*; **only once** seulement une fois; **it's only 9 o'clock** il n'est que 9 heures *[eel nay kuh]*; **I've only just arrived** je viens d'arriver *[juh v-yan dareevay]*

open ouvert *[oovair]*; **when do you open?** à quelle heure est-ce que vous ouvrez? *[a kel urr eskuh vooz oovray]*; **in the open** (*open air*) en plein air *[on plan air]*; **it won't open** je n'arrive pas à l'ouvrir *[juh nareev pa za loovreer]*

opening times les heures d'ouverture *[urr doovairtœr]*

open top (*car*) décapotable *[daykapot-abl]*

opera un opéra *[opayra]*

operation une opération *[opayras-yon]*

operator (*tel*) l'opératrice *[opayratreess]*

opportunity une occasion *[okaz-yon]*

opposite: opposite the church en face de l'église *[on fass duh]*; **it's directly opposite** c'est juste en face *[jœst on fass]*

oppressive (*heat*) étouffant *[aytoofon]*

optician un opticien *[opteess-yan]*

optimistic optimiste *[opteemeest]*

optional facultatif *[—teef]*

or ou *[oo]*

orange (*fruit*) une orange *[oronj]*; (*colour*) orange

orange juice (*fresh*) une orange pressée *[oronj pressay]*; (*fizzy*) une orangeade *[oronjad]*; (*diluted*) un sirop d'orange *[seero]*

orchestra un orchestre *[orkestr]*

order: could we order now? est-ce que nous pouvons commander? *[eskuh noo poovon komonday]*; **I've already ordered** j'ai déjà commandé *[jay dayja komonday]*; **I didn't order that** ce n'est pas ce que j'ai commandé *[suh nay pa suh kuh jay komonday]*; **it's out of order** (*lift etc*) il (elle) ne marche pas *[eel, el nuh marsh pa]*

ordinary ordinaire

organization une organisation *[organeezas-yon]*

organize organiser *[organeezay]*; **could you organize it?** pouvez-vous organiser cela? *[poovay-voo]*

original original *[oreejee-nal]*; **is it an original?** (*painting etc*) est-ce un original? *[es]*

ornament un bibelot *[beeblo]*

ostentatious prétentieux *[praytonseeuh]*

other: the other waiter l'autre garçon *[ohtr]*; **the other one** l'autre; **do you have any others?** est-ce que vous en avez d'autres? *[eskuh voo zon avay dohtr]*; **some other time, thanks** une autre fois, merci

otherwise autrement *[ohtruh-mon]*

ouch! aïe! *[eye]*

ought: he ought to be here soon il devrait arriver bientôt *[eel duhvray]*

ounce *see page 120*

our: our car notre voiture *[notr]*; **our children** nos enfants *[no zonfon]*; *see page 107*

ours le (la) nôtre *[nohtr]*; *see page 111*

out: he's out (*of building etc*) il est sorti *[eel ay sortee]*; **get out!** dehors! *[duh-or]*; **I'm out of money** je suis fauché *[juh swee fo-shay]*; **a few kilometres out of town** à quelques kilomètres de la ville

outboard (motor) un hors-bord *[or-bor]*

outdoors en plein air *[on plan air]*

outlet (*elec*) une prise de courant *[preez duh kooron]*

outside: can we sit outside? est-ce que nous pouvons nous mettre dehors? *[eskuh noo poovon noo metr duh-or]*

outskirts: on the outskirts of ... dans les faubourgs de ... *[don lay fo-boor]*

oven le four *[foor]*

over: over here par ici *[ee-see]*; **over there** là-bas *[laba]*; **over 100** plus de 100 *[plœ duh]*; **I ache all over** j'ai mal partout *[jay mal partoo]*; **the holiday's over** les vacances sont finies *[feenee]*

overcharge: you've overcharged me il y a une erreur dans la note *[eelya œn errurr don la not]*

overcoat un pardessus *[parduhsœ]*

overcooked trop cuit *[tro kwee]*

overdrive la vitesse surmultipliée *[veetess sœrmœlteepleeay]*

overexposed surexposé *[sœrexpozay]*

overheat: it's overheating (*car*) elle chauffe *[el shohf]*
overland par voie de terre *[vwa duh tair]*
overlook: overlooking the sea avec vue sur la mer *[voo soor la mair]*
overnight (*travel*) de nuit *[duh nwee]*
oversleep: I overslept j'ai dormi trop longtemps *[jay dormee tro lontom]*
overtake dépasser *[daypassay]*

overweight: I'm overweight j'ai des kilos en trop *[jay day keelo on tro]*
owe: how much do I owe you? qu'est-ce que je vous dois? *[keskuh juh voo dwa]*
own: my own ... mon propre ... *[propr]*; **are you on your own?** êtes-vous seul? *[et-voo surl]*; **I'm on my own** je suis seul
owner le propriétaire *[propreeaytair]*
oyster une huître *[weetr]*

P

pack: a pack of cigarettes un paquet de cigarettes *[pakay]*; **I'll go and pack** je vais aller faire mes bagages *[juh vay zalay fair may bagahj]*
package un colis *[kolee]*
package holiday des vacances organisées *[vakonss organeezay]*
package tour un voyage organisé *[vwy-ahj organeezay]*
packed lunch un casse-croûte *[kass-kroot]*
packed out: the place was packed out il y avait foule *[eel yavay fool]*
packet (*parcel*) un colis *[kolee]*; **a packet of cigarettes** un paquet de cigarettes *[pakay]*
paddle (*for boat*) une pagaie *[pagay]*
padlock un cadenas *[kadna]*
page (*of book*) la page *[pahj]*; **could you page him?** pourriez-vous le faire appeler? *[pooreeay-voo luh fair aplay]*
pain la douleur *[doolurr]*; **I have a pain here** j'ai mal ici *[jay mal ee-see]*
painful douloureux *[dooloruh]*
painkillers des analgésiques *[an-aljayzeek]*
paint (*noun*) la peinture *[pantoor]*; **I'm going to do some painting** je vais faire un peu de peinture *[juh vay fair]*
paintbrush le pinceau *[pan-so]*
painting un tableau
pair: a pair of ... une paire de ...
pajamas un pyjama *[peejama]*
Pakistan le Pakistan

Pakistani pakistanais *[—ay]*
pal un copain (une copine) *[kopan, —een]*
palace le palais *[palay]*
pale pâle *[pahl]*; **pale blue** bleu clair
palm tree un palmier *[palmyay]*
palpitations des palpitations *[—tas-yon]*
pancake une crêpe
panic: don't panic! ne vous affolez pas! *[nuh voo zafollay pa]*
panties un slip *[sleep]*
pants (*trousers*) un pantalon *[pontalon]*; (*underpants*) un slip *[sleep]*
pantyhose des collants *[kolon]*
paper du papier *[papyay]*; (*newspaper*) un journal *[joor-nal]*; **a piece of paper** un bout de papier *[boo]*
paper handkerchiefs des kleenex (*tm*)
paraffin du pétrole *[paytrol]*
paragliding le parachutisme ascentionnel *[—ees-muh asonseeonel]*
parallel: parallel to ... parallèle à ...
parasol (*over table*) le parasol
parcel un colis *[kolee]*
pardon (me)? pardon?
parents: my parents mes parents *[paron]*
park se garer *[suh garay]*; **where can I park?** où est-ce que je peux me garer? *[weskuh juh puh muh]*; **there's nowhere to park** il n'y a pas de place pour se garer *[eel nya pa duh plass]*
parka un parka
parking lights les feux de position *[fuh duh pozeess-yon]*
parking lot un parking *[—eeng]*

parking place: there's a parking place! voilà une place de stationnement! *[vwala œn plass duh stas-yonmon]*

part une partie *[partee]*

partner le partenaire *[partuhnair]*

party (*group*) le groupe; (*celebration*) une fête *[fet]*; **let's have a party** organisons une fête *[organeezon zœn]*

pass (*mountain*) le col; (*overtake*) dépasser *[daypassay]*; **he passed out** il s'est évanoui *[eel set ayvanwee]*; **he made a pass at me** il m'a draguée *[eel ma dragay]*

passable (*road*) praticable *[prateek-abl]*

passenger un passager *[passahjay]*

passport le passeport *[pass-por]*

past: in the past autrefois *[ohtruh-fwa]*; **just past the bank** juste après la banque *[jœst apray]*; *see page 118*

pastry la pâte *[paht]*; (*cake*) un gâteau

patch: could you put a patch on this? pourriez-vous rapiécer ceci? *[pooreeay-voo rap-yessay suhsee]*

pâté du pâté

path le sentier *[sont-yay]*

patient: be patient soyez patient *[swy-ay pas-yon]*

patio le patio

pattern (*on cloth etc*) le motif; **a dress pattern** un patron de robe *[pat-ron duh rob]*

paunch du ventre *[dœ vontr]*

pavement (*sidewalk*) le trottoir *[trotwa]*

pay payer *[payay]*; **can I pay, please?** l'addition, s'il vous plaît *[ladeess-yon]*; **it's already paid for** ça a déjà été réglé *[sa a day-ja aytay rayglay]*; **I'll pay for this** c'est moi qui paie *[say mwa kee pay]*

pay phone une cabine téléphonique *[kabeen taylayfoneek]*

peace and quiet le calme *[kalm]*

peach une pêche *[pesh]*

peanuts des cacahuètes *[kaka-wet]*

pear une poire *[pwahr]*

pearl une perle *[pairl]*

peas des petits pois *[ptee pwa]*

peculiar bizarre

pedal la pédale *[pay-dal]*

pedalo un pédalo *[pay-dalo]*

pedestrian un piéton *[p-yayton]*

pedestrian crossing un passage pour piétons *[passahj poor p-yayton]*

pedestrian precinct la zone piétonne *[zohn p-yayton]*

pee: I need to go for a pee j'aimerais aller aux toilettes *[jemray alay o twalet]*

peeping Tom un voyeur

peg (*for washing*) une pince à linge *[panss a lanj]*; (*for tent*) un piquet *[peekay]*

pen un stylo *[steelo]*; **do you have a pen?** avez-vous un stylo?

pencil un crayon

penfriend un correspondant *[—don]*; **shall we be penfriends?** voulez-vous correspondre avec moi? *[voolay-voo]*

penicillin de la pénicilline *[payneeseeleen]*

penknife un canif *[kaneef]*

penpal le correspondant *[—don]*

pensioner un retraité *[ruhtraytay]*

people les gens *[jon]*; **there were a lot of people** il y avait beaucoup de monde *[eel yavay bo-koo duh mond]*; **French people** les Français

pepper (*spice*) le poivre *[pwahvr]*; **green pepper** un poivron vert *[pwahvron vair]*; **red pepper** un poivron rouge

peppermint (*sweet*) un bonbon à la menthe *[mont]*

per: per night par nuit; **how much per hour?** quel est le prix par heure? *[kel ay]*

per cent pour cent *[poor son]*

perfect parfait *[parfay]*

perhaps peut-être *[puht-etr]*

period (*of time*) une période *[payree-od]*; (*woman's*) les règles *[regl]*

perm une permanente *[pairmanont]*

permit une autorisation *[otoreezas-yon]*

person une personne *[pairson]*

pessimist(ic) pessimiste *[—meest]*

petrol l'essence *[essonss]*

petrol can un bidon d'essence *[beedon dessonss]*

petrol station une station-service *[stas-yon-sairveess]*

petrol tank le réservoir *[rayzairvwahr]*

pharmacy une pharmacie *[farmasee]*

phone *see* **telephone**

photogenic photogénique *[—jayneek]*

photograph une photo; **would you take a photograph of us?** pourriez-vous nous prendre en photo? *[pooreeay-voo noo prondr on]*

photographer un photographe *[—graf]*

phrase: a useful phrase une expression utile *[expres-yon œteel]*

phrasebook un manuel de conversation

[manœel duh konvairsas-yon]
pianist un pianiste *[—eest]*
piano un piano
pickpocket un pickpocket
pick up: when can I pick them up? quand est-ce que je peux venir les chercher? *[konteskuh juh puh vuhneer lay shairshay]*; **will you come and pick me up?** pouvez-vous venir me chercher? *[poovay-voo]*
picnic un pique-nique *[peek-neek]*
picture (*drawing*) un dessin *[dessan]*; (*painting*) un tableau; (*photograph*) une photo
pie (*meat*) un pâté en croûte *[patay on kroot]*; (*fruit*) une tarte
piece un morceau *[morso]*; **a piece of ...** un morceau de ...
pig un cochon *[koshon]*
pigeon un pigeon *[peejon]*
piles (*med*) des hémorroïdes *[aymo-roeed]*
pile-up une collision en chaîne *[koleez-yon on shen]*
pill une pilule *[peelool]*; **I'm on the pill** je prends la pilule *[juh pron]*
pillarbox une boîte aux lettres *[bwat o letr]*
pillow un oreiller *[oray-yay]*
pillow case une taie d'oreiller *[tay doray-yay]*
pin une épingle *[aypangl]*
pineapple un ananas *[anana]*
pineapple juice un jus d'ananas *[jœ da-nana]*
pink rose *[roz]*
pint *see page 121*
pipe un tuyau *[twee-o]*; (*smoking*) une pipe *[peep]*
pipe cleaners des cure-pipes *[kœr-peep]*
pipe tobacco du tabac à pipe *[taba a peep]*
pity: it's a pity c'est dommage *[say do-mahj]*
pizza une pizza
place un endroit *[ondrwa]*; **is this place taken?** est-ce que cette place est prise? *[eskuh set plass ay preez]*; **would you keep my place for me?** pourriez-vous me garder ma place? *[pooreeay-voo muh garday]*; **at my place** chez moi *[shay mwa]*
plain (*food*) simple *[sam-pl]*; (*not patterned*) uni *[œnee]*

plane un avion *[avyon]*
plant une plante *[plont]*
plaster cast le plâtre *[plahtr]*
plastic le plastique *[—teek]*
plastic bag un sac en plastique *[on —teek]*
plate une assiette *[assyet]*
platform le quai *[kay]*; **which platform, please?** quel quai, s'il vous plaît? *[kel]*
play (*verb*) jouer *[jooay]*; (*in theatre*) une pièce de théâtre *[pyess duh tay-atr]*
playboy un playboy
playground un terrain de jeux *[terran duh juh]*
pleasant agréable *[agray-abl]*
please: could you please ...? pourriez-vous ..., s'il vous plaît? *[pooreeay-voo, seel voo play]*; **yes please** oui, merci *[wee, mairsee]*
plenty: plenty of ... beaucoup de ... *[bo-koo duh]*; **that's plenty thanks** merci, ça suffit *[sa soofee]*
pleurisy une pleurésie *[plurrayzee]*
pliers une pince *[panss]*
plonk du pinard *[peenar]*; (*cheap*) de la piquette *[peeket]*
plug (*elec*) une prise *[preez]*; (*car*) une bougie *[boojee]*; (*bathroom*) le bouchon *[booshon]*
plughole le trou d'écoulement *[troo day-koolmon]*
plum une prune *[prœn]*
plumber un plombier *[plombyay]*
plus plus *[plœss]*
p.m.: 4 p.m. 4 heures de l'après-midi *[urr duh lapray-meedee]*; **9 p.m.** 9 heures du soir *[dœ swahr]*
pneumonia une pneumonie *[p-nuh-monee]*
poached egg un œuf poché *[urf poshay]*
pocket la poche *[posh]*; **in my pocket** dans ma poche
pocketbook (*woman's*) un sac à main *[man]*
pocketknife un canif *[kaneef]*
point: could you point to it? pourriez-vous me l'indiquer? *[pooreeay-voo muh landeekay]*; **four point six** quatre virgule six *[... vergœl ...]*; **there's no point** ça ne sert à rien *[sa nuh sair a ree-an]*
points (*car*) les vis platinées *[veess pla-teenay]*
poisonous (*snake*) venimeux *[vuh-*

neemuh]; (*plant*) vénéneux [*vaynaynuh*]

police la police; **call the police!** appelez la police!

policeman un agent de police [*ajon*]

police station le poste de police [*posst*]

polish du cirage [*seerahj*]; **will you polish my shoes?** pourriez-vous cirer mes chaussures? [*pooreeay-voo seeray may*]

polite poli [*polee*]

politician un politicien [*—teess-yan*]

politics la politique [*poleeteek*]

polluted pollué [*polooay*]

pond un étang [*ayton*]

pony un poney [*ponay*]

pool (*swimming*) la piscine [*peeseen*]; (*game*) le billard américain [*bee-yar amayreekan*]

pool table une table de billard [*tabl duh bee-yar*]

poor (*not rich*) pauvre [*pohvr*]; (*quality etc*) médiocre [*maydeeokr*]; **poor old Pierre!** ce pauvre vieux Pierre! [*suh pohvr v-yuh*]

pope le pape [*pap*]

pop music la musique pop [*moozeek*]

pop singer un chanteur de musique pop [*shonturr duh moozeek*]

popular populaire [*popoolair*]

population la population [*popoolas-yon*]

pork le porc [*por*]

port (*for boats*) le port [*por*]; (*drink*) un porto

porter (*hotel*) le portier [*portyay*]; (*for luggage*) un porteur [*porturr*]

portrait le portrait [*portray*]

Portugal le Portugal [*portoo-gal*]

Portuguese portugais [*portoo-gay*]

poser (*phoney person*) un poseur

posh (*restaurant*) chic [*sheek*]; **posh people** les gens bien [*lay jon b-yan*]

possibility une possibilité [*poseebeeleetay*]

possible possible [*poseebl*]; **is it possible to …?** est-ce qu'on peut …? [*eskon puh*]

post (*mail*) le courrier [*kooreeay*]; **could you post this for me?** pourriez-vous me poster cette lettre? [*pooreeay-voo muh postay set letr*]

postbox une boîte aux lettres [*bwat o letr*]

postcard une carte postale [*kart poss-tal*]

poster une affiche [*afeesh*]

poste restante la poste restante

post office la poste [*posst*]

pot le pot [*po*]; **a pot of tea** du thé [*doo*

tay]; **pots and pans** des casseroles

potato une pomme de terre [*pom duh tair*]

potato chips des chips [*cheeps*]

potato salad la salade de pommes de terre [*sa-lad duh pom duh tair*]

pottery la poterie [*potree*]

pound (*money*) une livre (sterling) [*leevr*]; (*weight*) une livre; *see page 120*

pour: it's pouring down il pleut à verse [*eel pluh ta vairss*]

powder (*for face*) de la poudre [*poodr*]

powdered milk du lait en poudre [*lay on poodr*]

power cut une panne de courant [*pan duh kooron*]

power point une prise [*preez*]

power station une centrale [*son-tral*]

practise, practice: I need to practise (*sport*) je manque d'entraînement [*juh monk dontrenmon*]

pram un landau [*londo*]

prawn cocktail un cocktail de crevettes [*kruhvet*]

prawns des crevettes [*kruhvet*]

prefer: I prefer white wine je préfère le vin blanc [*juh prayfair*]

preferably: preferably not tomorrow de préférence pas demain [*duh prayfayronss*]

pregnant enceinte [*onsant*]

prescription une ordonnance [*ordononss*]

present: at present actuellement [*aktooelmon*]; **here's a present for you** voici un cadeau pour vous [*vwasee an kado*]

president le président [*prayzeedon*]

press: could you press these? pourriez-vous repasser ces vêtements? [*pooreeay-voo ruhpassay say vetmon*]

pretty joli [*jolee*]; **it's pretty expensive** c'est plutôt cher [*say plooto shair*]

price le prix [*pree*]

prickly heat une irritation due à la chaleur [*eereetas-yon doo ala shalurr*]

priest un prêtre [*pretr*]

prime minister le Premier ministre [*pruhmyay meeneestr*]

print (*picture*) une gravure [*gravoor*]

printed matter un imprimé [*ampreemay*]

priority (*in driving*) la priorité [*preeoreetay*]

prison la prison [*preezon*]

private privé [preevay]; **with private bath** avec salle de bain [sal duh ban]

prize un prix [pree]

probably probablement [prob-abluh-mon]

problem le problème [prob-lem]; **I have a problem** j'ai un problème

product un produit [prodwee]

program(me) le programme [prog-ram]

promise: I promise je vous le promets [juh voo luh promay]; **is that a promise?** est-ce que vous me le promettez? [eskuh voo muh luh prometay]

pronounce: how do you pronounce this word? comment est-ce que ça se prononce? [komont eskuh sas prononss]

properly: it's not repaired properly ce n'est pas bien réparé [suh nay pa b-yan rayparay]

prostitute une prostituée [prosteetœay]

protect protéger [protayjay]

protection factor (suncream) l'indice de protection [andeess duh protex-yon]

protein remover (for contact lenses) un dissolvant de protéines [deesolvon duh protay-een]

Protestant protestant [—ton]

proud fier [f-yair]

prunes des pruneaux secs [prœno sek]

public (adj) public [pœbleek]

public convenience des toilettes publiques [twalet pœbleek]

public holiday un jour férié [joor fay-reeay]

pudding (dessert) un dessert [dessair]

pull (verb) tirer [teeray]; **he pulled out without indicating** il a déboîté sans mettre son clignotant [eel a daybwatay son metr son kleen-yoton]

pullover le pull [pœl]

pump une pompe [pomp]

punctual: are the buses punctual? est-ce que les bus arrivent à l'heure? [eskuh lay bœss areev ta lurr]

puncture la crevaison [kruhvezzon]

punk punk

pure pur [pœr]

purple violet [veeolay]

purse le porte-monnaie [port-monay]; (handbag) le sac à main [man]

push (verb) pousser [poosay]; **don't push in!** (into queue) ne poussez pas! [nuh poos-say]

push-chair la poussette [pooset]

put: where did you put ...? où avez-vous mis ...? [oo avay-voo mee]; **where can I put ...?** où est-ce que je peux mettre ...? [weskuh juh puh metr]; **could you put the lights on?** pourriez-vous allumer la lumière? [pooreeay-voo alœmay]; **will you put the light out?** pourriez-vous éteindre la lumière? [... aytandr ...]; **you've put the price up** vous avez augmenté le prix [... ohgmontay ...]; **could you put us up for the night?** pourriez-vous nous héberger pour la nuit? [nooz aybairjay poor la nwee]

pyjamas un pyjama [peejama]

Q

quality la qualité [kaleetay]; **poor quality** de mauvaise qualité [mo-vez]; **good quality** de bonne qualité

quarantine la quarantaine [karonten]

quart see page 121

quarter un quart [kar]; **a quarter of an hour** un quart d'heure [durr]; see page 118

quay le quai [kay]

quayside: on the quayside sur les quais [sœr lay kay]

question la question [kest-yon]; **that's out of the question** il n'en est pas question [eel non ay pa]; see page 117

queue une file d'attente [feel datont]; **there was a big queue** il y avait beaucoup de gens qui faisaient la queue [eel yavay bo-koo duh jon kee fuhzay la kuh]

quick rapide *[rapeed]*; **that was quick** vous avez fait vite *[voo zavay fay veet]*; **which is the quickest way?** quel est le chemin le plus court? *[kel ay luh shuhman luh plœ koor]*
quickly vite *[veet]*
quiet tranquille *[tronkeel]*; **be quiet down there!** silence, là-bas! *[seelonss, la-ba]*
quinine la quinine *[keeneen]*
quite: quite a lot (of) pas mal (de) *[pa mal]*; **it's quite different** c'est très différent *[say tray]*; **I'm not quite sure** je ne suis pas tout à fait sûr *[juh nuh swee pa toota fay]*

R

rabbit le lapin *[lapan]*
rabies la rage *[rahj]*
race (*horses, cars*) la course *[koorss]*; **I'll race you there** faisons la course! *[fezzon]*
racket (*tennis etc*) une raquette *[raket]*
radiator le radiateur *[radeeaturr]*
radio la radio *[ra-deeo]*; **on the radio** à la radio
rag (*cleaning*) un chiffon
rail: by rail en train *[on tran]*
railroad, railway le chemin de fer *[shuhman duh fair]*
railroad crossing un passage à niveau *[passahj a neevo]*
rain la pluie *[plwee]*; **in the rain** sous la pluie *[soo]*; **it's raining** il pleut *[eel pluh]*
rain boots des bottes de caoutchouc *[bot duh kaoochoo]*
raincoat un imperméable *[ampairmay-abl]*
rape un viol *[veeol]*
rare rare *[rar]*; (*steak*) saignant *[sen-yon]*
rash (*on skin*) une éruption *[ayrœps-yon]*
raspberries des framboises *[frombwahz]*
rat un rat *[ra]*
rate (*for changing money*) le cours de change *[koor duh shonj]*; **what's the rate for the pound?** quel est le cours de la livre sterling? *[kel ay]*; **what are your rates?** (*car hire etc*) quels sont vos tarifs? *[tareef]*
rather: it's rather late il est plutôt tard *[eel ay plœto tar]*; **I'd rather have fish** je préfère du poisson *[juh prayfair]*
raw cru *[krœ]*
razor un rasoir *[razwahr]*

razor blades des lames de rasoir *[lahm duh razwahr]*
reach: within easy reach à proximité *[—tay]*
read lire *[leer]*; **I can't read it** je n'arrive pas à le lire *[juh nareev pa]*
ready: when will it be ready? quand est-ce que ce sera prêt? *[konteskuh suh suhra pray]*; **I'll go and get ready** je vais aller me préparer *[juh vay zalay muh prayparay]*; **I'm not ready yet** je ne suis pas encore prêt
real véritable *[vayreet-abl]*
really vraiment *[vraymon]*; **I really must go** il faut absolument que je m'en aille *[eel foht absolœmon kuh juh mon eye]*; **is it really necessary?** est-ce vraiment nécessaire? *[es]*
realtor une agence immobilière *[ajonss eemobeelee-air]*
rear: at the rear à l'arrière *[laree-air]*
rear wheels les roues arrière *[aree-air]*
rearview mirror le rétroviseur *[raytro-veezurr]*
reasonable raisonnable *[rezzon-abl]*; (*quite good*) acceptable *[axept-abl]*
receipt le reçu *[ruhsœ]*
recently récemment *[ray-samon]*
reception (*hotel*) la réception *[ray-seps-yon]*; (*for guests*) une réception
reception desk la réception *[ray-seps-yon]*
receptionist (*in hotel*) le (la) réceptionniste *[rayseps-yoneest]*
recipe la recette *[ruhset]*; **can you give me the recipe for this?** pouvez-vous me

donner la recette?

recognize reconnaître *[ruhkonetr]*; **I didn't recognize it** je ne l'avais pas reconnu *[juh nuh lavay pa ruhkonoo]*

recommend: could you recommend ...? pourriez-vous me recommander ...? *[pooreeay-voo muh ruhkomonday]*

record (*music*) un disque *[deesk]*

record player un électrophone *[aylektrofon]*

red rouge *[rooj]*

reduction (*in price*) un rabais *[rabay]*

red wine le vin rouge *[van rooj]*

refreshing rafraîchissant *[rafreshee-son]*

refrigerator le frigo *[freego]*

refund: do I get a refund? est-ce que je serai remboursé? *[eskuh juh suhray romboorsay]*

region la région *[rayjeeon]*

registered: by registered mail en recommandé *[on ruhkomonday]*

registration number (*of car*) le numéro d'immatriculation *[noomayro deematreekoolas-yon]*

relative: my relatives ma parenté *[parontay]*

relaxing: it's very relaxing c'est très délassant *[daylasson]*

reliable (*car*) sûr *[soor]*; **he's very reliable** on peut compter sur lui *[on puh komtay soor lwee]*

religion la religion *[ruhleejeeon]*

remains (*of old city etc*) les vestiges *[vesteej]*

remember: I don't remember je ne me souviens pas *[juh nuh muh soov-yan pa]*; **do you remember?** vous souvenez-vous? *[voo soovnay-voo]*

remote (*village etc*) isolé *[eezolay]*

rent (*for room etc*) le loyer *[lwy-ay]*; **I'd like to rent a bike/car** j'aimerais louer un vélo/une voiture *[jemray looay]*

rental car une voiture de location *[vwatoor duh lokas-yon]*

repair réparer *[rayparay]*; **can you repair this?** pouvez-vous réparer ceci? *[poovay-voo]*

repeat répéter *[raypetay]*; **would you repeat that?** pourriez-vous répéter? *[pooreeay-voo]*

representative (*of company*) un représentant *[ruhprayzonton]*

rescue sauver *[so-vay]*

reservation une réservation *[rayzairvas-yon]*; **I have a reservation** j'ai réservé *[jay rayzairvay]*

reserve réserver *[rayzairvay]*; **I reserved a room in the name of ...** j'ai réservé une chambre au nom de ... *[jay rayzairvay]*; **can I reserve a table for tonight?** j'aimerais réserver une table pour ce soir *[jemray]*

rest: I need a rest (*holiday etc*) j'ai besoin de repos *[jay buh-zwan duh ruhpo]*; **the rest of the group** le reste du groupe *[rest]*

restaurant un restaurant *[—ron]*

rest room les toilettes *[twalet]*

retired: I'm retired je suis retraité *[ruhtretay]*

return: a return to Chartres un aller-retour pour Chartres *[alay-ruhtoor]*; **I'll return it tomorrow** je le rapporterai demain *[juh luh raportuhray]*

returnable (*deposit*) qui sera retourné *[kee suhra ruhtoornay]*

reverse charge call: I'd like to make a reverse charge call j'aimerais téléphoner en PCV *[jemray taylayfonay on pay-say-vay]*

reverse gear la marche arrière *[marsh aree-air]*

revolting dégoûtant *[daygooton]*

rheumatism des rhumatismes *[roomateess-muh]*

rib une côte *[koht]*; **a cracked rib** une côte fêlée *[felay]*

ribbon (*for hair*) un ruban *[roobon]*

rice le riz *[ree]*

rich (*person*) riche *[reesh]*; **it's too rich** (*food*) c'est trop lourd *[say tro loor]*

ride: can you give me a ride into town? pouvez-vous m'emmener en ville? *[poovay-voo momnay]*; **thanks for the ride** merci de m'avoir ramené *[duh mavwahr ramnay]*

ridiculous: that's ridiculous c'est ridicule *[reedeekool]*

right (*correct*) exact; (*not left*) droit *[drwa]*; **you're right** vous avez raison *[voo zavay rezzon]*; **you were right** vous aviez raison *[voo zaveeay]*; **that's right** c'est juste *[say joost]*; **that can't be right** ce n'est pas possible *[suh nay pa poseebl]*; **right!** (*OK*) d'accord! *[dakor]*; **is this the right road for ...?** est-ce bien la route de ...? *[es*

b-yan *la root]*; **on the right** à droite
[drwat]; **turn right** tournez à droite
[toornay]; **not right now** pas maintenant
[pa mantnon]

right-hand drive la conduite à droite
[kondweet a drwat]

ring (*on finger*) une bague *[bag]*; (*on cooker*)
le brûleur *[brœlurr]*; **I'll ring you** je vous
appellerai *[juh vooz apelray]*

ring road le périphérique *[payreefayreek]*

ripe mûr *[mœr]*

rip-off: it's a rip-off c'est du vol organisé
[say dœ vol organeezay]; **rip-off prices**
des prix exorbitants *[pree exorbeeton]*

risky risqué *[reeskay]*; **it's too risky** c'est
trop risqué

river une rivière *[reev-yair]*; **by the river**
au bord de la rivière *[o bor]*

road la route *[root]*; **is this the road to ...?**
est-ce la bonne route pour aller à ...? *[es la
bon root poor alay]*; **further down the
road** plus loin sur cette route *[plœ lwan-
sœr]*

road accident un accident de la circulation *[axeedon duh la seerkœlas-yon]*

road hog un chauffard *[shofar]*

road map une carte routière *[kart root-
yair]*

roadside: by the roadside au bord de la
route *[o bor duh la root]*

roadsign le panneau de signalisation
[pano duh seen-yaleezas-yon]

roadwork(s) des travaux *[travo]*

roast beef un rôti de bœuf *[rotee duh burf]*

rob: I've been robbed j'ai été dévalisé *[jay
aytay dayvaleezay]*

robe (*housecoat*) un peignoir *[pen-wahr]*

rock (*stone*) le rocher *[roshay]*; **on the
rocks** (*with ice*) avec des glaçons *[avek
day glasson]*

rock climbing la varappe *[varap]*

rocky (*coast*) rocheux *[roshuh]*

roll (*bread*) un petit pain *[ptee pan]*

Roman Catholic catholique *[katoleek]*

romance une idylle *[eedeel]*

Rome: when in Rome ... à Rome, il faut
faire comme les Romains *[a rom eel fo fair
kom lay romman]*

roof le toit *[twa]*; **on the roof** sur le toit

roof rack (*on car*) la galerie *[galree]*

room une chambre *[shombr]*; **do you
have a room?** avez-vous une chambre de
libre? *[avay-voo œn shombr duh leebr]*; **a**

room for two people une chambre pour
deux personnes *[pairson]*; **a room for
three nights** une chambre pour trois
nuits *[nwee]*; **a room with bathroom**
une chambre avec salle de bains; **in my
room** dans ma chambre; **there's no
room** il n'y a pas de place *[eel nya pa duh
plass]*

room service le service des chambres
[sairveess day shombr]

rope une corde *[kord]*

rose une rose

rosé (*wine*) du rosé

rotary (*for traffic*) un sens giratoire *[sonss
jeeratwahr]*

rough (*sea*) houleux *[ooluh]*; **a rough
crossing** une mauvaise traversée *[mo-
vez travairsay]*; **the engine sounds a bit
rough** le moteur tousse *[luh moturr
tooss]*; **I've been sleeping rough** j'ai
dormi à la belle étoile *[jay dormee ala bel
aytwal]*

roughly (*approx*) environ *[onveeron]*

roulette la roulette

round (*adjective*) rond *[ron]*; **it's my
round** c'est ma tournée *[say ma toornay]*

roundabout le sens giratoire *[sonss jee-
ratwahr]*

round-trip: a round-trip ticket to ... un
aller-retour pour ... *[alay-ruhtoor]*

route un itinéraire *[eeteenayrair]*; **what's
the best route?** quel itinéraire nous conseillez-vous? *[noo konsay-ay-voo]*

rowboat, rowing boat un canot à rames
[kano a ram]

rubber (*material*) le caoutchouc
[kaoochoo]; (*eraser*) une gomme *[gom]*

rubber band un élastique *[aylasteek]*

rubbish (*waste*) les ordures; (*poor quality
items*) de la camelote *[kamlot]*; **rubbish!**
vous dites n'importe quoi! *[voo deet nam-
port kwa]*

rucksack un sac à dos *[do]*

rude grossier *[gross-yay]*; **he was very
rude** il a été très grossier *[eel a aytay]*

rug un tapis *[tapee]*

ruins les ruines *[rœeen]*

rum du rhum

rum and coke un rhum coca

run (*person*) courir *[kooreer]*; **I go running**
je fais du jogging *[juh fay dœ]*; **quick,
run!** dépêchez-vous! *[daypeshay-voo]*;
how often do the buses run? quelle est

la fréquence des bus? *[kel ay la fraykonss day bœss]*; **he's been run over** il s'est fait renverser (par une voiture) *[eel say fay ronvairsay (par œn vwatœr)]*; **I've run out of gas/petrol** je suis en panne sèche *[juh swee zon pan sesh]*

rupture (*med*) une hernie *[airnee]*
Russia la Russie *[rœsee]*
Russian russe *[rœss]*
rusty: my French is rather rusty mon français est plutôt rouillé *[mon fronsay ay plœto roo-yay]*

S

saccharine la saccharine *[—reen]*
sad triste *[treest]*
saddle la selle *[sel]*
safe (*not in danger*) en sécurité *[on say-kœreetay]*; (*not dangerous*) sûr *[sœr]*; **will the car be safe here?** est-ce que nous pouvons laisser la voiture ici? *[eskuh noo poovon lessay]*; **is the water safe to drink?** est-ce que cette eau est potable? *[eskuh set o ay pot-abl]*; **is it a safe beach for swimming?** n'est-il pas dangereux de se baigner ici? *[net-eel pa donjruh]*; **could you put this in your safe?** pourriez-vous mettre ceci dans votre coffre-fort? *[pooreeay-voo metr suhsee don votr kofr-for]*
safety pin une épingle de sûreté *[aypangl duh sœrtay]*
sail la voile *[vwal]*; **can we go sailing?** est-ce qu'on peut faire de la voile? *[eskon puh fair]*
sailboard une planche à voile *[plonsh a vwal]*
sailboarding: I like sailboarding j'aime la planche à voile *[jem la plonsh a vwal]*
sailor le marin *[maran]*; **I'm a keen sailor** je fais beaucoup de voile *[juh fay bo-koo duh vwal]*
salad la salade *[sa-lad]*
salad cream de la mayonnaise
salad dressing la vinaigrette
sale: is it for sale? est-ce à vendre? *[es a vondr]*; **it's not for sale** ce n'est pas à vendre
sales clerk le vendeur (la vendeuse) *[von-durr, vondurz]*
salmon le saumon *[so-mon]*

salt le sel
salty: it's too salty c'est trop salé *[say tro salay]*
same même *[mem]*; **one the same as this** un comme ça *[an kom sa]*; **the same again, please** la même chose, s'il vous plaît *[mem shohz seel voo play]*; **have a good day — same to you** bonne journée — à vous de même; **it's all the same to me** ça m'est égal *[sa met aygal]*; **thanks all the same** merci quand-même *[mair-see kon-mem]*
sand le sable *[sabl]*
sandal une sandale *[son-dal]*; **a pair of sandals** une paire de sandales
sandwich un sandwich *[sond-weetch]*; **a chicken sandwich** un sandwich au poulet *[o poolay]*
sandy: a sandy beach une plage de sable *[plahj duh sabl]*
sanitary napkin, sanitary towel une serviette hygiénique *[eejeeayneek]*
sarcastic sarcastique *[—teek]*
sardines des sardines
satisfactory satisfaisant *[sateesfuhzon]*; **this is not satisfactory** c'est inacceptable *[set eenaxept-abl]*
Saturday samedi *[samdee]*
sauce une sauce *[sohss]*
saucepan une casserole
saucer une soucoupe *[sookoop]*
sauna un sauna *[sona]*
sausage une saucisse *[soseess]*
sauté potatoes des pommes de terre sautées *[pom duh tair]*
save (*life*) sauver *[sovay]*
savo(u)ry salé *[salay]*

say: how do you say ... in French? comment dit-on ... en français? *[komon deeton]*; **what did you say?** qu'est-ce que vous avez dit? *[keskuh voo zavay dee]*; **what did he say?** qu'est-ce qu'il a dit?; **you can say that again** c'est le cas de le dire! *[say luh ka duh luh deer]*; **I wouldn't say no** je ne dis pas non *[juh nuh dee pa non]*

scald: he's scalded himself il s'est ébouillanté *[eel set ayboo-yontay]*

scarf (*neck*) une écharpe *[aysharp]*; (*head*) un foulard *[foolar]*

scarlet écarlate *[aykarlat]*

scenery le paysage *[payee-zahj]*

scent (*perfume*) un parfum *[parfam]*

schedule l'horaire *[orair]*

scheduled flight un vol de ligne *[vol duh leen]*

school l'école *[aykol]*; (*university*) l'université *[œneevairseetay]*; **I'm still at school** je suis encore au lycée *[leesay]*

science les sciences *[see-onss]*

scissors: a pair of scissors une paire de ciseaux *[seezo]*

scooter un scooter *[—tair]*

scorching: it's really scorching (*weather*) il fait une de ces chaleurs! *[eel fayt œn duh say shalurr]*

score: what's the score? où en est la partie? *[oo on ay la partee]*

scotch (*whisky*) un scotch

Scotch tape (*tm*) du scotch

Scotland l'Ecosse *[aykoss]*

Scottish écossais *[aykossay]*

scrambled eggs des œufs brouillés *[uh broo-yay]*

scratch une éraflure *[ayraflœr]*; **it's only a scratch** ce n'est qu'une égratignure *[suh nay kœn aygrateen-yœr]*

scream crier *[kreeay]*

screw une vis *[veess]*

screwdriver un tournevis *[toornuhveess]*

scrubbing brush une brosse à ongles *[bross a ongl]*

scruffy négligé *[naygleejay]*

scuba diving la plongée sous-marine *[plonjay soo-mareen]*

sea la mer *[mair]*; **by the sea** au bord de la mer *[o bor]*

sea air l'air marin *[air maran]*

seafood les fruits de mer *[frwee duh mair]*

seafood restaurant un restaurant spécialisé dans les fruits de mer *[spayseea-leezay don lay frwee duh mair]*

seafront le bord de la mer *[bor duh la mair]*; **on the seafront** au bord de la mer

seagull une mouette *[mwet]*

search fouiller *[fwee-yay]*; **I searched everywhere** j'ai fouillé partout *[jay fwee-yay partoo]*

search party une équipe de secours *[ay-keep duh suhkoor]*

seashell une coquillage *[kokeeyahj]*

seasick: I feel seasick j'ai le mal de mer *[jay luh mal duh mair]*; **I get seasick** je suis sujet au mal de mer *[juh swee sœjay]*

seaside: by the seaside au bord de la mer *[o bor duh la mair]*; **let's go to the seaside** allons au bord de la mer *[alon zo]*

season la saison *[sezzon]*; **in the high season** en haute saison *[on oht]*; **in the low season** pendant la morte-saison *[pondon]*

seasoning l'assaisonnement *[asezzon-mon]*

seat la siège *[see-ej]*; **is this anyone's seat?** est-ce que cette place est prise? *[eskuh set plass ay preez]*

seat belt la ceinture de sécurité *[santœr duh saykœreetay]*; **do you have to wear a seatbelt?** est-ce que le port de la ceinture de sécurité est obligatoire? *[eskuh luh por]*

sea urchin un oursin *[oorsan]*

seaweed les algues *[alg]*

secluded isolé *[eezolay]*

second (*adjective*) second *[suhgon]*; (*time*) une seconde *[suhgond]*; **just a second!** une seconde!; **can I have a second helping?** est-ce que je peux me resservir? *[eskuh juh puh muh ruhssairveer]*

second class (*travel*) en seconde *[on suhgond]*

second-hand d'occasion *[dokaz-yon]*

secret secret *[suhkray]*

security check le contrôle de sécurité *[duh saykœreetay]*

sedative un calmant *[kalmon]*

see voir *[vwahr]*; **I didn't see it** je ne l'avais pas vu *[juh nuh lavay pa vœ]*; **have you seen my husband?** avez-vous vu mon mari? *[avay-voo vœ]*; **I saw him this morning** je l'ai vu ce matin *[juh lay vœ]*; **can I see the manager?** j'aimerais parler au patron *[jemray parlay]*; **see**

you tonight! à ce soir! *[a suh swahr]*; **can I see?** est-ce que je peux voir?; **oh, I see** ah, je vois *[juh vwa]*; **will you see to it?** est-ce que vous pouvez vous en occuper? *[eskuh voo poovay voo zon okœpay]*

seldom rarement *[rar-mon]*

self-catering apartment un appartement (de vacances) *[apartmon (duh vakonss)]*

self-service self-service *[—sairveess]*

sell vendre *[vondr]*; **do you sell ...?** est-ce que vous vendez ...? *[eskuh voo vonday]*; **will you sell it to me?** j'aimerais vous l'acheter *[jemray voo lashtay]*

sellotape (*tm*) du scotch

send envoyer *[onvwy-ay]*; **I want to send this to England** j'aimerais envoyer ceci en Angleterre *[jemray]*; **I'll have to send this food back** ceci est immangeable, il faut le renvoyer à la cuisine *[suhsee et amonj-abl, eel fo luh ronvwy-ay]*

senior: Mr Jones senior Monsieur Jones père *[pair]*

senior citizen une personne du troisième âge *[pairson dœ trwaz-yem ahj]*

sensational sensationnel *[sonsas-yonel]*

sense: I have no sense of direction je n'ai pas le sens de l'orientation *[juh nay pa luh sonss duh loree-ontas-yon]*; **it doesn't make sense** ce n'est pas logique *[suh nay pa lojeek]*

sensible raisonnable *[rezzon-abl]*

sensitive sensible *[sonseebl]*

sentimental sentimental *[sonteemon-tal]*

separate (*room*) séparé *[sayparay]*; **can we have separate bills?** est-ce que nous pouvons avoir des notes séparées? *[eskuh noo poovon zavwahr day not sayparay]*

separated: I'm separated je suis séparé *[juh swee sayparay]*

September septembre *[septombr]*

septic infecté *[anfektay]*

serious sérieux *[sayree-uh]*; **I'm serious** je ne plaisante pas *[juh nuh plezzont pa]*; **you can't be serious!** vous plaisantez! *[voo plezzontay]*; **is it serious, doctor?** est-ce que c'est grave, docteur? *[eskuh say grahv]*

seriously: seriously ill gravement malade *[grahvmon malad]*

service: the service was excellent le service était parfait *[sairveess aytay parfay]*; **could we have some service,**

please! est-ce que vous pouvez nous servir, s'il vous plaît? *[eskuh voo poovay noo sairveer]*; (*church*) le service; **the car needs a service** la voiture a besoin d'être révisée *[buh-zwan detr rayveezay]*

service charge le service *[sairveess]*

service station une station-service *[stas-yon sairveess]*

serviette une serviette *[sair—]*

set: it's time we were setting off il faut que nous partions maintenant *[eel fo kuh noo parteeon mantnon]*

set menu le plat du jour *[pla dœ joor]*

settle up: can we settle up now? est-ce que nous pouvons faire nos comptes? *[eskuh noo poovon fair no komt]*

several plusieurs *[plœz-yurr]*

sew: could you sew this back on? pouvez-vous recoudre ceci? *[poovay-voo ruhkoodr suhsee]*

sex (*activity*) le sexe *[sex]*

sexist sexiste *[sexeest]*

sexy sexy

shade: in the shade à l'ombre *[lombr]*

shadow une ombre *[ombr]*

shake: the French shake hands more les Français se serrent la main plus souvent *[suh sair la man plœ soovon]*

shallow peu profond *[puh profon]*

shame: what a shame! quel dommage! *[kel domahj]*

shampoo un shampooing *[shompwan]*; **can I have a shampoo and set?** je voudrais un shampooing-mise en plis *[juh voodray zan shompwan-meez on plee]*

shandy un panaché *[panashay]*

share (*room, table*) partager *[partajay]*; **let's share the cost** partageons les frais *[partajon lay fray]*

shark un requin *[ruhkan]*

sharp (*knife etc*) tranchant *[tronshon]*; (*taste*) âpre *[apr]*; (*pain*) violent *[veeolon]*

shattered: I'm shattered (*very tired*) je suis complètement crevé *[juh swee kompletmon kruhvay]*

shave: I need a shave il faut que je me rase *[eel fo kuh juh muh raz]*; **can you give me a shave?** pouvez-vous me faire la barbe? *[poovay-voo muh fair la barb]*

shaver un rasoir *[razwahr]*

shaving brush un b'aireau *[blairo]*

shaving foam de la crème à raser *[krem a razay]*

shaving point une prise pour rasoirs [*preez poor razwahr*]

shaving soap du savon à barbe [*barb*]

shawl un châle [*shal*]

she elle [*el*]; **is she a friend of yours?** est-ce une amie à vous? [*es*]; *see page 108*

sheep un mouton [*mooton*]

sheet un drap [*dra*]

shelf une étagère [*aytajair*]

shellfish les crustacés [*krœstassay*]

sherry du sherry

shingles (*med*) le zona

ship un bateau [*bato*]; **by ship** en bateau

shirt une chemise [*shuhmeez*]

shock (*surprise*) un choc [*shok*]; **I got an electric shock from the ...** j'ai reçu une décharge en touchant ... [*jay ruhsœ œon daysharj on tooshon*]

shock-absorber l'amortisseur [*amortee-surr*]

shocking scandaleux [*skondaluh*]

shoelaces des lacets [*lassay*]

shoe polish du cirage [*seerahj*]

shoes des chaussures [*shohsœr*]; **a pair of shoes** une paire de chaussures

shop un magasin [*magazan*]

shopping: I'm going shopping je vais faire des courses [*juh vay fair day koorss*]

shop window la vitrine [*veetreen*]

shore (*of sea*) le rivage [*reevahj*]; (*lake*) la rive [*reev*]

short (*person*) petit [*ptee*]; **it's only a short distance** ce n'est pas loin [*suh nay pa lwan*]

short-change: you've short-changed me vous ne m'avez pas assez rendu [*voo nuh mavay pa zassay rondœ*]

short circuit un court-circuit [*koorseerkwee*]

shortcut un raccourci [*rakoorsee*]

shorts un short [*short*]; (*underwear*) des caleçons [*kalson*]

should: what should I do? que faut-il que je fasse? [*kuh fo-teel kuh juh fass*]; **he shouldn't be long** il devrait revenir bientôt [*eel duhvray*]; **you should have told me** vous auriez dû me le dire [*voo zoreeay dœ*]

shoulder l'épaule [*aypol*]

shoulder blade l'omoplate [*omoplat*]

shout crier [*kreeay*]

show: could you show me? pourriez-vous me montrer? [*pooreeay-voo muh montray*]; **does it show?** est-ce que ça se voit? [*eskuh sa suh vwa*]; **we'd like to go to a show** nous voudrions aller voir un spectacle [*noo voodreeon alay vwahr an spekt-akl*]

shower (*in bathroom*) la douche [*doosh*]; **with shower** avec douche

shower cap un bonnet de douche [*bonay*]

show-off: don't be a show-off arrête de crâner! [*aret duh kranay*]

shrimps des crevettes [*kruhvet*]

shrink: it's shrunk ça a rétréci [*sa a raytraysee*]

shut fermer [*fairmay*]; **when do you shut?** à quelle heure fermez-vous? [*a kel urr fairmay-voo*]; **when do they shut?** à quelle heure est-ce que ça ferme? [*eskuh sa fairm*]; **it was shut** c'était fermé [*saytay fairmay*]; **I've shut myself out** je me suis enfermé dehors [*juh muh sweez onfairmay duh-or*]; **shut up!** taisez-vous! [*tezzay-voo*]

shutter (*phot*) l'obturateur [*obtœraturr*]; (*of window*) le volet [*volay*]

shutter release le déclencheur d'obturateur [*dayklonshurr dobtœraturr*]

shy timide [*teemeed*]

sick malade [*malad*]; **I think I'm going to be sick** (*vomit*) je crois que je vais être malade [*juh krwa kuh juh vay zetr*]

side le côté [*kotay*]; (*in game*) le camp [*kom*]; **at the side of the road** au bord de la route [*o bor duh*]; **on the other side of town** de l'autre côté de la ville

side lights les feux de position [*fuh duh pozeess-yon*]

side salad une salade [*sa-lad*]

side street une petite rue [*pteet rœ*]

sidewalk le trottoir [*trotwahr*]

sidewalk café une terrasse de café

siesta la sieste [*see-est*]

sight: the sights of ... les endroits à voir à ...

sightseeing: sightseeing tour une excursion [*exkœrs-yon*]; **we're going sightseeing** nous allons visiter la ville [*noo zalon veezeetay*]

sign (*roadsign*) le panneau de signalisation [*pano duh seen-yaleezas-yon*]; (*notice*) un panneau; **where do I sign?** où est-ce que je dois signer? [*weskuh juh dwa seen-jay*]

signal: he didn't give a signal il n'a pas

mis son clignotant [eel na pa mee son kleen-yoton]

signature la signature [seen-yatoor]

signpost le poteau indicateur [poto andeekaturr]

silence le silence [seelons]

silencer le silencieux [seelons-yuh]

silk la soie [swa]

silly idiot [eed-yo]; **that's silly** c'est idiot

silver l'argent [arjon]

silver foil du papier d'aluminium [papyay]

similar semblable [sombl-abl]

simple simple [sam-pl]

since: since yesterday depuis hier [duhpwee]; **since we got here** depuis que nous sommes arrivés [areevay]

sincere sincère [sansair]

sing chanter [shontay]

singer un chanteur (une chanteuse) [shonturr, —urz]

single: a single room une chambre pour une personne [shombr poor œn pairson]; **a single to ...** un aller simple pour ... [alay sam-pl]; **I'm single** je suis célibataire [juh swee sayleebatair]

sink (kitchen) l'évier [layv-yay]; **it sank** il a coulé [eel a koolay]

sir Monsieur [muh-syuh]; **excuse me, sir** pardon, Monsieur

sirloin l'aloyau [alwy-o]; **a sirloin steak** un steak dans l'aloyau

sister: my sister ma sœur [surr]

sister-in-law: my sister-in-law ma belle-sœur [bel-surr]

sit: may I sit here? est-ce que je peux m'asseoir ici? [eskuh juh puh mass-wahr]; **is anyone sitting here?** est-ce que cette place est prise? [eskuh set plass ay preez]

site (campsite) un terrain [terran]

sitting: the second sitting for lunch le second service pour le déjeuner [suhgon sairveess poor luh dayjurnay]

situation la situation [seetœas-yon]

size la taille [tie]

sketch (drawing) le croquis [krokee]

ski le ski; (verb) skier [skeeay]; **a pair of skis** une paire de skis

ski boots des chaussures de ski [shohsoor]

skid: I skidded j'ai dérapé [jay dayrapay]

skiing le ski; **we're going skiing** nous allons faire du ski [noo zalon fair]

ski instructor un moniteur (de ski) [moneeturr]

ski-lift un remonte-pente [ruhmont-pont]

skin la peau [po]

skin-diving la plongée sous-marine [plonjay soo-mareen]; **I'm going skin-diving** je vais faire de la plongée [juh vay fair]

skinny maigrichon [megreeshon]

ski-pants un fuseau [fœzo]

ski pole un bâton de ski

skirt une jupe [jœp]

ski run une piste de ski

ski slope une pente de ski [pont]

ski wax du fart [far]

skull le crâne [kran]

sky le ciel [s-yel]

sleep: I can't sleep je n'arrive pas à dormir [juh nareev pa za dormeer]; **did you sleep well?** avez-vous bien dormi? [avay-voo b-yan dormee]; **I need a good sleep** j'ai besoin d'une bonne nuit de sommeil [jay buh-zwan dœn bon nwee duh somay]

sleeper (rail) une couchette

sleeping bag un sac de couchage [kooshahj]

sleeping car un wagon-couchettes

sleeping pill un somnifère [somneefair]

sleepy: I'm feeling sleepy j'ai sommeil [jay somay]

sleet de la neige fondue [nej fondœ]

sleeve la manche [monsh]

slice une tranche [tronsh]

slide (phot) une diapositive [deeapozeeteev]

slim mince [manss]; **I'm slimming** je suis au régime [juh swee zo rayjeem]

slip (under dress) la combinaison [—ezzon]; **I slipped** (on pavement etc) j'ai glissé [jay gleessay]

slipped disc: I've got a slipped disc je me suis déplacé une vertèbre [juh muh swee dayplassay œn vairtebr]

slippery glissant [gleeson]

slow lent [lon]; **slow down** ralentir [ralonteer]

slowly lentement [lontmon]; **could you say it slowly?** pourriez-vous parler plus lentement? [pooreeay-voo parlay plœ]

small petit [ptee]

small change de la monnaie [monay]

smallpox la variole [vareeol]

smart (*clothes*) chic [*sheek*]

smashing épatant [*aypaton*]

smell: there's a funny smell il y a une drôle d'odeur [*eel ya oon drohl dodurr*]; **what a lovely smell!** ça sent vraiment bon! [*sa son vraymon bon*]; **it smells** ça sent mauvais [*mo-vay*]

smile sourire [*sooreer*]

smoke la fumée [*foomay*]; **do you smoke?** vous fumez? [*voo foomay*]; **do you mind if I smoke?** est-ce que ça vous dérange si je fume? [*eskuh sa voo dayronj see juh foom*]; **I don't smoke** je ne fume pas

smooth lisse [*leess*]; (*sea*) calme [*kalm*]

smoothy un beau-parleur [*bo-parlurr*]

snack: I'd just like a snack j'aimerais manger un petit quelque chose [*jemray monjay an ptee kelkuh shohz*]

snackbar un snack

snails des escargots [*eskargo*]

snake un serpent [*sairpon*]

sneakers des tennis [*teneess*]

snob un snob

snorkel un tuba

snow la neige [*nej*]

so: it's so hot il fait tellement chaud! [*... telmon ...*]; **not so fast** pas si vite!; **thank you so much** merci mille fois [*meel fwa*]; **it wasn't — it was so!** ce n'est pas vrai — si! [*suh nay pa vray — see*]; **so am I** moi aussi [*mwa o-see*]; **so do I** moi aussi; **how was it? — so-so** comment c'était? — comme ci, comme ça [*komon saytay — kom see, kom sa*]

soaked: I'm soaked je suis trempé [*juh swee trompay*]

soaking solution (*for contact lenses*) une solution de trempage [*solooss-yon duh trompahj*]

soap du savon

soap-powder de la lessive [*lesseev*]

sober: I was completely sober je n'avais pas bu du tout [*juh navay pa boo doo too*]

sock la chaussette [*sho-set*]

socket (*elec*) une prise [*preez*]

soda: whisky soda un whisky soda

sofa le divan [*deevon*]

soft doux (douce) [*doo, dooss*]

soft drink une boisson non alcoolisée [*bwasson non alkoleezay*]

soft lenses des lentilles souples [*lontee soopl*]

soldier un soldat [*solda*]

sole (*of shoe*) la semelle [*suhmel*]; **could you put new soles on these?** pourriez-vous ressemeler ces chaussures? [*pooreeay-voo ruh-suhmuhlay say shohsoor*]

solid solide [*sol-eed*]

some: may I have some water? j'aimerais de l'eau, s'il vous plaît [*jemray*]; **do you have some matches?** avez-vous des allumettes? [*... day ...*]; **that's some wine!** quel fameux vin! [*kel famuh*]; **some of them** quelques-uns [*kelkuh-zan*]; **can I have some of them?** est-ce que je peux en avoir? [*eskuh juh puh on avwahr*]

somebody, someone quelqu'un [*kelkan*]

something quelque chose [*kelkuh shohz*]; **something to drink** quelque chose à boire

sometime: sometime this afternoon dans l'après-midi [*don*]

sometimes quelquefois [*kelkuh-fwa*]

somewhere quelque part [*kelkuh par*]

son: my son mon fils [*feess*]

song une chanson [*shonson*]

son-in-law: my son-in-law mon gendre [*jondr*]

soon bientôt [*b-yanto*]; **I'll be back soon** je reviens bientôt; **as soon as you can** dès que possible [*day kuh poseebl*]

sore: it's sore ça fait mal [*sa fay mal*]

sore throat: I have a sore throat j'ai mal à la gorge [*jay mal ala gorj*]

sorry: (I'm) sorry excusez-moi [*exkoozay-mwa*]; **sorry?** pardon?

sort: what sort of ...? quel genre de ...? [*kel jonr duh*]; **will you sort it out?** pouvez-vous vous en occuper? [*poovay-voo voo zon okoopay*]

soup de la soupe

sour acide [*aseed*]

south le sud [*sood*]; **to the south** vers le sud [*vair*]

South Africa l'Afrique du Sud [*afreek doo sood*]

South African sud-africain [*sood-afree-kan*]

southeast le sud-est [*sood-est*]; **to the southeast** vers le sud-est [*vair*]

southwest le sud-ouest [*sood-west*]; **to the southwest** vers le sud-ouest [*vair*]

souvenir un souvenir

spa une station thermale [*stas-yon tair-*]

mal]

space heater un radiateur [radeeaturr]

spade une pelle [pel]

Spain l'Espagne [espan]

Spaniard un Espagnol [espan-yol]

Spanish espagnol [espan-yol]; **a Spanish woman** une Espagnole

spanner une clé [klay]

spare part une pièce de rechange [p-yess duh ruhshonj]

spare tyre un pneu de rechange [p-nuh duh ruhshonj]

spark(ing) plug la bougie [boojee]

speak: do you speak English? parlez-vous l'anglais? [parlay-voo]; **I don't speak ...** je ne parle pas ... [juh nuh parl pa]; **can I speak to ...?** j'aimerais parler à ... [jemray parlay]; **speaking** (tel) c'est moi-même [say mwa-mem]

special spécial [spayss-yal]; **nothing special** rien de spécial

specialist un spécialiste [spayss-yaleest]

special(i)ty (in restaurant) une spécialité [spayss-yaleetay]; **the special(i)ty of the house** la spécialité de la maison

spectacles des lunettes [lœnet]

speed la vitesse [veetess]; **he was speeding** il roulait trop vite [eel roolay tro veet]

speedboat un hors-bord [or-bor]

speed limit la limitation de vitesse [lee-meetas-yon duh veetess]

speedometer le compteur [komturr]

spell: how do you spell it? comment est-ce que ça s'écrit? [komon teskuh sa saykree]

spend (money) dépenser [dayponsay]; **I've spent all my money** j'ai dépensé tout mon argent [jay dayponsay]

spice une épice [aypeess]

spicy: it's very spicy c'est très relevé [say tray ruhluhvay]

spider une araignée [aren-yay]

spin-dryer une essoreuse [esorurz]

splendid fantastique [fontasteek]

splint (for broken limb) une éclisse [ayk-leess]

splinter (in finger etc) une écharde [ay-shard]

splitting: I've got a splitting headache j'ai un mal de tête atroce [jay an mal duh tet atross]

spoke (in wheel) un rayon

sponge une éponge [ayponj]

spoon une cuillère [kwee-yair]

sport le sport [spor]

sport(s) jacket une veste sport [spor]

spot: will they do it on the spot? est-ce qu'ils peuvent le faire tout de suite? [es-keel purv luh fair toot sweet]; (on skin) un bouton [booton]

sprain: I've sprained my ... je me suis foulé ... [juh muh swee foolay]

spray (for hair) de la laque [lak]

spring (season) le printemps [prantom]; (of car, seat) le ressort [ruhsor]

square (in town) une place [plass]; **ten square metres** dix mètres carrés [karay]

squash (sport) le squash

stain (on clothes) une tache [tash]

stairs les escaliers [eskalyay]

stale pas frais (fraîche) [pa fray, fresh]; (bread) rassis [rasee]

stall: the engine keeps stalling le moteur cale sans arrêt [moturr kal son zaray]

stalls l'orchestre [orkestr]

stamp un timbre [tambr]; **a stamp for England please** un timbre pour l'Angleterre, s'il vous plaît

stand: I can't stand ... je ne supporte pas ... [juh nuh sœport pa]

standard (adjective) normal [nor-mal]

stand-by en stand-by

star une étoile [aytwal]

start le début [daybœ]; (verb) commencer [komonsay]; **when does the film start?** à quelle heure commence le film? [a kel urr komonss]; **the car won't start** la voiture refuse de démarrer [ruhfœz duh day-maray]

starter (car) le démarreur [daymarurr]; (food) l'entrée [ontray]

starving: I'm starving je meurs de faim [juh murr duh fam]

state (in country) l'Etat [ayta]; **the States** (USA) les Etats-Unis [ayta-zœnee]

station la gare [gar]

statue une statue

stay: we enjoyed our stay nous avons beaucoup aimé notre séjour [sayjoor]; **where are you staying?** où logez-vous? [oo lojay-voo]; **I'm staying at ...** je loge au ... [juh loj o]; **I'd like to stay another week** j'aimerais rester une semaine de plus [jemray restay]; **I'm staying in tonight** ce soir, je ne sors pas [juh nuh sor pa]

steak un steak

steal: my bag has been stolen on m'a volé mon sac *[on ma volay]*

steep *(hill)* raide *[red]*

steering *(car)* la direction *[deerex-yon]*; **the steering is slack** la direction est faussée *[fo-say]*

steering wheel le volant *[volon]*

stereo stéréo *[stayray-o]*

sterling une livre sterling *[leevr stair-leeng]*

stew un ragoût *[ragoo]*

steward *(on plane)* le steward

stewardess l'hôtesse de l'air *[otess]*

sticking plaster un sparadrap *[—dra]*

sticky collant *[kolon]*

sticky tape du scotch *(tm)*

still: I'm still waiting j'attends toujours *[toojoor]*; **will you still be open?** est-ce que le magasin sera encore ouvert? *[eskuh luh magazan suhra onkor]*; **he's still not here** il n'est pas encore arrivé *[eel nay pa zonkor]*; **that's still better** c'est encore mieux

sting: a bee sting une piqûre d'abeille *[peekœr dabay]*; **I've been stung** j'ai été piqué (par un insecte) *[jay aytay peekay (par an ansekt)]*

stink la puanteur *[pœ-onturr]*

stockings des bas *[ba]*

stolen: my wallet's been stolen on m'a volé mon portefeuille *[on ma volay]*

stomach l'estomac *[estoma]*; **do you have something for an upset stomach?** avez-vous quelque chose pour les indigestions? *[avay-voo kelkuh shohz poor layz andeejest-yon]*

stomach-ache des maux d'estomac *[mo destoma]*

stone *(rock)* une pierre; *see page 120*

stop *(bus stop)* un arrêt *[aray]*; **which is the stop for ...?** où est-ce que je dois descendre pour aller à ...? *[weskuh juh dwa desondr poor alay]*; **please stop here** *(to taxi driver etc)* arrêtez-moi ici, s'il vous plaît *[aretay-mwa ee-see]*; **do you stop near ...?** est-ce que vous vous arrêtez près de ...? *[eskuh voo voo zaretay pray duh]*; **stop doing that!** arrêtez!

stopover une halte *[alt]*

store un magasin *[magazan]*

storey un étage *[aytahj]*

storm une tempête *[tom-pet]*; *(thunder-*

storm) un orage *[orahj]*

story une histoire *[eestwahr]*

stove le fourneau *[foorno]*

straight *(road etc)* droit *[drwa]*; **it's straight ahead** c'est tout droit *[say too]*; **straight away** tout de suite *[toot sweet]*; **a straight whisky** un whisky sec

straighten: can you straighten things out? pouvez-vous arranger les choses? *[poovay-voo aronjay lay shohz]*

strange *(odd)* étrange *[aytronj]*; *(unknown)* inconnu *[ankonœ]*

stranger un étranger *[aytronjay]*; **I'm a stranger here** je ne suis pas d'ici *[juh nuh swee pa dee-see]*

strap *(on watch)* le bracelet *[braslay]*; *(suit-case)* la sangle *[songl]*; *(dress)* la bretelle *[bruhtel]*

strawberry une fraise *[frez]*

streak: could you put streaks in? *(in hair)* pourriez-vous me faire des mèches? *[poo-reeay-voo muh fair day mesh]*

stream un cours d'eau *[koor do]*

street une rue *[rœ]*; **on the street** dans la rue

street café une terrasse de café

streetcar un tramway

streetmap un plan de ville *[plon duh veel]*

strep throat: I've got a strep throat j'ai une angine *[jay œn onjeen]*

strike: they're on strike ils sont en grève *[eel son ton grev]*

string une ficelle *[feesel]*

striped *(shirt etc)* à rayures

striptease le strip-tease

stroke: he's had a stroke il a eu une attaque *[eel a œ œn atak]*

stroll: let's go for a stroll allons faire un tour *[alon fair an toor]*

stroller *(for babies)* une poussette *[pooset]*

strong fort *[for]*

stroppy peu aimable *[puh em-abl]*

stuck: the key's stuck la clé est coincée *[kwansay]*

student un(e) étudiant(e) *[aytœd-yon, —yont]*

stupid stupide *[stœpeed]*

sty *(in eye)* un orgelet *[orjuhlay]*

subtitles des sous-titres *[soo-teetr]*

suburb un faubourg *[fo-boor]*

subway le métro *[maytro]*

successful: was it successful? est-ce que ça a réussi? *[eskuh sa a rayœ-see]*

suddenly brusquement [brœskuhmon]

sue: I intend to sue je vais engager des poursuites [juh vay zongajay day poorsweet]

suede du daim [dam]

sugar le sucre [sœkr]

suggest: what do you suggest? que proposez-vous? [kuh propozay-voo]

suit un costume; **it doesn't suit me** (colour etc) ça ne me va pas [sa nuh muh va pa]; **it suits you** ça vous va bien [b-yan]; **that suits me fine** cela me convient très bien [suhla muh konv-yan tray]

suitable (time, place) propice [—peess]

sulk: he's sulking il fait la tête [eel fay la tet]

sultry (weather) lourd [loor]

summer l'été [aytay]; **in the summer** en été

sun le soleil [solay]; **in the sun** au soleil [o]; **out of the sun** à l'ombre [lombr]; **I've had too much sun** je suis resté trop longtemps au soleil [juh swee restay tro lontom]

sunbathe prendre des bains de soleil [prondr day ban duh solay]

sunblock un écran total [aykron toh-tal]

sunburn un coup de soleil [koo duh solay]

sunburnt: I am sunburnt j'ai pris un coup de soleil [jay pree an koo duh solay]

Sunday dimanche [deemonsh]

sunglasses des lunettes de soleil [lœnet duh solay]

sun lounger une chaise longue [shez long]

sunny: if it's sunny s'il y a du soleil [seelya dœ solay]

sunrise le lever du soleil [luhvay dœ solay]

sun roof (in car) le toit ouvrant [twa oovron]

sunset le coucher de soleil [kooshay duh solay]

sunshade (over table) un parasol

sunshine le soleil [solay]

sunstroke une insolation [ansolas-yon]

suntan le bronzage [bronzahj]

suntan lotion du lait solaire [lay]

suntanned bronzé [bronzay]

suntan oil de l'huile solaire [weel]

sun worshipper un fana de soleil [duh solay]

super super [sœpair]; **super!** fantastique! [fontasteek]

superb merveilleux [mairvay-uh]

supermarket le supermarché [sœpairmarshay]

supper le dîner [deenay]

supplement un supplément [sœplaymon]

suppose: I suppose so probablement [prob-abluhmon]

suppository un suppositoire [—twahr]

sure: I'm sure j'en suis sûr [jon swee sœr]; **are you sure?** vous êtes sûr?; **he's sure** il en est sûr; **sure!** d'accord! [dakor]

surf le surf

surfboard une planche de surf [plonsh]

surfing: to go surfing faire du surf

surname le nom de famille [duh famee]

surprise la surprise [sœrpreez]

surprising: that's not surprising ce n'est pas surprenant [pa sœrpruhnon]

suspension (on car) la suspension [sœspons-yon]

swallow (verb) avaler [avalay]

swearword un juron [jœron]

sweat (verb) transpirer [tronspeeray]; **all covered in sweat** en nage [on nahj]

sweater un pullover

sweet (taste) sucré [sœkray]; (dessert) le dessert [dessair]

sweets des sucreries [sœkruhree]

swelling une enflure [onflœr]

sweltering étouffant [aytoofon]

swerve: I had to swerve j'ai dû donner un coup de volant [jay dœ donay an koo duh volon]

swim: I'm going for a swim je vais me baigner [juh vay muh benyay]; **do you want to go for a swim?** voulez-vous venir vous baigner? [voolay-voo vuhneer]; **I can't swim** je ne sais pas nager [juh nuh say pa nahjay]

swimming la natation [natas-yon]; **I like swimming** j'aime la natation

swimming costume un maillot de bain [my-o duh ban]

swimming pool la piscine [peeseen]

swimming trunks un maillot de bain [my-o duh ban]

Swiss suisse [sweess]

switch l'interrupteur [antairœpturr]; **could you switch it on?** pourriez-vous l'enclencher? [pooreeay-voo lonklon-

shay]; **could you switch it off?** pourriez-vous l'éteindre? *[laytandr]*
Switzerland la Suisse *[sweess]*
swollen enflé *[onflay]*

swollen glands des ganglions *[gongleeon]*
synagogue une synagogue *[see—]*
synthetic synthétique *[santayteek]*

T

table la table *[tahbl]*; **a table for two** une table pour deux; **at our usual table** à notre table habituelle *[abeetœel]*
tablecloth la nappe
table tennis le ping-pong
table wine un vin ordinaire *[van]*
tactful diplomatique *[deeplomateek]*
tailback un bouchon *[booshon]*
tailor un tailleur *[tie-urr]*
take prendre *[prondr]*; **will you take this to room 12?** pourriez-vous apporter ceci à la chambre 12? *[pooreeay-voo aportay suhsee]*; **will you take me to Hotel ...?** à l'hôtel ..., s'il vous plaît; **do you take credit cards?** acceptez-vous les cartes de crédit? *[axeptay-voo]*; **OK, I'll take it** d'accord, je le prends *[juh luh pron]*; **how long does it take?** combien de temps est-ce que ça prend? *[komb-yan duh tom eskuh sa pron]*; **it took 2 hours** ça a pris deux heures *[sa a pree]*; **is this seat taken?** est-ce que cette place est occupée? *[eskuh set plass et okœpay]*; **I can't take too much sun** je ne supporte pas très bien le soleil *[juh nuh sœport pa]*; **to take away** *(food)* à emporter *[a omportay]*; **will you take this back, it's broken** pouvez-vous reprendre cet objet: il est cassé *[poovay-voo ruhprondr]*; **could you take it in at the waist?** pourriez-vous reprendre la taille? *[pooreeay-voo ruhprondr la tie]*; **when does the plane take off?** à quelle heure est-ce que l'avion décolle? *[daykol]*; **can you take a little off the top?** pouvez-vous couper un peu sur le dessus? *[koopay an puh sœr luh duhsœ]*
talcum powder du talc
talk parler *[parlay]*

tall grand *[gron]*
tampax *(tm)* un tampax *[tom—]*
tampons des tampons hygiéniques *[tompon eejeeayneek]*
tan *(noun)* le bronzage *[bronzahj]*; *(verb)* bronzer *[bronzay]*; **I want to get a good tan** je veux bronzer *[juh vuh]*
tank *(of car)* le réservoir *[rayzairvwahr]*
tap le robinet *[robeenay]*
tape *(for cassette)* la bande magnétique *[bond man-yayteek]*; *(sticky)* le scotch *(tm)*
tape measure un mètre *[metr]*
tape recorder un magnétophone *[man-yaytofon]*
taste le goût *[goo]*; **can I taste it?** est-ce que je peux goûter? *[eskuh juh puh gootay]*; **it has a peculiar taste** ça a un drôle de goût *[sa a an drohl duh goo]*; **it tastes very nice** c'est délicieux *[daylees-yuh]*; **it tastes revolting** c'est dégoûtant *[daygooton]*
taxi un taxi; **will you get me a taxi?** pouvez-vous m'appeler un taxi? *[poovay-voo maplay]*
taxi-driver le chauffeur de taxi
taxi rank la station de taxis *[stas-yon]*
tea *(drink)* le thé *[tay]*; **tea for two please** deux thés, s'il vous plaît *[duh tay]*; **could I have a cup of tea?** une tasse de thé, s'il vous plaît *[œn tass]*
teabag un sachet de thé *[sashay duh tay]*
teach: could you teach me? est-ce que vous pouvez m'apprendre? *[eskuh voo poovay maprondr]*; **could you teach me French?** est-ce que vous pourriez m'enseigner le français? *[... pooreeay monsenyay ...]*
teacher *(junior)* un instituteur (une ins-

titutrice) *[ansteetœturr, —treess]*; (*secondary*) le professeur

team une équipe *[aykeep]*

teapot une théière *[tay-yair]*

tea towel le torchon *[torshon]*

teenager un adolescent *[—son]*

teetotaller: he's a teetotaller il ne boit pas d'alcool *[nuh bwa pa dalkol]*

telegram un télégramme *[taylay—]*; **I want to send a telegram** je voudrais envoyer un télégramme *[juh voodray zonvwy-ay]*

telephone le téléphone *[taylay—]*; **can I make a telephone call?** j'aimerais téléphoner *[jemray taylayfonay]*; **could you talk to him for me on the telephone?** est-ce que vous pourriez lui téléphoner à ma place? *[eskuh voo pooreeay lwee ... plass]*

telephone box une cabine téléphonique *[kabeen taylayfoneek]*

telephone directory un annuaire du téléphone *[anœair dœ taylayfon]*

telephone number le numéro de téléphone *[nœmayro duh taylayfon]*; **what's your telephone number?** quel est votre numéro de téléphone? *[kel ay]*

telephoto lens le téléobjectif *[taylay—]*

television la télévision *[taylayveez-yon]*; **I'd like to watch television** j'aimerais regarder la télévision *[jemray ruhgarday]*; **is the match on television?** est-ce que le match est télédiffusé? *[eskuh ... taylaydeefœzay]*

tell: could you tell him ...? pourriez-vous lui dire ...? *[pooreeay-voo lwee deer]*; **I can't tell the difference** pour moi, il n'y a pas de différence *[poor mwa eel nya pa duh deefayrons]*

temperature la température *[tompayra-tœr]*; **he has a temperature** il a de la fièvre *[eel a duh la fee-evr]*

temporary temporaire *[temporair]*

tenant (*of apartment*) le locataire *[lokatair]*

tennis le tennis *[teneess]*

tennis ball la balle de tennis *[bal duh teneess]*

tennis court le court de tennis *[koor duh teneess]*; **can we use the tennis court?** est-ce que nous pouvons jouer au tennis dans le court? *[eskuh noo povon jooay o teneess don luh koor]*

tennis racket la raquette de tennis *[raket*

duh teneess]*

tent la tente *[tont]*

term (*school*) le trimestre *[treemestr]*

terminus le terminus *[tairmeenœss]*

terrace la terrace *[tair-ass]*; **on the terrace** sur la terrace

terrible épouvantable *[aypoovont-abl]*

terrific fantastique *[fontasteek]*

testicle le testicule *[testeekœl]*

than que *[kuh]*; **smaller than** plus petit que

thanks, thank you merci *[mairsee]*; **thank you very much** merci beaucoup *[bo-koo]*; **thank you for everything** merci pour tout; **no thanks** non, merci

that: that dog ce chien *[suh]*; **that woman** cette femme *[set]*; **that man** cet homme *[set]*; **that one** celui-ci (celle-ci) *[suhlwee-see, sel-see]*; **I hope that ...** j'espère que ... *[kuh]*; **that's perfect** c'est parfait *[say]*; **that's it** (*that's right*) c'est ça *[say sa]*; **is it that expensive?** c'est vraiment cher! *[say vraymon shair]*; **is that ...?** est-ce que c'est ...? *[eskuh say]*

the (*singular*) le (la) *[luh]*; (*plural*) les *[lay]*; *see page 103*

theater, theatre le théâtre *[tay-atr]*

their leur *[lurr]*; *see page 107*

theirs le (la) leur *[luh lurr]*; *see page 111*

them: I like them je les aime beaucoup *[juh layz em]*; **I gave it to them** je le leur ai donné *[juh luh lurr ay donnay]*; **for them** pour eux (elles) *[uh, el]*; *see page 108*

then alors *[alor]*

there là; **over there** là-bas *[la-ba]*; **up there** là-haut *[la-o]*; **there is ...** il y a ... *[eel ya]*; **there are ...** il y a ...; **is there ...?** y a-t-il ...? *[yateel]*; **are there ...?** y a-t-il ...?; **there you are** (*giving something*) voilà *[vwala]*

thermal spring une source thermale *[soorss tairm-al]*

thermometer un thermomètre *[tair-mometr]*

thermos flask un thermos (*tm*) *[tairmos]*

thermostat (*car*) le thermostat *[tairm—]*

these ces *[say]*; **can I have these?** j'aimerais ceux-ci, s'il vous plaît

they ils (elles) *[eel, el]*; **are they ready?** sont-ils (elles) prêt(e)s?; *see page 108*

thick épais *[aypay]*; (*stupid*) bouché *[boo-shay]*

thief le voleur *[volurr]*

thigh la cuisse *[kweess]*

thin mince *[manss]*

thing une chose *[shohz]*; **have you seen my things?** avez-vous vu mes affaires? *[may zafair]*; **first thing in the morning** dès demain matin *[day duhman matan]*

think penser *[ponsay]*; **what do you think?** qu'en pensez-vous? *[kon ponsay-voo]*; **I think so** je pense que oui *[juh ponss kuh wee]*; **I don't think so** je ne crois pas *[juh nuh krwa pa]*; **I'll think about it** je vais y réfléchir *[juh vay zee rayflesheer]*

third party: third party insurance une assurance au tiers *[o t-yair]*

thirsty: I'm thirsty j'ai soif *[jay swaf]*

this: this bridge ce pont *[suh]*; **this hotel** cet hôtel *[set]*; **this street** cette rue *[set]*; **this one** celui-ci (celle-ci) *[suhlwee-see, sel-see]*; **this is my wife** je vous présente ma femme *[juh voo prayzont ma fam]*; **this is my favo(u)rite café** voici mon bistrot préféré *[vwasee]*; **is this yours?** est-ce à vous? *[es a voo]*; **this is ...** (*on phone*) ici ... *[ee-see]*

those ces *[say]*; **not these, those** pas ceux-ci, ceux-là (pas celles-ci, celles-là) *[suh-see, suh-la, sel-see, sel-la]*

thread du fil *[feel]*

throat la gorge *[gorj]*

throat lozenges des pastilles pour la gorge *[pastee poor la gorj]*

throttle le papillon des gaz *[papeeyon day gaz]*

through à travers *[a travair]*; **does the train go through Paris?** est-ce que le train passe par Paris? *[eskuh luh tran pass par]*; **Monday through Friday** du lundi au vendredi *[dœ ... o ...]*; **go straight through the city centre** passez par le centre ville *[passay]*

through train un train direct *[tran dee-rekt]*

throw lancer *[lonsay]*; **don't throw it away** ne le jetez pas *[nuh luh juhtay pa]*; **I'm going to throw up** je vais être malade *[juh vay zetr malad]*

thumb le pouce *[pooss]*

thumbtack une punaise *[pœnez]*

thunder le tonnerre *[tonair]*

thunderstorm un orage *[orahj]*

Thursday jeudi *[jurdee]*

ticket le billet *[beeyay]*; (*bus, checkroom, cloakroom*) le ticket *[teekay]*

ticket office le guichet *[gheeshay]*

tide: at low tide à marée basse *[maray bas]*; **at high tide** à marée haute *[oht]*

tie (*necktie*) une cravate

tight (*clothes*) serré *[serray]*; **the waist is too tight** ça serre à la taille *[sa sair]*

tights des collants *[kollon]*

time le temps *[tom]*; **what's the time?** quelle heure est-il? *[kel urr eteel]*; **at what time do you close?** à quelle heure fermez-vous?; **there's not much time** il ne reste pas beaucoup de temps *[eel nuh rest pa bo-koo]*; **for the time being** pour le moment *[poor luh momon]*; **from time to time** de temps en temps *[duh tom zon tom]*; **right on time** à l'heure exacte *[a lurr]*; **this time** cette fois *[set fwa]*; **last time** la dernière fois; **next time** la prochaine fois; **four times** quatre fois; **have a good time!** amusez-vous bien! *[amœzay-voo b-yan]*; *see page 118*

timetable un horaire *[orair]*

tin (*can*) une boîte *[bwat]*

tinfoil du papier d'aluminium *[papyay]*

tin-opener un ouvre-boîte *[oovr-bwat]*

tint (*hair*) teindre *[tandr]*

tiny minuscule *[meenœskœl]*

tip le pourboire *[poorbwahr]*; **does that include the tip?** est-ce que le pourboire est compris? *[eskuh luh poorbwahr ay kompree]*

tire (*for car*) le pneu *[pnuh]*

tired fatigué *[fateegay]*; **I'm tired** je suis fatigué

tiring fatigant *[fateegon]*

tissues des kleenex (*tm*)

to: to Marseilles à Marseille; **to England** en Angleterre *[on]*; **to the airport** à l'aéroport; **here's to you!** (*toast*) à votre santé! *[a votr sontay]*; *see page 118*

toast du pain grillé *[pan greeyay]*; (*drinking*) le toast

tobacco le tabac *[taba]*

tobacconist, tobacco store le (bureau de) tabac *[taba]*

today aujourd'hui *[ojoordwee]*; **today week** aujourd'hui en huit *[on weet]*

toe un orteil *[ortay]*

toffee un caramel

together ensemble; **we're together** nous sommes ensemble; **can we pay to-**

gether? pouvons-nous payer ensemble? *[poovon-noo payay]*

toilet les toilettes *[twalet]*; **where's the toilet?** où sont les toilettes? *[oo son lay]*; **I have to go to the toilet** j'aimerais aller aux toilettes *[jemray alay o]*; **she's in the toilet** elle est aux toilettes

toilet paper du papier hygiénique *[papyay eejeeayneek]*

toilet water une eau de toilette *[o duh]*

toll le péage *[payahj]*; **motorway toll** le péage autoroutier *[otorooteeay]*

tomato la tomate *[tomat]*

tomato juice un jus de tomate *[joo duh tomat]*

tomato ketchup le ketchup

tomorrow demain *[duhman]*; **tomorrow morning** demain matin; **tomorrow afternoon** demain après-midi; **tomorrow evening** demain soir; **the day after tomorrow** après-demain *[apray]*; **see you tomorrow!** à demain!

ton une tonne *[ton]*; *see page 120*

toner une lotion tonique *[lo-syon toneek]*

tongue la langue *[long]*

tonic (water) un schweppes *(tm)*

tonight ce soir *[suh swahr]*; **not tonight** pas ce soir

tonsillitis une angine *[onjeen]*

tonsils les amygdales *[ameegdal]*

too trop *[tro]*; *(also)* aussi *[o-see]*; **too much** trop; **me too** moi aussi *[mwa]*; **I'm not feeling too good** je ne me sens pas très bien *[pa tray b-yan]*

tooth la dent *[don]*

toothache le mal de dents *[mal duh don]*

toothbrush une brosse à dents *[bross a don]*

toothpaste le dentifrice *[donteefreess]*

top: on top of ... sur ... *[soor]*; **on top of the car** sur le toit de la voiture *[soor luh twa]*; **on the top floor** au dernier étage *[o dairnyayr aytahj]*; **at the top** tout en haut *[tooton o]*; **at the top of the hill** au sommet de la colline *[o somay duh la koleen]*; **top quality** de qualité supérieure *[duh kaleetay soopayree-urr]*; **bikini top** un haut de bikini *[o duh]*

topless seins nus *[san noo]*; **topless beach** une plage seins nus

torch une lampe de poche *[lomp duh posh]*

total le total *[toh-tal]*

touch toucher *[tooshay]*; **let's keep in touch** restons en contact *[reston zon kontakt]*

tough *(meat)* coriace *[koreeass]*; **tough luck!** manque de pot! *[monk duh po]*

tour une excursion *[exkoors-yon]*; **is there a tour of ...?** y a-t-il une visite guidée de ...? *[yateel oon veezeet gheeday duh]*

tour guide le guide *[gheed]*

tourist le touriste *[tooreest]*

tourist office le syndicat d'initiative *[sandeeka deeneessee-ateev]*

touristy: somewhere not so touristy un endroit pas trop touristique *[an ondrwa pa tro tooreesteek]*

tour operator une agence de voyages *[ajonss duh vwy-ahj]*

tow: can you give me a tow? pourriez-vous me remorquer? *[pooreeay-voo muh ruhmorkay]*

toward(s) vers *[vair]*; **toward(s) Lorient** dans la direction de Lorient *[don la deerex-yon duh]*

towel une serviette *[sairvee-et]*

town une ville *[veel]*; **in town** en ville *[on]*; **which bus goes into town?** quel bus faut-il prendre pour se rendre en ville? *[kel boos fohteel prondr poor suh rondr]*

town hall la mairie *[mairee]*

tow rope une corde de dépannage *[kord duh daypanahj]*

toy le jouet *[jooay]*

track suit le survêtement de sport *[soorvetmon duh spor]*

traditional traditionnel *[tradeess-yonel]*; **a traditional French meal** un repas typiquement français *[... teepeekmon ...]*

traffic la circulation *[seerkoolas-yon]*

traffic circle le sens giratoire *[sons jeeratwahr]*

traffic cop un agent de la circulation *[ajon duh la seerkoolas-yon]*

traffic jam un embouteillage *[ombootayahj]*

traffic light(s) les feux *[fuh]*

trailer *(for carrying tent etc)* une remorque *[ruhmork]*; *(caravan)* une caravane

train le train *[tran]*; **when's the next train to ...?** quand part le prochain train pour ...? *[kon par]*; **by train** en train *[on]*

trainers *(shoes)* des chaussures de sport *[shohsoor duh spor]*

train station la gare [gar]

tram le tram

tramp (*person*) le clochard [kloshar]

tranquillizers des calmants [kalmon]

transatlantic transatlantique [tron-zatlonteek]

transformer un transformateur [tronz-formaturr]

transistor (radio) un transistor [tron-zeestor]

transit lounge la salle de transit [sal duh tronzeet]

translate traduire [tradweer]; **could you translate that?** pourriez-vous me traduire cela? [pooreeay-voo muh ... suhla]

translation une traduction [tradœx-yon]

transmission (*of car*) la transmission [tronzmeess-yon]

travel voyager [vwyahj-ay]; **we're travel(l)ing around** nous visitons la région [noo veezeeton la rayjeeon]

travel agent une agence de voyage [ajonss duh vwyahj]

travel(l)er le voyageur [vwyahjurr]

traveller's cheque, traveler's check le chèque de voyage [shek duh vwyahj]

tray un plateau

tree un arbre [arbr]

tremendous fantastique [fontasteek]

trendy à la mode

tricky (*difficult*) délicat [dayleeka]

trim: just a trim please pouvez-vous me les égaliser, s'il vous plaît? [poovay-voo muh lay zaygaleezay]

trip un voyage [vwyahj]; **I'd like to go on a trip to ...** j'aimerais faire une excursion à ... [jemray fair œn exkœrs-yon]; **have a good trip!** bon voyage!

tripod un trépied [trayp-yay]

tropical tropical

trouble des ennuis [on-nwee]; **I'm having trouble with ...** j'ai des problèmes de ... [jay day prob-lem]; **sorry to trouble you** désolé de vous déranger [dayzolay duh voo dayronjay]

trousers un pantalon [pontalon]

trouser suit un ensemble-pantalon [on-sombl-pontalon]

trout une truite [trweet]

truck un camion [kamyon]

truck driver un camionneur [ka-myonurr]

true vrai [vray]; **that's not true** ce n'est pas vrai

trunk (*car*) le coffre [kofr]

trunks (*swimming*) un maillot de bain [my-o duh ban]

truth la vérité [vayreetay]; **it's the truth** c'est la vérité

try essayer [esay-ay]; **please try** pouvez-vous essayer, s'il vous plaît? [poovay-voo]; **I've never tried it** (*food*) je n'en ai jamais goûté [juh non ay jamay gootay]; (*sport*) je n'ai jamais essayé [juh nay ja-mayz esay-ay]; **can I have a try?** est-ce que je peux essayer? [eskuh juh puh]; **may I try it on?** est-ce que je peux l'essayer?

T-shirt un T-shirt

tube (*for tyre*) une chambre à air [shombr a air]

Tuesday mardi [mardee]

tuition: I'd like tuition j'aimerais des leçons [jemray day luhson]

tulip une tulipe [tœleep]

tuna fish le thon [ton]

tune un air

tunnel le tunnel [tœnel]

Turkey la Turquie [tœrkee]

turn: it's my turn next c'est à mon tour [set a mon toor]; **turn left** tournez à gauche [toornay]; **where do we turn off?** où devons-nous bifurquer? [oo duhvon-noo beefœrkay]; **can you turn the air-conditioning on?** est-ce que vous pouvez mettre l'air climatisé? [es-kuh voo poovay]; **can you turn the air-conditioning off?** est-ce que vous pouvez arrêter l'air climatisé? [... aretay ...]; **he didn't turn up** il n'est pas venu [eel nay pa vuhnœ]

turning (*in road*) la bifurcation [bee-fœrkas-yon]

TV la télé [taylay]

tweezers une pince à épiler [panss a ay-peelay]

twice deux fois [duh fwa]; **twice as much** deux fois plus [plœss]

twin beds des lits jumeaux [lee jœmo]

twins des jumeaux (jumelles) [jœmo, jœ-mel]

twist: I've twisted my ankle je me suis tordu la cheville [juh muh swee tordœ la shuhvee]

type le type [teep]; **a different type of ...** une autre sorte de ... [ohtr sort duh]

typewriter une machine à écrire *[ma-sheen a aykreer]*
typhoid la typhoïde *[teefoeed]*

typical typique *[teepeek]*
tyre le pneu *[pnuh]*
tyre-lever un démonte-pneu *[daymont—]*

U

ugly laid *[lay]*
ulcer un ulcère *[oolsair]*
Ulster l'Irlande du Nord *[eerlond doo nor]*
umbrella un parapluie *[paraplwee]*
uncle: my uncle mon oncle *[onkl]*
uncomfortable (*chair*) peu confortable *[puh confort-abl]*
unconscious sans connaissance *[son ko-nessonss]*
under sous *[soo]*
underdone (*food*) mal cuit *[kwee]*
underground (*rail*) le métro *[maytro]*
underpants un slip *[sleep]*
undershirt un maillot de corps *[my-o duh kor]*
understand: I don't understand je ne comprends pas *[juh nuh kompron pa]*; **I understand** je comprends; **do you understand?** comprenez-vous? *[kompruhnay-voo]*
underwear des sous-vêtements *[soovetmon]*
undo (*clothes*) défaire *[dayfair]*
uneatable: it's uneatable c'est immangeable *[set amonj-abl]*
unemployed au chômage *[o shomahj]*
unfair: that's unfair ce n'est pas juste *[suh nay pa joost]*
unfortunately malheureusement *[malururzmon]*
unfriendly désagréable *[dayzagray-abl]*
unhappy malheureux *[maluruh]*
unhealthy malsain *[malsan]*
United States les Etats-Unis *[aytazoonee]*; **in the United States** aux Etats-Unis
university l'université *[—vairseetay]*
unlimited mileage le kilométrage illimité *[keelomaytrahj eeleemeetay]*
unlock ouvrir *[oovreer]*; **the door was unlocked** la porte n'était pas fermée à

clef *[la port naytay pa fairmay a klay]*
unpack défaire sa valise *[dayfair]*
unpleasant désagréable *[dayzagray-abl]*
untie défaire *[dayfair]*
until jusqu'à *[jooska]*; **until we meet again** jusqu'à la prochaine *[jooskala proshen]*; **not until Wednesday** pas avant mercredi *[pa zavon]*
unusual inhabituel *[eenabeetooel]*
up en haut *[on o]*; **further up the road** plus loin sur cette route *[ploo lwan soor set root]*; **up there** là-haut *[la-o]*; **he's not up yet** il n'est pas encore levé *[eel nay pa zonkor luhvay]*; **what's up?** que se passe-t-il? *[kuh suh pasteel]*
upmarket chic *[sheek]*
upset stomach: I have an upset stomach j'ai une indigestion *[jay oon andeejest-yon]*
upside down à l'envers *[a lonvair]*
upstairs en haut *[on o]*
urgent urgent *[oorjon]*; **it's very urgent** c'est très urgent
urinary tract infection une infection du canal urinaire *[anfex-yon doo kanal ooreenair]*
us nous *[noo]*; **with us** avec nous; **please help us** pouvez-vous nous aider, s'il vous plaît? *[poovay-voo]*; *see page 108*
use: may I use ...? puis-je me servir de ...? *[pweej muh sairveer duh]*
used: I used to swim a lot dans le temps, je faisais beaucoup de natation *[don luh tom juh fuhzay]*; **when I get used to the heat** lorsque je me serai habitué à la chaleur *[lorsk juh muh suhray abeetooay]*
useful utile *[ooteel]*
usual habituel *[abeetooel]*; **as usual** comme d'habitude *[kom dabeetood]*
usually d'habitude *[dabetood]*
U-turn un demi-tour *[duhmee-toor]*

V

vacancy: do you have any vacancies?
(*hotel*) avez-vous de la place? *[avay-voo
duh la plass]*
vacation les vacances *[vakonss]*; **we're
here on vacation** nous sommes ici en
vacances *[... on ...]*
vaccination la vaccination *[vaxeenas-
yon]*
vacuum cleaner un aspirateur *[aspee-
raturr]*
vacuum flask un thermos (*tm*) *[tairmos]*
vagina le vagin *[vajan]*
valid valable *[val-abl]*; **how long is it
valid for?** jusqu'à quand est-il valable?
[jɷska kon eteel]
valley la vallée *[valay]*
valuable de valeur *[duh valurr]*; **can I
leave my valuables here?** est-ce que je
peux laisser mes objets de valeur ici? *[...
objay ...]*
value la valeur *[valurr]*
van la camionnette *[kameeonet]*
vanilla la vanille *[vanee]*; **vanilla ice
cream** une glace à la vanille *[glass]*
varicose veins des varices *[vareess]*
variety show un spectacle de variétés
[spek-takl duh vareeaytay]
vary: it varies ça dépend *[sa daypon]*
vase un vase *[vahz]*
vaudeville un spectacle de variétés *[spek-
takl duh vareeaytay]*
VD une maladie vénérienne *[maladee vay-
nayree-en]*
veal le veau *[vo]*
vegetables les légumes *[laygɷm]*
vegetarian végétarien(ne) *[vayjaytaree-
an, —en]*; **I'm a vegetarian** je suis vé-
gétarien
velvet le velours
vending machine un distributeur au-

tomatique *[deestreebɷturr otomateek]*
ventilator le ventilateur *[vonteelaturr]*
verruca une verrue *[verɷ]*
very très *[tray]*; **just a very little French**
un tout petit peu de français *[an too ptee
puh]*; **just a very little for me** un tout
petit peu pour moi; **I like it very much**
ça me plaît beaucoup *[sa muh play bo-
koo]*
vest un maillot de corps *[my-o duh kor]*;
(*waistcoat*) un gilet *[jeelay]*
via par
video vidéo *[veedayo]*
video recorder un magnétoscope *[ma-
nyaytoskop]*
view la vue *[vɷ]*; **what a superb view!**
quelle vue magnifique! *[man-yeefeek]*
viewfinder le viseur *[veezurr]*
villa une villa *[veela]*
village le village *[veelahj]*
vine la vigne *[veen]*
vinegar le vinaigre *[veenegr]*
vine-growing area une région viticole
[rayjeeon veeteekol]
vineyard le vignoble *[veen-yobl]*
vintage le millésime *[meelayzeem]*; **vintage wine** un grand vin *[gron van]*
visa le visa
visibility la visibilité *[veezeebeeleetay]*
visit visiter *[veezeetay]*; **I'd like to visit ...**
j'aimerais visiter ... *[jemray]*; **come and
visit us** venez nous voir *[vuhnay noo
vwahr]*
vital: it's vital that ... il faut absolument
que ... *[eel foht absolɷmon]*
vitamins les vitamines *[veetameen]*
vodka une vodka
voice la voix *[vwa]*
voltage le voltage *[volt-ahj]*
vomit vomir *[vomeer]*

W

waist la taille *[tie]*

waistcoat le gilet *[jeelay]*

wait attendre *[atondr]*; **wait for me!** attendez-moi! *[atonday-mwa]*; **don't wait for me** ne m'attendez pas *[nuh]*; **it was worth waiting for** ça valait la peine d'attendre *[sa valay la pen datondr]*; **I'll wait till my wife comes** je vais attendre le retour de ma femme *[juh vay zatondr luh ruhtoor duh ma fam]*; **I'll wait a little longer** je vais attendre encore un moment *[onkor an momon]*; **can you do it while I wait?** pouvez-vous le faire tout de suite? *[poovay-voo luh fair toot sweet]*

waiter le serveur *[sairvurr]*; **waiter!** garçon! *[garson]*

waiting room la salle d'attente *[sal datont]*

waitress la serveuse *[sairvurz]*; **waitress!** s'il vous plaît! *[seel voo play]*

wake: will you wake me up at 6.30? pouvez-vous me réveiller à 6 heures 30? *[poovay-voo muh rayvayay]*

Wales le Pays de Galles *[payee duh gal]*

walk: let's walk there allons-y à pied *[alon-zee a p-yay]*; **is it possible to walk there?** peut-on y aller à pied? *[puhton ee alay]*; **I'll walk back** je vais rentrer à pied *[juh vay rontray]*; **is it a long walk?** est-ce loin à pied? *[es lwan]*; **it's only a short walk** c'est à deux pas d'ici *[set a duh pa dee-see]*; **I'm going out for a walk** je vais faire un tour *[juh vay fair an toor]*; **let's take a walk around town** que diriez-vous d'une promenade en ville? *[kuh deereeay-voo doon promnad]*

walking: I want to do some walking j'aimerais faire de la marche *[jemray fair duh la marsh]*

walking boots des chaussures de marche *[shohsœr duh marsh]*

walking stick une canne

walkman (*tm*) un walkman

wall (*inside*) la paroi *[parwa]*; (*outside*) le mur *[mœr]*

wallet le portefeuille *[portfuh-ee]*

wander: I like just wandering around j'aime bien flâner *[jem b-yan flanay]*

want: I want a ... j'aimerais un ... *[jemray]*; **I don't want any ...** je ne veux pas de ... *[juh nuh vuh pa duh]*; **I want to go home** j'aimerais rentrer à la maison; **I don't want to** non, je ne veux pas; **he wants to ...** il veut ... *[eel vuh]*; **what do you want?** que voulez-vous? *[kuh voolay-voo]*

war la guerre *[gair]*

ward (*in hospital*) la salle *[sal]*

warm chaud *[sho]*; **it's so warm today** il fait tellement chaud aujourd'hui *[eel fay telmon]*; **I'm too warm** j'ai trop chaud *[jay tro]*

warning un avertissement *[avairteesmon]*

was: it was ... c'était ... *[saytay]*; **was it ...?** était-ce ...? *[aytayss]*; *see page 113*

wash laver *[lavay]*; **I need a wash** j'aimerais me débarbouiller *[jemray muhdaybarboouyay]*; **can you wash the car?** pouvez-vous laver la voiture? *[poovay-voo]*; **can you wash these?** pouvez-vous laver ceci, s'il vous plaît?; **it'll wash off** (*stain etc*) ça partira au lavage *[sa parteera o lavahj]*

washcloth un gant de toilette *[gon duh twalet]*

washer (*for bolt etc*) un joint *[jwan]*

washhand basin le lavabo

washing (*clothes*) la lessive *[leseev]*; **where can I hang my washing?** où puis-je faire sécher ma lessive? *[oo pweej fair sayshay ma leseev]*; **can you do my washing for me?** pourriez-vous faire laver ce linge? *[pooreeay-voo fair lavay suh lanj]*

washing machine la machine à laver

[la lavay]
washing powder la poudre à lessive *[poodr a leseev]*
washing-up: I'll do the washing-up je ferai la vaisselle *[juh fuhray la ves-el]*
washing-up liquid du lave-vaisselle *[lav-ves-el]*
wasp une guêpe *[ghep]*
wasteful: that's wasteful quel gaspillage! *[kel gaspee-yahj]*
wastepaper basket une corbeille à papier *[korbay a papyay]*
watch (*wrist-*) une montre *[montr]*; **will you watch my things for me?** pourriez-vous me garder mes affaires, s'il vous plaît? *[pooreeay-voo muh garday]*; **I'll just watch** je préfère regarder *[juh prayfair ruhgarday]*; **watch out!** attention! *[atons-yon]*
watch strap le bracelet-montre *[braslaymontr]*
water l'eau *[o]*; **waiter, may I have some water?** pourriez-vous m'apporter de l'eau, s'il vous plaît? *[pooreeay-voo maportay]*
watercolour une aquarelle
waterproof imperméable *[ampairmayabl]*
waterski: I'd like to learn to waterski j'aimerais apprendre à faire du ski nautique *[jemray zaprondr a fair doo skee noteek]*
waterskiing le ski nautique *[skee noteek]*
water sports les sports nautiques *[spor noteek]*
water wings des flotteurs de natation *[flotturr duh natas-yon]*
wave (*sea*) la vague *[vag]*
way: which way is it? par où est-ce? *[par oo es]*; **it's this way** c'est par ici *[say par ee-see]*; **it's that way** c'est par là; **could you tell me the way to …?** pouvez-vous m'indiquer le chemin de …? *[poovay-voo mandeekay luh shuhman]*; **is it on the way to Nice?** est-ce sur la route de Nice? *[es soor la root duh]*; **you're blocking the way** vous bouchez le passage *[voo booshay luh pas-ahj]*; **is it a long way to …?** est-ce que c'est loin d'ici à …? *[eskuh say lwan dee-see]*; **would you show me the way to do it?** pouvez-vous me montrer comment faire? *[muh montray komon fair]*; **do it this way** faites comme

ceci *[fet kom suhsee]*; **we want to eat the French way** nous aimerions manger à la française *[ala fronsez]*; **no way!** pas question! *[pa kestyon]*
we nous *[noo]*; *see page 108*
weak faible *[febl]*
wealthy riche *[reesh]*
weather le temps *[tom]*; **what foul weather!** quel temps épouvantable! *[aypoovont-abl]*; **what beautiful weather!** quel temps magnifique! *[man-yeefeek]*
weather forecast les prévisions météorologiques *[prayveez-yon maytay-orolojeek]*
wedding un mariage *[mareeahj]*
wedding anniversary l'anniversaire de mariage *[duh mareeahj]*
wedding ring une alliance *[aleeonss]*
Wednesday mercredi *[mairkruhdee]*
week une semaine *[suhmen]*; **a week (from) today** aujourd'hui en huit *[ojoordwee on weet]*; **a week (from) tomorrow** demain en huit; **Monday week** lundi en huit
weekend: at/on the weekend ce weekend
weight le poids *[pwa]*; **I want to lose weight** j'aimerais perdre du poids *[jemray pairdr doo pwa]*
weight limit le poids limite *[pwa leemeet]*
weird étrange *[aytronj]*
welcome: welcome to … bienvenue à … *[b-yan-vuhnoo]*; **you're welcome** je vous en prie *[juh voo zon pree]*
well: I don't feel well je ne me sens pas bien *[juh nuh muh son pa b-yan]*; **I haven't been very well** j'ai été peu bien *[jay aytay puh b-yan]*; **she's not well** elle ne se sens pas bien *[… son …]*; **how are you? — very well, thanks** comment allez-vous — très bien, merci *[tray b-yan]*; **you speak English very well** vous parlez très bien l'anglais; **me as well** moi aussi *[mwa o-see]*; **well done!** bravo!; **well, …** eh bien, …; **well well!** tiens! *[t-yan]*
well-done (*steak*) bien cuit *[b-yan kwee]*
wellingtons des bottes en caoutchouc *[bot on kaoochoo]*
Welsh gallois *[galwa]*
were *see page 113*
west l'ouest *[west]*; **to the west** vers l'ouest *[vair]*

West Indian antillais *[onteeyay]*
West Indies les Antilles *[ontee]*
wet mouillé *[mooyay]*; **it's all wet** il est tout mouillé; **it's been wet all week** il a plu toute la semaine *[eel a plœ toot la suhmen]*
wet suit une combinaison de plongée *[kombeenezzon duh plonjay]*
what? quoi? *[kwa]*; **what's that?** qu'est-ce que c'est? *[keskuh say]*; **what are you drinking?** *(can I get you one?)* que buvez-vous? *[kuh bœvay-voo]*; **I don't know what to do** je ne sais que faire *[kuh fair]*; **what a view!** quelle vue magnifique! *[kel]*
wheel la roue *[roo]*
wheelchair un fauteuil roulant *[fotuh-ee roolon]*
when? quand? *[kon]*; **when we get back** à notre retour *[a notr ruhtoor]*; **when does it start?** à quelle heure est-ce que ça commence? *[a kel urr]*
where? où? *[oo]*; **where is …?** où est …? *[oo ay]*; **I don't know where he is** je ne sais pas où il est; **this is where I left it** c'est ici que je l'ai laissé *[set ee-see kuh juh lay lessay]*
which: which bus? quel bus? *[kel]*; **which one?** lequel (laquelle)? *[luhkel, lakel]*; **which is yours?** quel(le) est le (la) vôtre?; **I forget which it was** j'ai oublié lequel c'était; **the one which …** celui (celle) qui … *[suhlwee (sel) kee]*
while: while I'm here pendant que je suis ici *[pondon kuh]*
whipped cream de la crème fouettée *[krem fooetay]*
whisky le whisky
whisper chuchoter *[shœshotay]*
white blanc(he) *[blon, blonsh]*
white wine du vin blanc *[van blon]*
Whitsun la Pentecôte *[pontkot]*
who? qui? *[kee]*; **who was that?** qui était-ce? *[kee aytayss]*; **the man who …** l'homme qui …
whole: the whole week toute la semaine *[toot]*; **two whole days** deux jours entiers *[ontyay]*; **the whole lot** le tout *[luh too]*
whooping cough la coqueluche *[kok-lœsh]*
whose: whose is this? à qui est ceci? *[a kee ay suhsee]*

why? pourquoi? *[poorkwa]*; **why not?** pourquoi pas? *[pa]*; **that's why it's not working** voilà pourquoi ça ne marche pas *[vwala]*
wide large *[larj]*
wide-angle lens un objectif grand angle *[objekteef grond ongl]*
widow une veuve *[vurv]*
widower un veuf *[vurf]*
wife: my wife ma femme *[fam]*
wig une perruque *[perœk]*
will: will you give this to him? pourriez-vous lui donner ceci? *[pooreeay-voo]*; *see page 116*
win gagner *[ganyay]*; **who won?** qui est-ce qui a gagné? *[kee eskee a ganyay]*
wind le vent *[von]*
window la fenêtre *[fuhnetr]*; *(of shop)* la vitrine *[veetreen]*; **near the window** près de la fenêtre; **in the window** *(of shop)* en vitrine *[on]*
window seat une place près de la fenêtre *[plass pray duh la fuhnetr]*
windscreen, windshield le pare-brise *[par-breez]*
windscreen wipers, windshield wipers les essuie-glace *[eswee-glass]*
windsurf: I'd like to windsurf j'aimerais faire de la planche à voile *[jemray fair duh la plonsh a vwal]*
windsurfing la planche à voile *[plonsh a vwal]*
windy: it's so windy il y a beaucoup de vent *[eelya bo-koo duh von]*
wine le vin *[van]*; **can we have some more wine?** encore un peu de vin, s'il vous plaît *[onkor an puh]*
wine glass un verre à vin *[vair a van]*
wine list la carte des vins *[kart day van]*
wine-tasting la dégustation de vin *[day-gœstas-yon duh van]*
wing une aile *[el]*
wing mirror le rétroviseur *[raytro-veezurr]*
winter l'hiver *[eevair]*; **in the winter** en hiver *[on]*
winter holiday les vacances d'hiver *[va-konss deevair]*
winter sports les sports d'hiver *[spor dee-vair]*
wire le fil de fer *[feel duh fair]*; *(elec)* le fil
wireless une radio *[rad-yo]*
wiring *(in house)* l'installation électrique

[anstalas-yon aylektreek]

wish: wishing you were here je m'ennuie de vous [juh mon-nwee duh voo]; **best wishes** meilleurs vœux [mayurr vuh]

with avec [avek]; **I'm staying with …** j'habite chez … [jabeet shay]

without sans [son]

witness le témoin [taymwan]; **will you be a witness for me?** voulez-vous me servir de témoin? [voolay-voo muh sairveer duh]

witty (person) spirituel [speereetœel]

wobble: the wheel wobbles la roue est voilée [la roo ay vwalay]

woman une femme [fam]; **women** les femmes

wonderful merveilleux [mairvayuh]

won't: the engine won't start le moteur refuse de démarrer [refœz duh daymaray]; see page 116

wood (material) le bois [bwa]

woods (forest) la forêt [foray]

wool la laine [len]

word le mot [mo]; **what does that word mean?** que signifie ce mot?; **you have my word** je vous donne ma parole [juh voo don]

work travailler [tra-vy-ay]; **how does it work?** comment est-ce que ça fonctionne? [komon eskuh sa fonx-yon]; **it's not working** ça ne marche pas [sa nuh marsh pa]; **I work in an office** je travaille dans un bureau [juh trav-eye]; **do you have any work for me?** avez-vous du travail pour moi? [avay-voo dœ trav-eye]; **when do you finish work?** à quelle heure quittez-vous votre travail? [a kel urr keetay-voo]

world le monde [mond]

worn-out (person) épuisé [aypweezay]; (clothes, shoes) usé [œzay]

worry: I'm worried about her je me fais du souci pour elle [juh muh fay dœ soosee poor el]; **don't worry** ne vous faites pas de souci [nuh voo fet pa]

worse: it's worse c'est pire [say peer]; **it's getting worse** ça empire [sa ompeer]

worst le pire [luh peer]

worth: it's not worth 50 ça ne vaut pas 50 [sa nuh vo pa]; **it's worth more than that** ça vaut plus que ça [plœss kuh sa]; **is it worth a visit?** est-ce que ça vaut le détour? [eskuh sa vo luh daytoor]

would: would you give this to …? pourriez-vous donner ceci à …? [pooreeay-voo donay suhsee]; **what would you do?** que feriez-vous à ma place? [kuh fuhreeay-voo a ma plass]

wrap: could you wrap it up? pourriez-vous me l'emballer? [pooreeay-voo muh lombalay]

wrapping un emballage [ombalahj]

wrapping paper du papier d'emballage [papyay dombalahj]

wrench (tool) une clef anglaise [klay onglez]

wrist le poignet [pwanyay]

write écrire [aykreer]; **could you write it down?** pouvez-vous me l'écrire? [poovay-voo muh laykreer]; **how do you write it?** comment est-ce que ça s'écrit? [komont eskuh sa saykree]; **I'll write to you** je vous écrirai [juh voo zaykreeray]; **I wrote to you last month** je vous ai écrit le mois passé [juh voo zay aykree]

write-off (car) bon pour la ferraille [poor la fair-eye]

writer un écrivain [aykreevan]

writing paper du papier à lettres [papyay a letr]

wrong: you're wrong vous vous trompez [voo voo trompay]; **the bill's wrong** il y a une erreur dans la facture [eelya œn erurr don la faktœr]; **sorry, wrong number** excusez-moi, je me suis trompé de numéro [juh muh swee trompay duh nœmayro]; **I'm on the wrong train** je me suis trompé de train; **I went to the wrong room** je me suis trompé de chambre; **that's the wrong key** ce n'est pas la bonne clef [suh nay pa la bon klay]; **there's something wrong with …** … ne marche pas bien [nuh marsh pa b-yan]; **what's wrong?** qu'y a-t-il? [kyateel]; **what's wrong with it?** quel est le problème? [kel ay luh prob-lem]

X Y Z

X-ray les rayons X *[rayon eex]*

yacht le voilier *[vwalyay]*
yacht club le club de voile *[vwal]*
yard: in the yard dans le jardin *[jardan]*;
see page 119
year une année *[anay]*
yellow jaune *[jo-n]*
yellow pages les pages jaunes *[pahj jo-n]*
yes oui *[wee]*; (*answering negative question*) si!
[see]
yesterday hier *[yair]*; **yesterday morning** hier matin; **yesterday afternoon** hier après-midi; **the day before yesterday** avant-hier *[avont-yair]*
yet: has it arrived yet? est-il arrivé? *[eteel areevay]*; **not yet** pas encore *[pa zonkor]*
yobbo un voyou *[vwy-oo]*
yog(h)urt un yaourt *[yaoor]*
you vous *[voo]*; (*to close friend*) tu *[too]*; **for you** pour vous; (*to close friend*) pour toi

[twa]; *see pages 108, 109*
young jeune *[jurn]*
young people les jeunes *[jurn]*
your votre; (*familiar form*) ton (ta); **your friends** vos amis *[vo zamee]*; (*familiar form*) tes amis *[tay]*; **is this your camera?** est-ce votre/ton appareil-photo?;
see page 107
yours le (la) vôtre *[luh (la) vohtr]*;
(*familiar form*) le tien (la tienne) *[t-yan, t-yen]*; (*plural*) les vôtres/les tiens (tiennes); *see page 111*
youth hostel une auberge de jeunesse *[obairj duh jur-ness]*
youth hostelling: we're youth hostelling nous dormons dans des auberges de jeunesse *[noo dormon don day zobairj duh jur-ness]*
Yugoslavia la Yougoslavie *[—slavee]*

zero zéro *[zayro]*; **it's below zero** la température est au-dessous de zéro degré *[duh zayro duhgray]*
zip, zipper la fermeture éclair *[fairmtoor ayklair]*; **could you put a new zip on?**

pourriez-vous mettre une nouvelle fermeture éclair? *[pooreeay-voo maitr oon noovel]*
zoo le zoo *[zo]*
zoom lens le zoom

French–English

A

à consommer avant le ... eat by ..., best before ...

à emporter to take away, to go

à l'ancienne *[a lons-yen]* traditional style

à la provençale *[provonsahl]* with tomatoes, garlic and herbs

à louer to let, for rent

à moitié prix half price

à point *[a pwan]* medium

à prendre ... fois par jour to be taken ... times a day

à prendre à jeun to be taken on an empty stomach

à prendre après les repas to be taken after meals

à prendre avant le coucher to be taken before going to bed

à tout à l'heure *[a toota lurr]* see you later

à usage externe for external use

à utiliser avant ... use before ...

à vendre for sale

abats *[aba]* offal

abonnements season tickets

abricot *[abreeko]* apricot

accès autorisé pour livraisons deliveries only

accès aux quais to platforms/tracks

accès interdit no entry

accès réservé au personnel staff entrance only

accès réservé aux riverains no entry except for access

accès réservé aux voyageurs munis de billets ticket holders only

accueil reception

achat buying rate

adressez-vous à la réception ask at reception

affranchissements letters and postcards

agent conservateur preservative

agiter avant l'emploi shake before use

agneau *[anyo]* lamb

aiguillette de bœuf *[ay-gwee-yet duh burf]* piece of beef

ail *[eye]* garlic

ailloli *[eye-olee]* garlic mayonnaise

air conditionné air-conditioning

aire de repos rest area

alimentation food; grocer

alimentation générale grocer

aller-retour return/round trip ticket

allez vous faire foutre! *[alay voo fair footr]* go to hell!

allez vous faire voir! *[alay voo fair vwar]* go to hell!

allumez vos phares switch on your lights

allumez vos veilleuses switch on your sidelights/parking lights

alose *[alohz]* shad *(type of fish)*

amande *[amond]* almond

ambassade embassy

ameublement furniture

analgésique pain killer

ananas *[a-nana]* pineapple

anchois *[onshwa]* anchovies

ancien franc old French franc (= *1 centime*)

andouillette *[ondoo-yet]* small sausage

Anglais English

Angleterre England

anguille *[onghee]* eel

annulé cancelled

antiquités antiques

août August

appellation contrôlée mark guaranteeing the quality of a wine

appellation d'origine contrôlée mark guaranteeing the quality of a wine

appuyer ici press here

après-midi afternoon

araignée de mer *[aren-yay duh mair]* spider crab

argent money; silver

argent massif solid silver

arôme naturel/artificiel natural/artificial flavo(u)ring

arrêt stop
arrêt facultatif request stop
arrêtez votre moteur switch off your engine
arrivée arrivals
arrondissement district of Paris
artichaut *[arteesho]* artichoke
articles de camping camping accessories
articles de sport sports goods
articles de voyage travel accessories
artisanat crafts
arts ménagers household goods
ascenseur lift, elevator
asperge *[aspairj]* asparagus
aspic de volaille *[vol-eye]* chicken in aspic
assiette anglaise *[assyet onglez]* selection of cold meat, cold cuts
assure la correspondance avec … connects with …
attachez vos ceintures fasten your seat belt
attendez votre ticket wait for your ticket
attendre la sonorité wait for the dialling tone

attention caution
attention à la marche mind the step
attention, chien méchant beware of the dog
attention, enfants caution, children
attention, fermeture automatique des portières caution, doors close automatically
attention, peinture fraîche wet paint
au choix choice of
au vin blanc *[o van blon]* in white wine
auberge inn
auberge de jeunesse youth hostel
aubergine *[obairjeen]* aubergine, eggplant
autocar coach, bus
autocar postal post bus (*Switzerland*)
autoroute motorway, highway
autoroute à péage toll motorway/highway
auto-stop hitch-hiking
autres destinations other destinations
avec des glaçons with ice
avis notice
avocat *[avoka]* avocado
avril April

B

baba au rhum *[o ram]* rum baba
bagages à main hand baggage
baguette *[bag-et]* stick of bread
baignade dangereuse danger, do not swim here
baignade interdite no swimming
bains douches municipaux public baths
bal du 14 juillet open air dance on the French national holiday
banane *[ba-nan]* banana
bananes flambées *[ba-nan flombay]* bananas flambéd in brandy
bande de cons! *[bond duh kon]* stupid idiots!
banque bank
barbue *[barboo]* brill (*fish*)

barrière de dégel road closed to heavy vehicles during thaw
barrières automatiques automatic gates
bateau boat
bateau-mouche sightseeing boat
bavaroise *[bavarwahrz]* light mousse
bavette à l'échalote *[bavet a layshalot]* grilled beef with shallots
bd boulevard
BD (bande dessinée) comic strip
béarnaise *[bay-arnez]* sauce made with egg yolk, lemon juice or vinegar, butter and herbs
bécasse *[baykass]* woodcock
béchamel *[bayshamel]* thick white sauce made of cream, butter and flour
beignet *[benyay]* fritter, doughnut

beignet aux pommes [benyay o pom] apple fritter

belge Belgian

Belgique Belgium

betterave [betrahv] beetroot

beurre [burr] butter

beurre d'anchois [burr donch-wa] anchovy paste

beurre d'estragon [burr destragon] butter with tarragon

beurre noir [burr nwahr] dark melted butter

bibliothèque municipale public library

bien cuit [byan kwee] well done (meat)

bienvenue à … welcome to …

bière [bee-air] beer

bière blonde [bee-air blond] lager

bière brune [bee-air broon] bitter, dark beer

bière panachée [bee-air panashay] shandy

bifteck [beeftek] steak

bifteck de cheval [beeftek duh shval] horsemeat steak

bijouterie jewel(l)er

bijoux jewel(l)ery

billet de banque banknote, bill

billets tickets

billets internationaux international tickets

billets périmés used tickets

biscuit de Savoie [beesskwee duh savwa] sponge cake

bisque d'écrevisses [beesk daykruh-veess] freshwater crayfish soup

bisque de homard [beesk duh omar] lobster bisque

bisque de langoustines [beesk duh longoosteen] saltwater crayfish soup

blanc [blon] white wine

blanc de blancs [blon duh blon] white wine from white grapes

blanchisserie laundry

blanquette de Limoux [blonket duh lee-moo] sparkling white wine from Languedoc

blanquette de veau [blonket duh vo] veal stew

bleu [bluh] very rare

bleu d'Auvergne [bluh dovairn] blue cheese from Auvergne

bœuf [burf] beef

bœuf à la ficelle [burf ala feesel] beef cooked in stock

bœuf bourguignon [burf boor-gheen-yon] beef cooked in red wine

bœuf braisé [burf brezay] braised beef

bœuf en daube [burf on dohb] beef casserole

bœuf miroton [burf meeroton] boiled beef with onions

bœuf mode [burf mod] beef stew with carrots

boissons pilotes most common drinks (low priced)

boîte de nuit night club

bolet [bolay] boletus (mushroom)

bottin telephone directory

bouchée à la reine [booshay ala ren] vol-au-vent

boucherie butcher

boucherie chevaline horsemeat butcher

boucherie-charcuterie butcher

boudin [boodan] black pudding, blood sausage

bouillabaisse [booya-bess] fish soup from the south of France

bouillon [booyon] broth

bouillon de légumes [booyon duh lay-goom] vegetable stock

bouillon de poule [booyon duh pool] chicken stock

boulangerie bakery

boulangerie-pâtisserie baker and confectioner

boulette [boolet] meatball

bouquet rose [bookay roz] prawn

Bourgogne [boor-gon] wine from the Burgundy area

bourride [booreed] fish soup

boutique small shop/store

boutique de mode clothes boutique

boutique hors-taxe duty free shop/store

BP (boîte postale) PO Box

braisé [brezay] braised

brandade de morue [brondad duh mo-roo] cod in cream and garlic

brasserie pub, bar

Bretagne Brittany

bricolage do-it-yourself

brioche [bree-osh] round bun

britannique British

brocante secondhand goods

brochet [broshay] pike

brochette [broshet] kebab

Brouilly [broo-ee] red wine from the

Beaujolais area
brugnon *[brœn-yon]* nectarine
brûlot *[brœlo]* flamed brandy

brushing blow-dry
bureau d'accueil reception centre/center
bureautique electronic office equipment

C

cabillaud *[kabeeyo]* cod
cabinet dentaire dentist
cabinet médical doctor's surgery/office
cadeaux gifts
cadeaux-souvenirs gift shop/store
café *[kafay]* coffee; café, bar
café au lait *[kafay o lay]* white coffee
café crème *[kafay krem]* white coffee
café glacé *[kafay glassay]* iced coffee
café viennois *[kafay vee-enwa]* iced coffee with cream
cagouilles *[kagwee]* snails
caille *[ky]* quail
caisse till, cashier's desk
caisse d'épargne savings bank
cake *[kayk]* fruit cake
calmant tranquillizer
calmar squid
calvados apple brandy from Normandy
camomille *[kamomee]* camomile tea
camping campsite
camping interdit no camping
camping-caravaning site for camping and caravans
canapé *[kanapay]* small open sandwich, canapé
canard *[kanar]* duck
canard à l'orange *[kanar a loronj]* duck in orange sauce
canard aux navets *[kanar o navay]* duck with turnips
canard laqué *[kanar lakay]* Chinese roast duck
canard rôti *[kanar rotee]* roast duck
caneton *[kanton]* duckling
cantal hard cheese from the Auvergne, similar to cheddar
canton administrative district of Switzerland
capiteux *[kapeetuh]* heady (*wine*)

car coach, bus
carbonnade *[karbonad]* (meat) cooked on charcoal
cardon cardoon, vegetable similar to celery, eaten blanched in white sauce
carnet de tickets book of tickets
carotte *[karot]* carrot
carottes Vichy *[karot veeshee]* carrots in butter and parsley
carpe *[karp]* carp
carrelet *[karlay]* plaice
carrosserie garage that does repairs
carte *[kart]* menu
carte de crédit credit card
carte des vins *[kart day van]* wine list
carte d'identité bancaire banker's card
carte orange season ticket
carte vermeille senior citizen's railcard
carte verte green card
casse-croûte *[kass-kroot]* snacks
cassis *[kassees]* blackcurrant
cassoulet *[kassoolay]* casserole with pork, sausages and beans
ça va? *[sa va]* how's things?
CCP (compte de chèques postaux) giro account
cédez le passage give way, yield
CEE (Communauté économique européenne) EEC (European Economic Community)
céleri *[selree]* celeriac
céleri en branches *[selree on bronsh]* celery
céleri rave *[selree rahv]* celeriac
céleri rémoulade *[selree raymoolahd]* celeriac in mustard dressing
centime centime (*1/100 franc*)
centre commercial shopping centre/center
centre d'action culturelle arts

centre/center
centre ville city centre/center
cèpe *[sep]* cepe (*mushroom*)
cerise *[suhreez]* cherry
cerises à l'eau de vie *[suhreez a lo duh vee]* cherries in brandy
cervelas *[sairvuhla]* saveloy (*sausage*)
cervelle *[sairvel]* brains
cette cabine peut être appelée à ce numéro incoming calls may be made to this number
CFF (Chemins de fer fédéraux) Swiss railways/railroad
CH (Confoederatio Helvetica) Switzerland
chabichou *[shabeeshoo]* goat and cow's milk cheese
Chablis *[shablee]* dry white wine from Burgundy
chambré *[shombray]* kept at room temperature (*wine*)
chambre pour deux personnes double room
chambre pour une personne single room
chambres rooms
champagne *[shompan]* champagne
champagnisé *[shompanyizay]* sparkling
champignon *[shompeen-yon]* mushroom
champignon de Paris *[shompeen-yon duh paree]* champignon (*cultivated mushroom*)
champignons à la grecque *[shompeen-yon ala grek]* mushrooms in olive oil and herbs
change exchange
changement à ... change at ...
changer à ... change at ...
changeur de monnaie change machine
chanterelle chanterelle (*mushroom*)
chantier roadworks, roadwork
chantilly *[shontee-yee]* whipped cream
chapeaux hats
chapellerie hat shop/store
charcuterie *[sharkootree]* sausages, ham and patés; pork butcher
chariot obligatoire take a trolley/cart
charlotte cream with fruit and biscuits/cookies
Chartreuse *[shartrurz]* herb liqueur
chasse gardée private hunting grounds
chasselas *[shassla]* white grape

château castle
château fort fortified castle
Château-Margaux *[shato margo]* red wine from the Bordeaux area
Châteauneuf-du-Pape *[shatonurf doo pap]* red wine from the Rhone valley
chaud warm, hot
chaudrée *[shodray]* fish soup
chauffage heating
chauffage central central heating
chauffard! *[shofar]* learn to drive!
chauffeur du dimanche *[doo deemonsh]* Sunday driver
chaussée déformée uneven road surface
chaussée glissante slippery road
chaussée rétrécie road narrows
chaussée verglacée icy road
chausson aux pommes *[shoson o pom]* apple turnover
chaussures shoes
chemiserie menswear
chèque cheque, check
chèque de voyage traveller's cheque, traveler's check
cheval *[shuh-val]* horse
chèvre *[shevr]* goat's cheese
chevreuil *[shevruh-ee]* venison
chez Marcel/Mimi (*restaurant*) Marcel's/Mimi's
chicorée *[sheekoray]* endive, chicory
chicorée frisée *[sheekoray freezay]* curly endive, chicory
chiffonnade d'oseille *[sheefonad dozay]* seasoned sorrel cooked in butter
chocolat chaud *[shokola sho]* hot chocolate
chocolat glacé *[shokola glassay]* iced chocolate drink
chocolatine *[shokolateen]* chocolate filled bun
chou *[shoo]* cabbage
chou à la crème *[shoo ala krem]* cream puff
chou de Bruxelles *[shoo duh broo-sel]* Brussels sprout
chou rouge *[shoo rooj]* red cabbage
choucroute *[shookroot]* sauerkraut with sausages etc
chou-fleur *[shooflurr]* cauliflower
chou-fleur au gratin *[shooflurr o gratan]* cauliflower cheese
chutes de pierre falling rocks
cidre bouché *[seedr booshay]* fine cider

cidre doux *[seedr doo]* sweet cider
cimetière cemetery
cinémathèque film theatre, movie theater
circuit touristique scenic route
circulation alternée single line traffic
circule le ... runs on ...
circulez! *[seerkoolay]* move along!
circulez sur une file single line traffic
cité universitaire university halls of residence
citron *[seetron]* lemon
citron pressé *[seetron pressay]* fresh lemon juice
civet de lièvre *[seevay duh lee-evr]* jugged hare
clafoutis *[klafootee]* fruit pudding done in the oven
climatisation air-conditioning
climatisé air-conditioned
clôture électrifiée electric fence
cochon de lait *[koshon duh lay]* sucking pig
cocktail de crevettes *[kruhvet]* prawn cocktail
cœur *[kurr]* heart
cœur d'artichaut *[kurr darteesho]* artichoke heart
coiffeur hairdresser
coiffure hairdresser
coing *[kwan]* quince
col fermé pass closed
col ouvert pass open
colin *[kolan]* hake
colis parcels, packages
comment? *[komon]* sorry?, pardon me?
commissariat de police police station
complet no vacancies, full
composer le numéro dial the number
composez le ... dial ...
composition contents
compostez votre billet validate/punch your ticket in the machine
compote *[kompot]* stewed fruit, compote
comprimé tablet
comprimé effervescent effervescent tablet
comté *[kontay]* hard cheese from the Jura area
concessionnaire ... ... agent
concierge caretaker
concombre *[konkombr]* cucumber
confiserie confectioner

confit d'oie *[konfee dwa]* goose preserve
confiture *[konfeetoor]* jam
congé annuel annual holiday/vacation
congre *[kongr]* conger eel
conserver au frais (et au sec) keep in a cool (dry) place
conservez votre titre de transport jusqu'à la sortie keep your ticket till you leave the vehicle
consigne left-luggage, baggage checkroom
consigne automatique left-luggage lockers, baggage lockers
consommé *[konsommay]* clear soup, consommé
consommer avant le ... eat by ..., best before ...
consulat consulate
contenu contents
contre les ... for ...
contre-indications contra-indications
contrôles radar radar speed checks
convoi exceptionnel long vehicle
coq au vin *[kok o van]* chicken in red wine
coque *[kok]* cockle
coquelet *[koklay]* cockerel
coquille Saint-Jacques *[kokee san-jak]* scallop
Corail intercity train
cordonnier cobbler
correspondance connection
Corse Corsica
côte de porc *[koht duh por]* pork chop
côté non stabilisé soft verge/shoulder
côtelette *[kotlet]* chop
coton cotton
cotriade bretonne *[kotree-ad breton]* fish soup from Brittany
couchette couchette, bunk bed
coulis *[koolee]* creamy sauce or soup
coulis de framboises *[koolee duh frombwahz]* raspberry sauce
coulis de langoustines *[koolee duh longoosteen]* saltwater crayfish soup
couloir bus et taxis lane for buses and taxis
coulommiers *[koolomee-ay]* rich semi-hard cheese
coupe *[koop]* ice cream dessert dish; haircut
coupe Danemark *[koop danmark]* vanilla ice cream with hot chocolate sauce
courgette courgette, zucchini

cours de change exchange rate

court-bouillon *[koor booyon]* stock for poaching fish

couscous *[kooskoos]* semolina with meat, vegetables and hot spicy sauce

couvent convent

couvert cover charge

crabe *[krab]* crab

crème *[krem]* cream; creamy sauce; dessert; white coffee

crème à la vanille *[krem ala vanee]* vanilla custard

crème anglaise *[krem onglez]* custard

crème Chantilly *[krem shontee-yee]* whipped cream

crème d'asperges *[krem daspairj]* cream of asparagus soup

crème de bolets *[krem duh bolay]* cream of mushroom soup

crème de volaille *[krem duh vol-eye]* cream of chicken soup

crème d'huîtres *[krem dweetr]* cream of oyster soup

crème fouettée *[krem foo-etay]* whipped cream

crème pâtissière *[krem pateessee-air]* fine custard

crème renversée *[krem ronvairsay]* cream dessert in a mould

crémerie dairy

crêpe pancake

crêpes aux champignons *[krep o shompeen-yon]* mushroom pancakes

crêpes aux épinards *[krep ohz aypeenar]* spinach pancakes

crêpes Suzette flamed orange pancakes

crépinette *[krepeenet]* sausage

cresson cress

crevette grise *[kruhvet greez]* shrimp

crevette rose *[kruhvet roz]* prawn

croisement junction, intersection

croque-madame *[krok madam]* toasted cheese sandwich with ham and egg

croque-monsieur *[krok muhs-yuh]* toasted cheese sandwich with ham

crottin de Chavignol *[krotan duh shaveen-yol]* small goat's cheese

croustade *[kroostad]* crusty paté

croûte au fromage *[kroot o fromahj]* toasted cheese

croûte aux champignons *[kroot o shompeen-yon]* mushrooms on toast

CRS (Compagnie républicaine de sécurité) special riot control police

cru *[kroo]* raw; vintage

cru classé high quality wine

crudités *[kroodeetay]* chopped raw vegetables

crustacés *[kroostassay]* shellfish

cuir leather

cuisses de grenouille *[kweess duh gruhnwee]* frogs' legs

cuissot de chevreuil *[kweeso duh shuhvruh-ee]* haunch of venison

culte à ... (church) service at ...

cycles cycle shop/store

D

d'accord! *[dakor]* ok!

dames ladies, ladies' restrooms

dancing dance hall, night club

danger, verglas danger, ice

dartois *[dartwa]* pastry with jam

date limite de vente sell-by date

daurade *[dorad]* gilt-head *(fish)*

de retour dans une heure back in an hour

décembre December

déconseillé aux personnes sensibles unsuitable for people of a nervous disposition

découpez suivant le pointillé cut along the dotted line

défense d'afficher stick no bills

défense de ... sous peine d'amende ... will be fined

défense de cracher no spitting

défense de déposer des ordures no

litter, no tipping

défense de fumer no smoking

défense d'entrer no entrance

défense de laisser des bagages dans le couloir bags must not be left in the corridor

défense de marcher sur la pelouse keep off the grass

défense de parler au conducteur do not talk to the driver

défense de stationner no parking

défense de traverser les voies it is forbidden to cross the railway/railroad lines

dégustation (de vin) wine tasting

déjeuner lunch

délimité de qualité supérieure superior quality wine

demandez à la caisse ask at the cash desk

demi [duhmee] half litre of wine; small beer

demi-pension half board, American plan

dentiste dentist

départ departures

département administrative district of France

désinfectant antiseptic

destinataire addressee

détaxe à l'exportation tax refund on export goods

déviation diversion

diabolo menthe [mont] mint cordial with lemonade

diététique health food shop/store

digestif [dee-jesteef] liqueur

diluer dans un peu d'eau dissolve in water

dimanche Sunday

dimanches et jours fériés Sundays and holidays

dinde [dand] turkey

dîner dinner

disquaire record shop/store

disque obligatoire parking disk compulsory

disques records

distributeur (automatique) de billets (de banque) autobank, cash point

distributeur de billets ticket machine

distributeur de boissons drink vending machine

d'occasion secondhand

dolmen megalithic tomb

domicile home address

dose pour adultes/enfants dose for adults/children

douane customs

douche(s) shower(s)

doux [doo] sweet

droguerie drugstore, *sells aspirin etc, toiletries, household goods*

droite right

du ... au ... du mois from the ... to the ... of the month

durée de conservation ... keeps for ...

E

eau minérale [o meenayral] mineral water

eau minérale gazeuse [o meenayral gazurz] sparkling mineral water

eau non potable not drinking water

échalote [ayshalot] shallot

échange/remboursement exchange/refund

école school

Ecosse Scotland

écrevisse [aykruhveess] freshwater crayfish

écrevisses à la nage [aykruhveess ala nahj] freshwater crayfish in wine and vegetable broth

église church

électroménager household appliances

embarquement immédiat boarding now

émincé de veau [aymansay duh vo] finely cut veal in cream sauce

Empire Napoleon's reign (1804–14)

empruntez le passage souterrain use the underpass

en cas d'incendie in the event of fire

en cas d'urgence in an emergency

en dérangement out of order

en panne out of order, broken down

en vente ici available here

endive *[ondeev]* chicory, endive

endives au jambon *[ondeev o jombon]* endives with ham done in the oven

endives braisées *[ondeev brezay]* braised endives

enregistrement des bagages baggage registration, check-in

ensemblier-décorateur interior decorator

entracte interval

entrecôte *[ontr-koht]* rib steak

entrecôte au poivre *[ontr-koht o pwahvr]* steak in pepper sauce

entrecôte maître d'hôtel *[ontr-koht metr dotel]* steak with butter and parsley

entrée entrance; starter, first course

entrée de service tradesman's entrance

entrée des artistes stage door

entrée interdite no admission

entrée libre admission free

entremets *[ontruhmay]* dessert

entrez! *[ontray]* come in!

entrez sans frapper enter without knocking

entrez sans sonner enter without ringing the bell

épaule d'agneau farcie *[aypohl dan-yo farsee]* stuffed shoulder of lamb

éperlan *[aypairlon]* smelt (*fish*)

épicerie grocery

épicerie fine delicatessen

épinards à la crème *[aypeenar ala krem]* spinach with cream

épinards en branches *[aypeenar on bronsh]* leaf spinach

escalier roulant escalator

escalope à la crème *[ala krem]* escalope in cream sauce

escalope panée *[panay]* breaded escalope

escargot *[eskargo]* snail

espadon *[espadon]* swordfish

espèce de con! *[espess duh kon]* you stupid bastard!

esquimau *[eskeemo]* ice on a stick

essence petrol, gas

est east

estouffade de bœuf *[estoofad duh burf]* beef casserole

Etats-Unis United States of America

été summer

éteignez vos phares switch off your lights

éteignez vos veilleuses switch off your sidelights/parking lights

étranger abroad; foreigner

excusez-moi *[exkoozay mwa]* sorry, excuse me

exigez votre reçu ask for a receipt

expéditeur sender

exposition exhibition

F

fabriqué en/au … made in …

faisan *[fezon]* pheasant

fait main hand-made

faites l'appoint have the right change ready

faites vérifier votre niveau d'huile have your oil checked

farci *[farsee]* stuffed

FB (franc belge) Belgian franc

Fendant *[fondon]* Swiss dry white wine

fenouil *[fuh-nwee]* fennel

fermé closed

fermé jusqu'au … closed until …

fermer la grille close the outside door

fermeture annuelle annual holiday/vacation

fermeture hebdomadaire closed on …

fête de village village fair

fête des vendanges grape harvest festival
feux d'artifice fireworks
feux de camp interdits no campfires
février February
FF (franc français) French franc
fibres naturelles natural fibres/fibers
filet *[feelay]* fillet
filet de bœuf Rossini *[feelay duh burf]* fillet of beef with foie gras
filet de perche *[feelay duh pairsh]* perch fillet
fin de ... end of ...
fin de série oddment
financière *[feenonsee-air]* rich sauce (*served with sweetbread, dumplings etc*)
fine *[feen]* fine brandy
flageolet *[flajolay]* kidney bean
flambé *[flombay]* flambé, flamed
flan *[flon]* crème caramel, custard tart
flétan *[flayton]* halibut
Fleurie *[fluree]* red wine from Beaujolais
fleuriste florist
foie de veau *[fwa duh vo]* veal liver
foie gras *[fwa gra]* fine liver pâté
foies de volaille *[fwa duh vol-eye]* chicken livers
fonds d'artichaut *[fon darteesho]* artichoke hearts

fondue *[fondoo]* Swiss dish of cheese melted in white wine
fondue bourguignonne *[fondoo boorgheen-yon]* meat fondue
fourreur furrier
fraise *[frez]* strawberry
framboise *[frombwaz]* raspberry
franc belge Belgian franc
franc français French franc
franc léger old French franc
franc lourd new French franc
franc suisse Swiss franc
frangipane *[fronjeepan]* almond pastry
frappez avant d'entrer knock before entering
frit *[free]* deep fried
frites *[freet]* chips, French fries
froid cold
fromage *[fromahj]* cheese
fromage blanc *[fromahj blon]* soft white cheese
fromage de chèvre *[fromahj duh shevr]* goat's cheese
fromager, fromages cheese shop/store
FrS (franc suisse) Swiss franc
fruité *[frweetay]* fruity
fruits de mer *[frwee duh mair]* seafood
fumeurs smokers

G

galantine *[galanteen]* cold meat in aspic
galerie d'art art gallery
galette *[galet]* flat round cake
gallo-romain civilization following Roman conquest of Gaul
ganterie glove shop/store
gare railway/railroad station
gare routière bus station
gare SNCF French railway/railroad station
garni *[garnee]* with potatoes and vegetables
gas-oil fuel
gâteau *[gato]* cake
gauche left

gaufre *[gohfr]* wafer
Gaulois Gauls (*original inhabitants of France*)
gelée *[juhlay]* jelly
gélule capsule
gendarmerie police station
génisse *[jayneess]* meat from heifer
génoise *[jaynwaz]* sponge cake
Gewurztraminer *[guh-woorz-tramee-nair]* white wine from Alsace
gibelotte de lapin *[jeeblot duh lapan]* rabbit stewed in white wine
gibier *[jeebyay]* game
gigot d'agneau *[jeego danyo]* leg of lamb
gigue de chevreuil *[jeeg duh shevruh-ee]* haunch of venison

girolle *[jeerol]* chanterelle (*mushroom*)

gîte rural holiday accommodation(s) in the countryside

glace *[glass]* ice cream

glacier glacier; ice-cream shop/store

glaçon *[glason]* ice-cube

Golfe de Gascogne Bay of Biscay

goujon *[goojon]* gudgeon (*fish*)

gouttes drops

grand cru *[gron kroo]* fine vintage

grand magasin department store

Grande-Bretagne Great Britain

grandes lignes main lines

gratin *[gratan]* baked cheese dish

gratin dauphinois *[gratan dofeenwa]* baked cheese dish with potatoes

gratin de langoustines *[gratan duh longoosteen]* saltwater crayfish au gratin

gratin de queues d'écrevisses *[gratan duh kuh daykruhveess]* freshwater crayfish au gratin

gratinée *[grateenay]* baked onion soup

gratuit free

Graves *[grahv]* red wine from the Bordeaux area

grillade *[greeyad]* grilled meat

grive *[greev]* thrush

grondin *[grondan]* gurnard (*fish*)

groseille blanche *[groz-eye blonsh]* white currant

groseille rouge *[groz-eye rooj]* red currant

grotte cave

gruyère *[grooyair]* hard Swiss cheese

guichet box office, counter

guichet fermé position closed

H

hachis parmentier *[ashee parmonteeay]* shepherd's pie

hall d'arrivée arrivals

hall (de) départ departures

halte stop

handicapés disabled

hareng mariné *[arong mareenay]* marinated herring

haricot *[areeko]* (green) bean

haricot blanc *[areeko blon]* haricot bean

haricot de mouton *[areeko duh mooton]* mutton stew with beans

haricot vert *[areeko vair]* green bean

hauteur limitée à ... maximum height ...

heures des levées collection

hiver winter

HLM (habitation à loyer modéré) council flat, public housing unit

homard *[omar]* lobster

homard à l'américaine *[omar a lamerreeken]* lobster with tomatoes and white wine

hôpital hospital

horaire timetable, schedule

horaires d'ouverture opening times

horlogerie watchmaker

horlogerie-bijouterie watchmaker and jewe(l)ler

horodateur parking meter

hors saison off season

hors service out of order

hors-d'œuvre *[or duvr]* starter

hôtel de ville city hall

huître *[weetr]* oyster

hypermarché *[eepairmarshay]* supermarket

I

ici here
il est interdit de ... ... is prohibited
il est interdit de déposer des ordures no litter, no tipping
il est interdit de donner à manger aux animaux do not feed the animals
île island
île flottante *[eel flotont]* floating islands
imbécile! *[ambayseel]* idiot!
impasse cul-de-sac, dead end
indicatif dialling code, area code
infusion *[anfooz-yon]* herb tea
institut de beauté beauty salon
interdiction de stationner no parking
interdit prohibited
interdit à tous véhicules no access to any vehicle
interdit aux forains et aux nomades no gypsies
interdit aux mineurs no admittance to those under 18 years of age
interdit aux moins de ... ans children under ... not admitted
introduire insert
introduisez votre pièce ici insert coin here
Irlande Ireland
itinéraire bis alternative route
itinéraire conseillé recommended route
itinéraire de délestage alternative route
itinéraire obligatoire compulsory route (*for heavy vehicles etc*)

J

jambon *[jombon]* ham
jambon au madère *[jombon o madair]* ham in Madeira wine
janvier January
jardin public public gardens, park
jardin zoologique zoo
jarret de veau *[jarray duh vo]* shin of veal
je vous en prie *[juh vooz on pree]* don't mention it, you're welcome
jeton telephone token
jeudi Thursday
jeux interdits aux moins de 16 ans use of gaming machines forbidden for those under 16
jouets toys
journaux newspapers, stationer
jours ouvrables weekdays
jours pairs/impairs parking allowed only on even/odd days of the month
juillet July
juin June
julienne *[joolee-en]* soup with chopped vegetables
jus de pommes *[joo duh pom]* apple juice
jus d'orange *[joo doronj]* orange juice

K

kermesse fair
kiosque à journaux newspaper stand
kir [keer] white wine with blackcurrant

liqueur
kirsch cherry brandy
kugelhof [kooglof] cake from Alsace

L

la maison n'accepte pas les chèques
we do not accept cheques/checks
la maison ne fait pas crédit we do not
give credit
lait [lay] milk
lait grenadine [lay gruhnadeen] milk with
grenadine cordial
laiterie dairy (Switzerland)
laitue [lettoo] lettuce
lampes lamps
langouste [longoost] lobster
langoustine [longoosteen] saltwater
crayfish
langue de bœuf [long duh burf] ox
tongue
lapereau [lapro] young rabbit
lapin [lapan] rabbit
lapin à la moutarde [lapan ala mootard]
rabbit in mustard sauce
lapin aux pruneaux [lapan o proono]
rabbit with prunes
lapin de garenne [lapan duh garren]
wild rabbit
lard [lar] bacon
lavage à la main hand wash
lave-auto car wash
laver séparément wash separately
laverie automatique launderette, laundromat
lavomatic launderette, laundromat

layette babywear
le compostage des billets est obligatoire tickets are valid only if punched
léger light
légume [laygoom] vegetable
lentille [lontee] lentil
les articles soldés ne sont ni repris ni
échangés no refund or exchange of reduced price goods
les chèques ne sont acceptés qu'à partir de 100 F cheques/checks accepted
for amounts over F100 only
les chèques ne sont pas acceptés we do
not accept cheques/checks
les chiens doivent être tenus en laisse
dogs must be kept on the leash
les toilettes sont dans la cour the toilet/
restroom is in the back yard
lettres letters
librairie bookshop, bookstore
libre vacant, free
libre-service self-service
libre-service bancaire autobank, cash
point
lièvre [lee-evr] hare
lignes de banlieue suburban lines
limande [leemond] dab, lemon sole
limonade [leemonad] lemonade
lin linen
linge de maison household linen

literie bed linen
livarot *[leevaro]* strong cheese from the north of France
livraison à domicile home deliveries
livraisons interdites de ... à ... no deliveries between ... and ...
livre sterling pound sterling
livres et journaux books and newspapers
location à la semaine charge per week
location de vélos bicycles for hire/rent

location de voitures car hire/rental
loges des artistes artists' dressing rooms
longe *[lonj]* loin
lotte *[lot]* burbot (*fish*)
loup au fenouil *[loo o fuh-nwee]* bass with fennel
lundi Monday
l'usage des WC est interdit pendant l'arrêt du train en gare do not use the toilet while the train is in a station
lycée secondary/high school

M

M (métro) underground, subway
M. (Monsieur) Mr
macaroni au gratin *[o gratan]* macaroni cheese
macédoine de légumes *[massaydwan duh laygoom]* mixed vegetables
mâche *[mash]* lamb's lettuce
Mâcon *[makon]* wine from Burgundy
magasin shop, store
magasin de santé health food shop/store
magasin diététique health food shop/store
magret de canard *[magray duh kanar]* duck breast
mai May
mairie town hall
maison de la culture arts centre/center
maison des jeunes youth club
Manche the English Channel
mandats postaux postal orders
maquereau au vin blanc *[makro o van blon]* mackerel in white wine sauce
marc grape brandy
marcassin *[marcassan]* young wild boar
marchand de vin off-licence, liquor store
marché market
mardi Tuesday
maroquinerie leather goods
marque déposée registered trademark
marron chestnut
mars March
massepain *[masspan]* marzipan

matin morning
médecin doctor
Médoc *[maydok]* red wine from the Bordeaux area
melon *[muhlon]* melon
menhir standing stone
menthe *[mont]* peppermint
menthe à l'eau *[mont a lo]* mint cordial
menu gastronomique gourmet menu
menu touristique economy menu
mercerie haberdasher, notions store
mercredi Wednesday
merde! *[maird]* shit!
merlan au vin blanc *[mairlon o van blon]* whiting in white wine
messe à ... mass at ...
messieurs gents, men's restroom
métro underground, subway
meublé furnished accommodation(s)
Meursault *[murrso]* wine from Burgundy
midi midday
Midi South of France
millefeuille *[meel-fuh-ee]* cream slice
millésime *[meelayzeem]* vintage
mise en fourrière immédiate illegally parked cars will be removed
MLF (Mouvement de libération de la femme) women's lib
Mlle (Mademoiselle) Miss
Mme (Madame) Mrs
mode d'emploi directions for use
modes ladies' fashions

mont-blanc *[mon-blon]* chestnut sweet/candy topped with whipped cream

monument aux morts war memorial

morille *[moree]* morel (*mushroom*)

morue *[morœ]* cod

moules à la poulette *[mool ala poolet]* mussels in rich white wine sauce

moules marinière *[mool mareen-yair]* mussels in white wine

mousse au chocolat *[o shokola]* chocolate mousse

mousse de foie *[duh fwa]* a light liver pâté

moutarde *[mootard]* mustard

mouton *[mooton]* mutton

moyen âge Middle Ages

mulet *[moolay]* mullet

munster *[manstair]* strong cheese from eastern France

mûre *[moor]* blackberry

Muscadet *[mooskaday]* white wine from the Nantes area

muscat *[mooska]* sweet white wine

musée museum, art gallery

muséum natural history museum

myrtille *[meertee]* bilberry

N

nature *[natœr]* plain

navarin *[navaran]* mutton stew with vegetables

navet *[navay]* turnip

navette shuttle service

ND (Notre Dame) Our Lady

ne circule pas le samedi/dimanche does not run on Saturdays/Sundays

ne contient pas de ... contains no ...

ne pas avaler do not swallow

ne pas congeler do not freeze

ne pas dépasser ... comprimés par jour do not take more than ... tablets a day

ne pas dépasser la dose prescrite do not exceed the prescribed dose

ne pas déranger do not disturb

ne pas essorer do not spin dry

ne pas laisser à la portée des enfants keep out of the reach of children

ne pas repasser do not iron

ne pas se pencher au dehors do not lean out of the window

ne pas se pencher par la fenêtre do not lean out of the window

ne pas tordre do not wring

ne pas toucher à ... do not touch ...

ne quittez pas *[nuh keetay pa]* hold on (*telephone*)

ne rien jeter dans les WC do not attempt to flush sanitary towels or other items down the toilet

ne rien jeter par la fenêtre do not throw anything out of the window

nettoyage à sec dry cleaner, dry clean only

névralgies headaches

nocturne late night opening

Noël Christmas

noisette *[nwahzet]* hazelnut

noix *[nwa]* walnut

nom name

nom de famille surname, family name

non fumeurs no smoking

nord north

normale 2 star petrol, regular (gas)

n'oubliez pas de composter votre billet do not forget to punch/validate your ticket

n'oubliez pas le guide don't forget to tip the guide

nouilles *[nwee]* noodles

nous acceptons les cartes de crédit credit cards welcome

nouveau new

nouveau franc new French franc (*100 old francs*)

novembre November

Nuits-Saint-Georges *[nwee san jorj]* red wine from Burgundy

O

objets trouvés lost property, lost and found

objets volumineux large parcels/packages

occasions bargains

occupé engaged, occupied

octobre October

œuf à la coque [urf a la kok] boiled egg

œuf dur [urf door] hard-boiled egg

œuf en gelée [urf on juhlay] egg in aspic

œuf mollet [urf molay] soft-boiled egg

œuf poché [urf poshay] poached egg

œuf sur le plat [urf soor luh pla] fried egg

œufs à la neige [uh ala nej] floating islands

œufs au lait [uh o lay] egg custard

œufs brouillés [uh brooyay] scrambled eggs

office du tourisme tourist office

offre spéciale special offer

oie [wa] goose

oignon [onyon] onion

omelette au fromage [o fromahj] cheese omelet(te)

omelette au jambon [o jombon] ham omelet(te)

omelette au naturel [o natoorel] plain omelet(te)

omelette aux champignons [o shompeen-yon] mushroom omelet(te)

omelette aux fines herbes [o feenz airb] omelet(te) with herbs

omelette aux foies de volaille [o fwa duh vol-eye] omelet(te) with chicken liver

omelette paysanne [payzan] omelet(te) with potatoes and bacon

on demande des vendangeurs we need grape-pickers

on peut apporter son manger you may eat your own food here

optique optician

or massif solid gold

orange [oronj] orange

orange givrée [oronj geevray] orange sorbet served in the orange skin

orange pressée [oronj pressay] fresh orange juice

orangeade [oronjad] orangeade

orchestre stalls

oseille [ozeye] sorrel

ouest west

oursin [oorsan] sea urchin

ouvert open

ouvert de ... à ... open from ... to ...

ouverture des guichets hours of opening

ouvreuse usherette

ouvrir ici open here

ovomaltine (tm) ovaltine (tm)

P

P & T (Postes et télécommunications) post office (with telephone)

pain [pan] bread

palais palace

palette de porc [palet duh por] shoulder of pork

palourde *[paloord]* clam
pamplemousse *[pompluhmooss]* grapefruit
panaché *[panashay]* shandy
panade *[panad]* bread soup
pané *[panay]* breaded
papeterie stationer
papiers papers; litter
Pâques Easter
par arrêté préfectoral by order
parapluies umbrellas
parcotrain parking for train users
pardon *[par-don]* excuse me, pardon me; thank you
parfait (glacé) *[parfay glassay]* frozen dessert
parfumerie perfume shop/store
parking non gardé unsupervised parking
parking payant pay to park here
parking privé private car park
parking réservé aux clients de l'hôtel parking for hotel guests only
parking souterrain underground car park/parking lot
parler ici talk here
parterre stalls, orchestra
passage à niveau gardé/non gardé manned/unmanned level crossing/railroad crossing
passage piétons pedestrian crossing
passage souterrain subway, underpass
Passe-Tout-Grain *[pass too gran]* red wine from Burgundy
pastis *[pastees]* aniseed-flavoured alcoholic drink
pâté de canard *[duh kanar]* duck pâté
pâté de foie de volailles *[duh fwa duh vol-eye]* chicken liver pâté
pâte feuilletée *[paht fuh-ee-tay]* puff pastry
pâtes *[paht]* pasta
patinoire ice-rink
pâtisserie cake shop/store
paupiettes de veau *[popee-yet duh vo]* rolled-up stuffed slices of veal
payez à la caisse pay at the cash desk
payez à la sortie pay on your way out
Pays de Galles Wales
PCV collect call, reverse charge call
péage toll
pêche *[pesh]* peach
pêche interdite no fishing

peinture fraîche wet paint
pension guesthouse
pension complète full board, European plan
pension de famille guesthouse
perdreau *[pairdro]* young partridge
perdrix *[pairdree]* partridge
périphérique ring road
permis de conduire driving licence, driver's license
pétanque bowls game
pétillant *[paytee-yon]* sparkling
petit déjeuner breakfast
petit pain *[ptee pan]* roll
petit pois *[ptee pwa]* pea
petit suisse *[ptee sweess]* light white cream cheese
petite friture *[pteet freetœr]* whitebait
petits fours *[ptee foor]* small fancy pastries
pharmacie chemist, pharmacy
pharmacie de garde duty chemist/pharmacy
photographe camera shop/store
pièces rejetées rejected coins
pied de cochon/porc *[p-yay duh koshon/por]* pigs' trotters
pigeon *[peejon]* pigeon
pigeonneau *[peejono]* young pigeon
pignatelle *[peen-yatel]* cheese fritter
pilaf *[peelaf]* rice dish with meat, pilaf
pilaf de mouton *[duh mooton]* mutton pilaf
pintade *[pantad]* guinea fowl
pipérade *[peepayrad]* Basque egg dish with tomatoes
piscine swimming pool
pissaladière *[peessaladee-yair]* Provençal dish similar to pizza
pissenlit *[peessonlee]* dandelion
pissoir public urinal
piste cyclable cycle track
place square
place réservée aux ... this seat is intended for ...
places assises seats
places debout standing passengers
plage beach
plan de ville map of the town
plan du quartier map of the district
planning familial family planning
plat du jour *[pla dœ joor]* today's set menu

plateau de fromages *[plato duh fro-mahj]* cheese board

plateaux-repas light meals served on trains

PMU betting on horses

pochouse *[poshooz]* fish casserole with white wine

poids lourds heavy vehicles

poids maximum maximum weight

poids net net weight

point de rencontre meeting point

point de vue viewpoint

poire *[pwar]* pear

poire belle-Hélène *[pwar bel aylen]* pear in chocolate sauce

poireau *[pwaro]* leek

poisson *[pwasson]* fish

poissonnerie *[pwassonree]* fishmonger

poivron *[pwavron]* pepper

police secours emergency services

pomme *[pom]* apple

pommes dauphine *[pom dofeen]* potato fritters

pommes de terre *[pom duh tair]* potatoes

pommes de terre à l'anglaise *[pom duh tair a longlez]* boiled potatoes

pommes (de terre) en robe de chambre *[pom duh tair on rob duh shombr]* jacket potatoes

pommes (de terre) en robe des champs *[pom duh tair on rob day shon]* jacket potatoes

pommes (de terre) sautées *[pom duh tair sotay]* sauté potatoes

pommes frites *[pom freet]* chips, French fries

pommes paille *[pom pie]* finely cut chips/French fries

pommes vapeur *[pom vapurr]* boiled potatoes

pompiers fire brigade

pont bridge

pont à péage toll bridge

porc *[por]* pork

port harbo(u)r

port de pêche fishing port

porto Port (*wine*)

posologie directions for use, dosage

poste post office

poste restante poste restante, general delivery

potage *[potaj]* soup

potage bilibi *[potaj beeleebee]* fish and oyster soup

potage Crécy *[potaj kraysee]* carrot and rice soup

potage cressonnière *[potaj kressonee-air]* watercress soup

potage Esaü *[potaj ay-za-∞]* lentil soup

potage parmentier *[potaj parmontee-ay]* leek and potato soup

potage printanier *[potaj prantanee-ay]* fine vegetable soup

potage Saint-Germain *[potaj san-jair-man]* split pea soup

potage velouté *[potaj vuhlootay]* creamy soup

pot-au-feu *[potofuh]* beef and vegetable stew

potée *[potay]* vegetable and meat hotpot/ stew

Pouilly-Fuissé *[poo-yee-fweessay]* white wine from Burgundy

poularde *[poolard]* fattened chicken

poule au pot *[pool o po]* boiled chicken

poule au riz *[pool o ree]* chicken with rice

poulet à l'estragon *[poolay a lestragon]* chicken in tarragon sauce

poulet basquaise *[poolay baskez]* chicken with ham, tomatoes and peppers

poulet chasseur *[poolay shassurr]* chicken with mushrooms and white wine

poulet créole *[poolay kray-ohl]* chicken in white sauce served with rice

poulet rôti *[poolay ro-tee]* roast chicken

pour entrer, ... to enter, ...

pour tous renseignements, s'adresser à ... for enquiries, please see ...

pourboire interdit please do not tip

pousser push

poutargue *[pootarg]* smoked fish eggs

praire *[prair]* clam

précautions d'emploi instructions for use

préfecture local government offices

préfecture de police police headquarters

premier (*UK*) first floor, (*USA*) second floor

première première; first class

prenez un caddy take a trolley/cart

prenez un chariot take a trolley/cart

prenez un panier take a basket

prenez un ticket take a ticket

prénom Christian/first name

préparez votre monnaie have your change ready

pressing dry cleaner

pression *[pressee-on]* draught beer

prêt-à-porter clothes

prière de ... please ...

prière de frapper avant d'entrer please knock before entering

prière de ne pas déranger please do not disturb

prière de ne pas faire de bruit après 22 heures please be quiet after 10 pm

prière de ne pas fumer please do not smoke

prière de refermer la porte please close the door

prière de s'essuyer les pieds avant d'entrer please wipe your feet

prière de tenir les chiens en laisse keep dogs on a lead

primeurs fruit shop/store

priorité à droite right of way for traffic coming from the right

prise en charge minimum charge

privé private

prix price

prix cassés reduced prices

prix coûtant at cost price

prix des places ticket prices

prix par jour price per day

prix par personne price per person

prix par semaine price per week

prix réduits reduced prices

prix sacrifiés prices slashed

prochaine séance à ... heures next performance at ...

produit toxique poison

produits d'entretien household items

produits naturels health food

promenades à cheval horse riding

propriété privée private property

provenance from

prune *[proon]* plum

pruneau *[proono]* prune

PTT (Postes, télégraphes, téléphones) post office (*with telephone*)

pudding plum pudding

pure laine vierge pure new wool

purée *[pooray]* mashed potatoes

purée de marrons *[pooray duh marron]* chestnut purée

purée de pommes de terre *[pooray duh pom duh tair]* mashed potatoes

PV (procès-verbal) fine

Q

quai platform, track

quart quarter

quatre-quarts *[katr kahr]* pound cake

quenelle *[kuhnel]* dumpling

queue de bœuf *[kuh duh burf]* oxtail

quiche lorraine quiche with egg and bacon

quincaillerie ironmonger, hardware store

quoi? *[kwa]* what?

R

rabais discount

râble de lièvre [rabl duh lee-evr] saddle of hare

raclette [raklet] Swiss dish of melted cheese

ragoût [ragoo] stew

raie [ray] skate (fish)

raie au beurre noir [ray o burr nwahr] skate fried in butter

raifort [rayfor] horse radish

raisin [rezan] grape

ralentissez slow down

rappel reminder sign

rascasse [raskass] scorpionfish

ratatouille [rata-too-ee] Mediterranean vegetables cooked in olive oil

RATP (Régie autonome des transports parisiens) Paris public transport company

ravigote [raveegot] dressing with shallots and herbs

rayon department

reblochon [ruhbloshon] strong cheese from Savoy

réclamations complaints

recommandés recorded delivery

réductions familles nombreuses special rates for large families

règlement regulation

reine-claude [ren-klohd] greengage

relâche closure

relais routier transport café

remise reduction

remonte-pente ski-lift

rémoulade [raymoolad] dressing with mustard and herbs

renseignements information

renseignements internationaux international directory enquiries

représentation performance

reprise revival

RHR (Réseau express régional) fast, limited-stop métro line in Paris

réservation obligatoire booking essential

réservé reserved

réserve de chasse hunting preserve

respectez le silence de ces lieux please respect the sanctity of this place

respectez les pelouses please do not walk on the grass

retard delay

retirez votre reçu d'opération take your receipt

retirez votre argent take your money

retour de suite back soon

retrait des bagages baggage claim

revêtement temporaire temporary road surface

rez-de-chaussée (UK) ground floor, (USA) first floor

RF (République française) French Republic

rien à déclarer nothing to declare

rigotte [reegot] small goat's cheese from the Lyons area

rillettes [reeyet] potted pork/goose meat

ris de veau [ree duh vo] veal sweetbread

rissole meat pie

riverains autorisés no entry except for access

riz [ree] rice

riz à l'impératrice [ree a lampayratreess] sweet rice dish

riz pilaf [ree peelaf] spicy rice with meat or seafood

RN (route nationale) national highway

rognon [ronyon] kidney

rognons au madère [ron-yon o madair] kidneys in Madeira wine

Roi-Soleil [rwa solay] Louis XIV (The Sun King)

roman Romanesque

rond-point roundabout, traffic circle

roquefort [rokfor] blue ewe's milk cheese from the south of France

rosé *[rozay]* rosé wine
rosette de Lyon *[rozet duh lee-on]* dry sausage meat
rôti *[rotee]* joint, roast
rôti de porc *[rotee duh por]* roast pork
rouge *[rooj]* red wine
rouget *[roojay]* mullet
rouille *[roo-ee]* sauce accompanying bouillabaisse

roulez sur une file single lane traffic
route road
route barrée road blocked
route départementale secondary road
route du vin route taking in vineyards
route nationale national highway
rue street
rue piétonne pedestrian precinct
rue piétonnière pedestrian precinct

S

SA (société anonyme) Ltd, Inc
sabayon *[saba-yon]* dessert with egg yolks and white wine
sablé *[sablay]* shortbread
sables mouvants quicksand
s'adresser à ... ask ...
saignant *[senyon]* rare
Saint-Amour *[santamoor]* red wine from Beaujolais
Saint-Emilion *[sant-aymeelee-on]* red wine from the Bordeaux area
saint-honoré *[sant-onoray]* cake with cream and choux pastry decoration
saint-marcellin *[san-marsuhlan]* semi-soft cheese
salade salad, lettuce
salade de tomates *[duh tomaht]* tomato salad
salade niçoise *[neess-wahz]* salad with olives, tomatoes, anchovies
salade russe *[rooss]* salad with diced vegetables in mayonnaise
salade verte *[vairt]* green salad
salaud *[salo]* bastard
salle à manger dining room
salle climatisée dining room with air conditioning
salle d'attente waiting room
salle de bain bathroom
salmis *[salmee]* game stew
salon de coiffure hairdresser
salon de thé tearoom
salon d'essayage fitting room
salsifis *[salseefee]* oyster plant, salsify

samedi Saturday
sandwich au jambon *[sondweetch o jom-bon]* ham roll
sandwich au saucisson *[sondweetch o soseeson]* salami roll
sanglier *[son-glee-ay]* wild boar
sans agent de conservation contains no preservatives
sans alcool non-alcoholic
sans issue no through road, dead end
sans plomb lead-free
santé! *[sontay]* cheers!
SARL (société à responsabilité limitée) Ltd, Inc
sauce aurore *[o-ror]* white sauce with tomato purée
sauce aux câpres *[o kapr]* white sauce with capers
sauce béarnaise *[bayarnez]* sauce made from egg yolks, lemon juice or vinegar, butter and herbs
sauce blanche *[blonsh]* white sauce
sauce grand veneur *[gron vuhnurr]* sauce for game
sauce gribiche *[greebeesh]* dressing with hard boiled eggs, capers and herbs
sauce hollandaise *[olondez]* rich sauce served with fish
sauce madère *[madair]* Madeira sauce
sauce matelote *[matloht]* wine sauce
sauce Mornay béchamel sauce with cheese
sauce mousseline *[moossleen]* sauce hollandaise with cream

sauce poulette *[poolet]* sauce with mushrooms, egg yolks and wine

sauce ravigote *[raveegot]* dressing with shallots and herbs

sauce rémoulade *[raymoolad]* dressing with mustard and herbs

sauce suprême *[sœprem]* creamy sauce

sauce tartare mayonnaise with herbs, gherkins and capers

sauce veloutée *[vuhlootay]* white sauce with egg yolks and cream

sauce vinot *[veeno]* wine sauce

saucisse *[soseess]* sausage

saucisse de Francfort *[soseess duh fronkfor]* frankfurter

saucisson *[soseeson]* salami-type sausage

sauf indication contraire du médecin unless otherwise stated by your doctor

sauf le ... except on ...

sauf riverains access only

saumon *[somon]* salmon

saumon fumé *[somon fœmay]* smoked salmon

Sauternes *[sotairn]* fruity white wine from the Bordeaux area

savarin *[savaran]* crown shaped rum baba

se conserve au moins ... après la date-limite de vente keeps for at least ... after the sell-by date

sec dry, neat

second (*UK*) second floor, (*USA*) third floor

seconde second class

Secours routier français French motoring organization

seiche *[sesh]* cuttlefish

sel salt

selon arrivage depending on availability

sens giratoire roundabout, traffic circle

sens interdit no entry

sens unique one-way

septembre September

serrez à droite keep to the right

service *[sairveess]* not at all (*Switzerland*)

service 12% inclus 12% service charge included

service d'urgence emergencies

service (non) compris service (not) included

servir frais serve cool

shampooing-mise en plis wash and set

s'il vous plaît *[seel voo play]* please; excuse me

sirop cough mixture; cordial

site historique place of historical interest

snack snack bar

SNCB (Société nationale des chemins de fer belges) Belgian railways/railroad

SNCF (Société nationale des chemins de fer français) French railways/railroad

société company

soie silk

soirée evening performance

soldé reduced

soldes sale

sommet summit

somnifère sleeping pill

sonnette d'alarme alarm bell

sonnette de nuit night bell

sortie exit, way out

sortie de camions vehicle exit

sortie de secours emergency exit

soufflé au chocolat *[o shokola]* chocolate soufflé

soufflé au fromage *[o fromahj]* cheese soufflé

soufflé au Grand Marnier *[o gron marnee-ay]* soufflé with orange liqueur

soufflé au jambon *[o jom-bon]* ham soufflé

soufflé aux épinards *[ohz aypeenar]* spinach soufflé

soupe *[soop]* thick soup

soupe à l'ail *[al eye]* garlic soup

soupe à la tomate *[ala tomat]* tomato soup

soupe à l'oignon *[a lonyon]* onion soup

soupe à l'oseille *[a loz-eye]* sorrel soup

soupe au pistou *[o peestoo]* thick vegetable soup with basil

soupe aux choux *[o shoo]* cabbage soup

soupe aux moules *[o mool]* mussel soup

soupe aux poireaux et aux pommes de terre *[o pwaro ay o pom duh tair]* leek and potato soup

soupe de légumes *[duh laygœm]* vegetable soup

soupe de poissons *[duh pwasson]* fish soup

sous réserve de toute modification subject to modifications

sous-sol basement

sous-titré with subtitles

spectacle show
stade stadium
station thermale spa
stationnement alterné parking on alternate sides on alternate days of the week
stationnement en épis interdit no angle parking
stationnement gênant no parking
stationnement interdit no parking
stationnement limité à 30 minutes parking restricted to 30 minutes
stationnement payant pay to park here
stationnement réglementé limited parking
stationnement toléré 2 minutes parking only for 2 minutes
station-service petrol/gas station
steak au poivre *[o pwavr]* pepper steak

steak frites *[freet]* steak and chips/French fries
steak haché *[ashay]* minced meat, ground beef
steak tartare *[tartar]* raw minced/ground beef with a raw egg
substance dangereuse dangerous substance
sucre *[sookr]* sugar
sud south
Suisse Switzerland
Suisse romande French-speaking Switzerland
super 4 star petrol, premium (gas)
supermarché supermarket
supplément extra fare, extra charge
surgelés frozen foods
SVP (s'il vous plaît) please
syndicat d'initiative tourist information centre/center

T

tabac, tabac-journaux tobacconist and newsagent, tobacco store and news vendor (*also sells stamps*)
taille size
tailleur tailor
talon-minute heel bar
tanche *[tonsh]* tench (*fish*)
tarif des consommations price list
tarif normal first class mail
tarif réduit reduced fare; second class mail
tarte *[tart]* tart, pie
tarte aux fraises *[o frez]* strawberry tart/pie
tarte aux pommes *[o pom]* apple tart/pie
tarte frangipane *[fron-jeepan]* almond cream tart/pie
tarte Tatin *[tatan]* baked apple dish
tartelette *[tartuhlet]* small tart/pie
tartine *[tarteen]* buttered slice of bread
taxes comprises inclusive of taxes
taxis – tête de station taxi rank
TCF (Touring club de France) French automobile association

TEE (Trans-Europe-Express) first class trans-European train
teinturerie dry cleaner
téléphérique cable-car
téléphone interurbain long-distance telephone
télésiège chairlift
téléski ski tow
temple Protestant church
tendrons de veau *[tondron duh vo]* veal breast
terrain de camping campsite
terrine *[terren]* pâté
terrine du chef *[terreen doo shef]* chef's special pâté
tête de station taxi rank
tête de veau *[tet duh vo]* veal's head
TGV (Train à grande vitesse) high-speed train
thé *[tay]* tea
thé à la menthe *[tay ala mont]* mint tea
thé au lait *[tay o lay]* tea with milk
thé citron *[tay seetron]* lemon tea
thon *[ton]* tuna fish

tickets de quai platform/track tickets
tiède lukewarm
tilleul *[tee-yurl]* lime tea
timbres stamps
tirer pull
tissus fabrics
toilettes toilets, restrooms
tomate *[tomat]* tomato
tomates farcies *[tomat farsee]* stuffed tomatoes
tomme de Savoie *[tom duh savwa]* white cheese from Savoy
tonnage limité weight limit
tour tower
tour de France cycle race around France
tournedos *[toornuhdo]* round beef steak
tourte *[toort]* pie
tourteau *[toorto]* kind of crab
tout compris all inclusive
toute personne prise en flagrant délit de vol sera poursuivie all shoplifters will be prosecuted
toutes directions all directions
train auto-couchettes motorail

train direct fast train
train en partance pour ... train leaving for ...
train express fast train
train omnibus slow train
train rapide express train
train supplémentaire extra train
trains au départ departures
traiteur delicatessen
travaux roadworks, roadwork
tribunal court
tricots knitwear
tripes *[treep]* tripe
truite au bleu *[trweet o bluh]* poached trout
truite aux amandes *[trweet ohz amond]* trout with almonds
truite meunière *[trweet murnee-air]* fried trout
TTC (toutes taxes comprises) all taxes included
tunnel de lavage car-wash tunnel
turbot *[toorbo]* turbot (*fish*)
TVA (taxe sur la valeur ajoutée) VAT

U

un comprimé par jour pendant trois semaines one tablet a day for three weeks
un train peut en cacher un autre there may be another train hidden behind this one
urgences emergencies
urinoir public urinal
usage externe for external use
utiliser avant ... use before ...

V

vacances annuelles annual holiday/vacation
vacherin *[vashran]* strong cheese from the Jura area
vacherin glacé *[vashran glassay]* ice cream meringue

valable jusqu'au ... valid until ...

veau [vo] veal

velouté d'asperges [vuhlootay daspairj] cream of asparagus soup

velouté de tomate [vuhlootay duh tom-at] cream of tomato soup

velouté de volaille [vuhlootay duh vol-eye] cream of chicken soup

velouté d'huîtres [vuhlootay dweetr] cream of oyster soup

vendanges wine harvest

vendredi Friday

vendu uniquement sur ordonnance sold on prescription only

vente sale; selling rate

vérifiez votre monnaie check your change

vermicelle [vairmeesel] very fine pasta used in soups

versement payment

version originale in the original language

verveine [vairven] verbena tea

vestiaire cloakroom, checkroom

vêtements dames ladies' fashions

vêtements enfants children's wear

vêtements messieurs menswear

vétérinaire veterinary surgeon

veuillez établir votre chèque à l'ordre de ... please make cheques/checks payable to ...

veuillez éteindre votre moteur please switch off engine

veuillez fermer la porte please close the door

veuillez remplir le formulaire please fill out the form

viande [veeond] meat

viandox (tm) [veeondox] beef stock

vichyssoise [veesheeswaz] cold vegetable soup

vidange oil change

vieille ville old town

ville jumelée avec ... twin town ...

vin de pays [van duh payee] regional wine

vin de table [van duh tabl] table wine

vinaigrette French dressing

vins et spiritueux wine merchant

virage dangereux dangerous bend

virages sur ... km bends for ... km

virement transfer

visite guidée guided tour

visitez ... visit ...

vitesse limitée à ... speed limit ...

VO (version originale) in the original language

voie platform, track

voiture de queue rear carriage/car

voiture de tête front carriage/car

volaille [vol-eye] poultry

vos papiers, s'il vous plaît [vo papeeay seel voo play] your identity papers, please

Vosne-Romanée [vohn-romanay] red wine from Burgundy

vous êtes ici you are here

W Y Z

wagon-lit sleeper, sleeping car

wagon-restaurant dining car

yaourt [ya-oor] yogurt

Yvorne [eevorn] Swiss dry white wine

zone bleue restricted parking area

zone piétonne pedestrian precinct

Reference Grammar

NOUNS

GENDER
All nouns in French are either masculine or feminine in gender. The gender of nouns is largely unpredictable.

PLURALS
The plurals of most nouns are formed by adding **-s** to the singular. The following cases are exceptions to this rule:

ending of noun

-s, **-z** or **-x**	no change
-au, **-eau**, **-eu**, **-ou**	add **-x**
-al	change **-al** to **-aux**

For example:

le vélo	**les vélos**	the bicycle(s)
le poisson	**les poissons**	the fish
le bas	**les bas**	the stocking(s)
le nez	**les nez**	the nose(s)
le prix	**les prix**	the price(s)
le tuyau	**les tuyaux**	the pipe(s)
le bateau	**les bateaux**	the boat(s)
le cheveu	**les cheveux**	the hair
le chou	**les choux**	the cabbage(s)
le journal	**les journaux**	the newspaper(s)

There are exceptions to these rules and some words have irregular plurals:

l'œil	**les yeux**	the eye(s)
le monsieur	**les messieurs**	the gentleman (gentlemen)

ARTICLES

THE DEFINITE ARTICLE (THE)

The form of the definite article depends on whether the noun is masculine or feminine, singular or plural:

	sing.	pl.
m.	le	les
f.	la	les

For words starting with a vowel or a mute (unpronounced) H, the articles **le** and **la** are shortened to **l'** to avoid the clash of two vowels.
For example:

le restaurant	**les restaurants**	the restaurant(s)
la plage	**les plages**	the beach(es)
l'avion (m.)	**les avions**	the plane(s)
l'hôtel (m.)	**les hôtels**	the hotel(s)
l'arrivée (f.)	**les arrivées**	the arrival(s)
l'huître (f.)	**les huîtres**	the oyster(s)

The definite article changes its form when combined with the words **à** (to) and **de** (of):

	le	la	les
à +	au	à la	aux
de +	du	de la	des

For example:

je vais au café	I am going to the café
à côté du restaurant	next to the restaurant
je l'ai donné aux enfants	I gave it to the children
le parasol des Dupont	the Duponts' beach umbrella

Unlike English, French does not omit the articles **le**, **la** and **les** in generalizations:

la vie est trop courte   life is too short

Note that **du** and **de la** may be used to translate 'some' and 'any' in the singular:

avez-vous du beurre?	have you any butter?
j'aimerais de la confiture	I would like some jam

THE INDEFINITE ARTICLE (A, AN, SOME)

This also varies according to whether the noun is masculine or feminine, singular or plural:

	sing.	pl.
m.	**un**	**des**
f.	**une**	**des**

For example:

un château	**des châteaux**	a castle (castles *or* some castles)
une voiture	**des voitures**	a car (cars *or* some cars)

ADJECTIVES

Adjectives in French usually follow the noun they refer to (except for a few common ones), and change their form according to whether the noun is masculine or feminine, singular or plural.

To find the feminine form of most adjectives, add **-e** to the masculine form. Adjectives ending in **-e** remain the same. The following are exceptions to the general rule:

masculine endings	change to
-f	-ve
-eux	-euse
-eur	-euse
-os	-osse
-as	-asse
-el	-elle
-eil	-eille
-et	-ette
-on	-onne
-en	-enne
-er	-ère

For example:

neuf	neuve	new
heureux	heureuse	happy
trompeur	trompeuse	deceptive
gros	grosse	fat
gras	grasse	greasy
artificiel	artificielle	artificial
pareil	pareille	similar
violet	violette	purple
bon	bonne	good
moyen	moyenne	medium
cher	chère	expensive

Some common adjectives with irregular feminine forms are:

beau	**belle**	beautiful
vieux	**vieille**	old
frais	**fraîche**	fresh
doux	**douce**	soft, sweet
nouveau	**nouvelle**	new

The plurals of adjectives are formed according to the rules which apply to nouns. For example:

la table réservée	**les tables réservées**	the reserved table(s)
le beau jardin	**les beaux jardins**	the beautiful garden(s)

COMPARATIVES (BIGGER, BETTER etc)
Comparatives are formed by placing **plus** in front of the adjective:

cher	expensive	**plus cher**	more expensive

To say that something is 'more... than...' use **plus... que...**:

mon sac est plus lourd que le sien   my bag is heavier than his

To say that something is 'as... as...' use **aussi... que...**:

elle est aussi bronzée que sa sœur   she is as tanned as her sister

SUPERLATIVES (BIGGEST, BEST etc)
Superlatives are formed by placing **le** or **la plus** in front of the adjective:

cher expensive   **plus cher** more expensive   **le plus cher** or
la plus chère the
most expensive

Note that 'in' following a superlative in English is expressed by **de** in French:

le restaurant le plus cher de la ville   the most expensive restaurant in
town

A few adjectives have irregular comparatives and superlatives:

bon	good	**meilleur**	better	**le meilleur**	the best
mauvais	bad	**pire**	worse	**le pire**	the worst

POSSESSIVE ADJECTIVES (MY, YOUR etc)

As with other adjectives, their form depends on the gender and number of the noun they refer to. The possessive adjectives are:

	m. sing.	f. sing.	m. pl.	f. pl.
my	mon	ma	mes	mes
your (sing. familiar)	ton	ta	tes	tes
his/her/its	son	sa	ses	ses
our	notre	notre	nos	nos
your (pl. familiar; sing. and pl. formal)	votre	votre	vos	vos
their	leur	leur	leurs	leurs

For example:

tes valises	your suitcases
leur chambre	their room
mes amis	my friends

PRONOUNS

PERSONAL PRONOUNS

	subject	direct object		indirect object	
je	I	**me**	me	**me**	to me
tu	you (sing. familiar)	**te**	you	**te**	to you
il	he/it	**le**	him/it	**lui**	to him/it
elle	she/it	**la**	her/it	**lui**	to her/it
nous	we	**nous**	us	**nous**	to us
vous	you (pl. familiar; sing. and pl. formal)	**vous**	you	**vous**	to you
ils	they (m.)	**les**	them	**leur**	to them
elles	they (f.)	**les**	them	**leur**	to them

Personal pronouns usually come before the verb:
> **je leur achète un cadeau**   I am buying them a present
> **il nous emmène à Paris**   he is giving us a lift to Paris

However, when they are used with a command, the object pronouns follow the verb and are joined to it by a hyphen:
> **dis-moi!**   tell me!
> **aidez-nous!**   help us!

Note that some pronouns contract before a vowel or a mute (unpronounced) H:
> je → j'
> me → m'
> te → t'
> le → l'
> la → l'

For example:
> **j'habite à Paris**   I live in Paris
> **il l'aime**   he loves him/her

YOU

There are two ways of expressing 'you' in French. They are:

tu	used to address friends, relatives and children. The plural of **tu** is **vous**.
vous	used to address people the speaker doesn't know well. It is used with the second person plural of the verb.

For example:

qu'est-ce que tu bois?	what are you drinking?
vous vous êtes trompé	you made a mistake

USE OF 'ON'

The pronoun **on** is often used in French. It is used in three different ways:

1. To translate 'somebody':
   on vous demande au téléphone there is somebody on the phone for you
2. In generalizations:
   on ne sait jamais you never know
3. To replace **nous** (we) in spoken French:
   on reviendra demain we'll come back tomorrow

EMPHATIC PRONOUNS

These are:

moi	I or me
toi	you (sing. familiar)
lui	he or him
elle	she or he
nous	we or us
vous	you (pl. familiar; sing. and pl. formal)
eux	they or them (m.)
elles	they or them (f.)

These pronouns are used to emphasize the subject of a sentence, or when the subject pronoun stands on its own, or after **c'est** (it is):

moi, j'aime la pluie	*I* like rain
qui veut venir? – moi	who wants to come? – me
c'est moi	it's me

They are also used with **même** (self):

moi-même	myself
toi-même	yourself (sing. familiar)
vous-même	yourself (sing. formal)
lui-même	himself
elle-même	herself
nous-mêmes	ourselves
vous-mêmes	yourselves (pl. familiar and formal)
eux-mêmes	themselves (m.)
elles-mêmes	themselves (f.)

For example:

elle l'a fait elle-même	she did it herself

Other uses are after prepositions or after **que** in comparisons:

pour moi	for me
sans toi	without you
il est plus grand que moi	he is taller than me

REFLEXIVE PRONOUNS (MYSELF, YOURSELF etc)
Reflexive verbs are those in which the object is the same as the subject, e.g. I wash (myself). The verb is made reflexive by using it with one of the following pronouns:

me (m')	myself
te (t')	yourself (sing. familiar)
vous	yourself (sing. formal)
se (s')	himself/herself
nous	ourselves
vous	yourselves (pl. familiar and formal)
se (s')	themselves

French uses many more verbs reflexively than English.
For example:

je me rase tous les matins	I shave every morning
nous nous lavons à l'eau froide	we wash with cold water
elle s'habille	she is getting dressed
je me lève à sept heures	I get up at seven
elle s'ennuie	she is bored
il s'appelle Gérard	he is called Gérard

POSSESSIVE PRONOUNS (MINE, YOURS etc)
The possessive pronouns are:

	m. sing.	f. sing.	m. pl.	f. pl.
mine	**le mien**	**la mienne**	**les miens**	**les miennes**
yours (sing. familiar)	**le tien**	**la tienne**	**les tiens**	**les tiennes**
his/hers	**le sien**	**la sienne**	**les siens**	**les siennes**
ours	**le nôtre**	**la nôtre**	**les nôtres**	**les nôtres**
yours (pl. familiar; sing. and pl. formal)	**le vôtre**	**la vôtre**	**les vôtres**	**les vôtres**
theirs	**le leur**	**la leur**	**les leurs**	**les leurs**

Like possessive adjectives, possessive pronouns agree in gender and number with the object possessed:

ce n'est pas votre valise, c'est la mienne
this isn't your suitcase, it's mine

ce n'est pas mon passeport, c'est le vôtre
it isn't my passport, it's yours

VERBS

French verbs are divided into three groups:

Those ending in **-er**	e.g. **chanter** – to sing
those ending in **-ir**	e.g. **finir** – to finish
those ending in **-re**	e.g. **vendre** – to sell

THE PRESENT TENSE

To form the present tense, take off the **-er**, **-ir** or **-re** ending and add the present tense endings:

chanter		
je	chant-e	I sing
tu	chant-es	you sing (sing. familiar)
il/elle	chant-e	he/she/it sings
nous	chant-ons	we sing
vous	chant-ez	you sing (pl. familiar; sing. and pl. formal)
ils/elles	chant-ent	they sing

finir		
je	fin-is	I finish
tu	fin-is	you finish (sing. familiar)
il/elle	fin-it	he/she/it finishes
nous	fin-issons	we finish
vous	fin-issez	you finish (pl. familiar; sing. and pl. formal)
ils/elles	fin-issent	they finish

vendre		
je	vend-s	I sell
tu	vend-s	you sell (sing. familiar)
il/elle	vend	he/she/it sells
nous	vend-ons	we sell
vous	vend-ez	you sell (pl. familiar; sing. and pl. formal)
ils/elles	vend-ent	they sell

Most verbs are regular and follow and the above pattern, but some common verbs are irregular:

être (to be)	**avoir** (to have)	**aller** (to go)	**faire** (to make/do)
je suis	j'ai	je vais	je fais
tu es	tu as	tu vas	tu fais
il/elle est	il/elle a	il/elle va	il/elle fait
nous sommes	nous avons	nous allons	nous faisons
vous êtes	vous avez	vous allez	vous faites
ils/elles sont	ils/elles ont	ils/elles vont	ils/elles font

THE PAST TENSE

Two past tenses are in common use.

The IMPERFECT TENSE is used to express an action which was repeated over a period of time (like the meaning of 'used to' in English), or an action taking place in the past over a longer period of time (like the meaning of 'was ...ing'). The forms of the imperfect are:

chanter	**finir**	**vendre**
je chant-ais	je fin-issais	je vend-ais
tu chant-ais	tu fin-issais	tu vend-ais
il/elle chant-ait	il/elle fin-issait	il/elle vend-ait
nous chant-ions	nous fin-issions	nous vend-ions
vous chant-iez	vous fin-issiez	vous vend-iez
ils/elles chant-aient	ils/elles fin-issaient	ils/elles vend-aient

The following common verbs have irregular imperfect tenses:

être	**avoir**	**faire**
j'étais	j'avais	je faisais
tu étais	tu avais	tu faisais
il/elle était	il/elle avait	il faisait
nous étions	nous avions	nous faisions
vous étiez	vous aviez	vous faisiez
ils/elles étaient	ils/elles avaient	ils/elles faisaient

For example:

quand j'étais jeune, je faisais beaucoup de sport
when I was young, I used to do a lot of sport

nous dormions quand le lit s'est écroulé
we were sleeping when the bed collapsed

The PERFECT TENSE is used to express a completed action in the past. It is formed by using the present tense of the verb **avoir**, or occasionally **être**, and the past participle of the verb.

Past participles of regular verbs are formed by adding the following endings:

chanter	**chant-é**	sung
finir	**fin-i**	finished
vendre	**vend-u**	sold

For example:

nous avons fini notre repas	we have finished our meal
ils ont vendu leur maison	they have sold their house
vous avez oublié votre clef	you forgot your key

A few verbs have irregular past participles:

avoir	to have	**eu**
comprendre	to understand	**compris**
connaître	to know (people, places)	**connu**
croire	to believe	**cru**
devoir	to have to	**dû**
dire	to say	**dit**
disparaître	to disappear	**disparu**
être	to be	**été**
faire	to make/do	**fait**
interdire	to forbid	**interdit**
lire	to read	**lu**
mettre	to put	**mis**

mourir	to die	mort
naître	to be born	né
offrir	to offer	offert
ouvrir	to open	ouvert
permettre	to allow	permis
plaire	to please	plu
pouvoir	to be able to	pu
prendre	to take	pris
recevoir	to receive	reçu
s'asseoir	to sit down	assis
savoir	to know (facts)	su
venir	to come	venu
voir	to see	vu
vouloir	to want	voulu

A few verbs form their perfect using **être** instead of **avoir**. Most of these express movement from one place to another. The most common are:

aller	to go	je suis allé
arriver	to arrive	je suis arrivé
descendre	to go/come down	je suis descendu
entrer	to go/come in	je suis entré
monter	to go/come up	je suis monté
naître	to be born	je suis né
partir	to go away	je suis parti
passer	to pass	je suis passé
rentrer	to go/come back	je suis rentré
rester	to stay	je suis resté
retourner	to return	je suis retourné
sortir	to go/come out	je suis sorti
tomber	to fall	je suis tombé
venir	to come	je suis venu

THE FUTURE TENSE

The future is formed by adding the following endings to the **-er**, **-ir** or **-re** forms:

chanter	finir	vendre
je chanter-ai	je finir-ai	je vendr-ai
tu chanter-as	tu finir-as	tu vendr-as
il/elle chanter-a	il/elle finir-a	il/elle vendr-a
nous chanter-ons	nous finir-ons	nous vendr-ons
vous chanter-ez	vous finir-ez	vous vendr-ez
ils/elles chanter-ont	ils/elles finir-ont	ils/elles vendr-ont

Note that verbs ending in **-re** drop the **-e** before adding these endings.

A few verbs add these endings to a modified form of the verb:

avoir	j'aurai	I will have
devoir	je devrai	I will have to
être	je serai	I will be
faire	je ferai	I will make/do
pouvoir	je pourrai	I will be able to
savoir	je saurai	I will know
venir	je viendrai	I will come
voir	je verrai	I will see

MAKING THE VERB NEGATIVE

Verbs are made negative in French by putting **ne** before the verb and **pas** after it:

> **je ne fume pas** — I don't smoke
> **il ne veut pas aller à la plage** — he doesn't want to go to the beach

THE IMPERATIVE (GIVING COMMANDS)
The forms used to people addressed as **tu** are:

chant-e!	**fin-is!**	**vend-s!**

For people addressed as **vous** the forms are:

chant-ez!	**fin-issez!**	**vend-ez!**

For example:

mange ta soupe!	eat your soup!
n'arrêtez pas!	don't stop!

Pronouns are placed after the imperative. However, when the imperative is negative this rule does not apply:

achetez-le!	buy it!
ne l'achetez pas!	don't buy it!

QUESTIONS
There are three ways of asking questions in French:
1. Put **est-ce que** at the beginning of the sentence:

vous avez faim	you are hungry
est-ce que vous avez faim?	are you hungry?
il est anglais	he is English
est-ce qu'il est anglais?	is he English?

2. If the subject is a pronoun, change the order of verb and pronoun and join them with a hyphen:

vouz avez faim	you are hungry
avez-vous faim?	are you hungry?

If the subject is a noun, place the verb with the relevant pronoun after the noun:

votre ami est anglais	your friend is English
votre ami est-il anglais?	is your friend English?

3. Use the positive sentence and change the intonation, raising your voice at the end:

vous avez faim	you are hungry
vous avez faim?	are you hungry?

TELLING THE TIME

what time is it?	quelle heure est-il? *[kel urr eteel]*

it is ...	il est ... *[eel ay]*

one o'clock	une heure *[ɶn urr]*
seven o'clock	sept heures *[set urr]*
one a.m.	une heure du matin *[ɶn urr dɶ matan]*
seven a.m.	sept heures du matin
one p.m.	une heure de l'après-midi *[duh lapray-meedee]*
seven p.m.	sept heures du soir *[dɶ swahr]*
midday	midi *[meedee]*
midnight	minuit *[meenwee]*
five past eight	huit heures cinq
five to eight	huit heures moins cinq *[... mwan ...]*
half past ten	dix heures et demie *[ay duhmee]*
quarter past eleven	onze heures et quart *[ay kar]*
quarter to eleven	onze heures moins le quart *[mwan luh kar]*

CONVERSION TABLES

1. LENGTH

centimetres, centimeters
1 cm = 0.39 inches

metres, meters
1 m = 100 cm = 1000 mm
1 m = 39.37 inches = 1.09 yards

kilometres, kilometers
1 km = 1000 m
1 km = 0.62 miles = 5/8 mile

km	1	2	3	4	5	10	20	30	40	50	100
miles	0.6	1.2	1.9	2.5	3.1	6.2	12.4	18.6	24.9	31.1	62.1

inches
1 inch = 2.54 cm

feet
1 foot = 30.48 cm

yards
1 yard = 0.91 m

miles
1 mile = 1.61 km = 8/5 km

miles	1	2	3	4	5	10	20	30	40	50	100
km	1.6	3.2	4.8	6.4	8.0	16.1	32.2	48.3	64.4	80.5	161

2. WEIGHT

gram(me)s
1 g = 0.035 oz

g	100	250	500
oz	3.5	8.75	17.5 = 1.1 lb

kilos
1 kg = 1000 g
1 kg = 2.20 lb = 11/5 lb

kg	0.5	1	1.5	2	3	4	5	6	7	8	9	10
lb	1.1	2.2	3.3	4.4	6.6	8.8	11.0	13.2	15.4	17.6	19.8	22

kg	20	30	40	50	60	70	80	90	100
lb	44	66	88	110	132	154	176	198	220

tons
1 UK ton = 1018 kg
1 US ton = 909 kg

tonnes
1 tonne = 1000 kg
1 tonne = 0.98 UK tons = 1.10 US tons

ounces
1 oz = 28.35 g

pounds
1 pound = 0.45 kg = 5/11 kg

lb	1	1.5	2	3	4	5	6	7	8	9	10	20
kg	0.5	0.7	0.9	1.4	1.8	2.3	2.7	3.2	3.6	4.1	4.5	9.1

stones
1 stone = 6.35 kg

stones	1	2	3	7	8	9	10	11	12	13	14	15
kg	6.3	12.7	19	44	51	57	63	70	76	83	89	95

hundredweights
1 UK hundredweight = 50.8 kg
1 US hundredweight = 45.36 kg

3. CAPACITY

litres, liters
1 l = 7.6 UK pints = 2.13 US pints
½ l = 500 cl
¼ l = 250 cl

pints
1 UK pint = 0.57 l
1 US pint = 0.47 l

quarts
1 UK quart = 1.14 l
1 US quart = 0.95 l

gallons
1 UK gallon = 4.55 l
1 US gallon = 3.79 l

4. TEMPERATURE

centigrade/Celsius
$C = (F - 32) \times 5/9$

C	−5	0	5	10	15	18	20	25	30	37	38
F	23	32	41	50	59	64	68	77	86	98.4	100.4

Fahrenheit
$F = (C \times 9/5) + 32$

F	23	32	40	50	60	65	70	80	85	98.4	101
C	−5	0	4	10	16	20	21	27	30	37	38.3

NUMBERS

0	zéro *[zayro]*		
1	un *[an]*	1st	premier (feminine: première) *[pruhmyay, pruhmyair]*
2	deux *[duh]*	2nd	second (feminine: seconde) *[suhgon, suhgond]*
3	trois *[trwa]*	3rd	troisième *[trwazee-em]*
4	quatre *[katr]*	4th	quatrième *[katree-em]*
5	cinq *[sank]*	5th	cinquième *[sankee-em]*
6	six *[seess]*	6th	sixième *[seezee-em]*
7	sept *[set]*	7th	septième *[setee-em]*
8	huit *[weet]*	8th	huitième *[weetee-em]*
9	neuf *[nuhff]*	9th	neuvième *[nuhvee-em]*
10	dix *[deess]*	10th	dixième *[deezee-em]*

11 onze *[onz]*
12 douze *[dooz]*
13 treize *[trez]*
14 quatorze *[katorz]*
15 quinze *[kanz]*
16 seize *[sez]*
17 dix-sept *[dee-set]*
18 dix-huit *[deezweet]*
19 dix-neuf *[deeznuhff]*
20 vingt *[van]*
21 vingt et un *[vantay-an]*
22 vingt-deux *[vanduh]*
23 vingt-trois *[vantrwa]*
etc

30 trente *[tront]*
40 quarante *[karont]*
50 cinquante *[sankont]*
60 soixante *[swassont]*
70 soixante-dix *[—deess]*
80 quatre-vingts *[katr-van]*
90 quatre-vingt-dix *[—deess]*
91 quatre-vingt-onze *[—onz]*
92 quatre-vingt-douze *[—dooz]*
etc

100 cent *[son]*
101 cent un *[son an]*
200 deux cents *[duh son]*
201 deux cent un
1000 mille *[meel]*
1987 mille neuf cent quatre-vingt-sept *[meel nuhff son katr-van-set]*
2000 deux mille